ELECTRIC LIGHTING
of the 20's & 30's
Vol. 1

edited by
JAMES EDWARD BLACK

© 1994

5th Printing 1998

Published by:

L-W Book Sales

P.O. Box 69
Gas City, IN 46933

Printed in the U.S.A. by Image Graphics, Paducah, KY

TABLE OF CONTENTS

PRICING

This is only a guide and should be used as such. All prices are for lighting in good condition. Lamps that are mint (as in box), or the brass is polished as new, would bring much more. Any chip or crack in glass will bring price down 50% or more. A dealer will not pay full retail. So you should consider 40% or less if you sell to a dealer. L-W, Inc. will not be responsible for gains or losses in using this book.

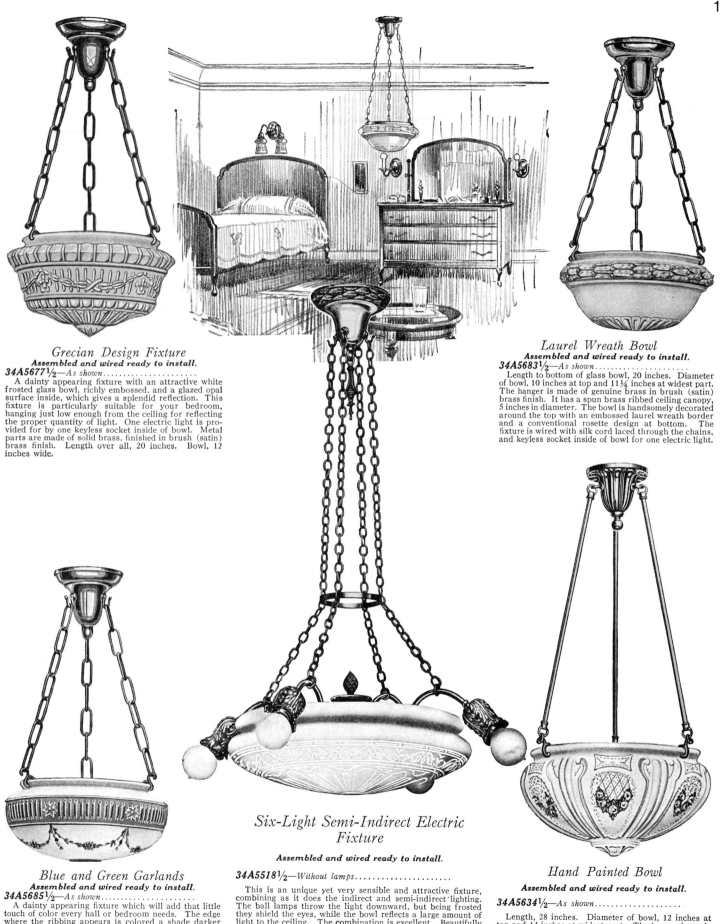

Grecian Design Fixture
Assembled and wired ready to install.
34A5677½—As shown......................

A dainty appearing fixture with an attractive white frosted glass bowl, richly embossed, and a glazed opal surface inside, which gives a splendid reflection. This fixture is particularly suitable for your bedroom, hanging just low enough from the ceiling for reflecting the proper quantity of light. One electric light is provided for by one keyless socket inside of bowl. Metal parts are made of solid brass, finished in brush (satin) brass finish. Length over all, 20 inches. Bowl, 12 inches wide.

Laurel Wreath Bowl
Assembled and wired ready to install.
34A5683½—As shown......................

Length to bottom of glass bowl, 20 inches. Diameter of bowl, 10 inches at top and 11¼ inches at widest part. The hanger is made of genuine brass in brush (satin) brass finish. It has a spun brass ribbed ceiling canopy, 5 inches in diameter. The bowl is handsomely decorated around the top with an embossed laurel wreath border and a conventional rosette design at bottom. The fixture is wired with silk cord laced through the chains, and keyless socket inside of bowl for one electric light.

Blue and Green Garlands
Assembled and wired ready to install.
34A5685½—As shown......................

A dainty appearing fixture which will add that little touch of color every hall or bedroom needs. The edge where the ribbing appears is colored a shade darker than sky blue. Six pretty garlands of tiny purple flowers and green leaves seem to hang from the blue border. The background of the entire bowl is satin white. One electric light is provided for by one keyless socket inside of bowl. Metal parts are made of solid brass and are finished in satin brass. Length, over all, 22 inches. Diameter of bowl, 12 inches at widest part.

Six-Light Semi-Indirect Electric Fixture
Assembled and wired ready to install.
34A5518½—Without lamps......................

This is an unique yet very sensible and attractive fixture, combining as it does the indirect and semi-indirect lighting. The ball lamps throw the light downward, but being frosted they shield the eyes, while the bowl reflects a large amount of light to the ceiling. The combination is excellent. Beautifully etched blown glass iridescent bowl in white satin finish. Inside of the bowl are keyless sockets for two electric lights and over the side extend keyless sockets for four electric lights. The round frosted lamps are not included in the price. We recommend using our 34A6825 Lamps shown on page 78. Metal parts are made of genuine brass in brush (satin) brass and black finish. Length, 35 inches. Diameter of bowl, 17 inches.

Hand Painted Bowl
Assembled and wired ready to install.
34A5634½—As shown......................

Length, 28 inches. Diameter of bowl, 12 inches at top and 14 inches at widest part. The hanger is made of genuine brass in brush (satin) brass and black finish. Ceiling canopy, 4½ inches in diameter, fitted with three brass reeded rods ⅜ inch in diameter. The bowl is beautifully embossed in panel design. These panels are exquisitely hand painted with delicately colored pink rosebuds and latticework design. The fixture is wired with silk cord run through the rods and has keyless socket inside of bowl for one electric light.

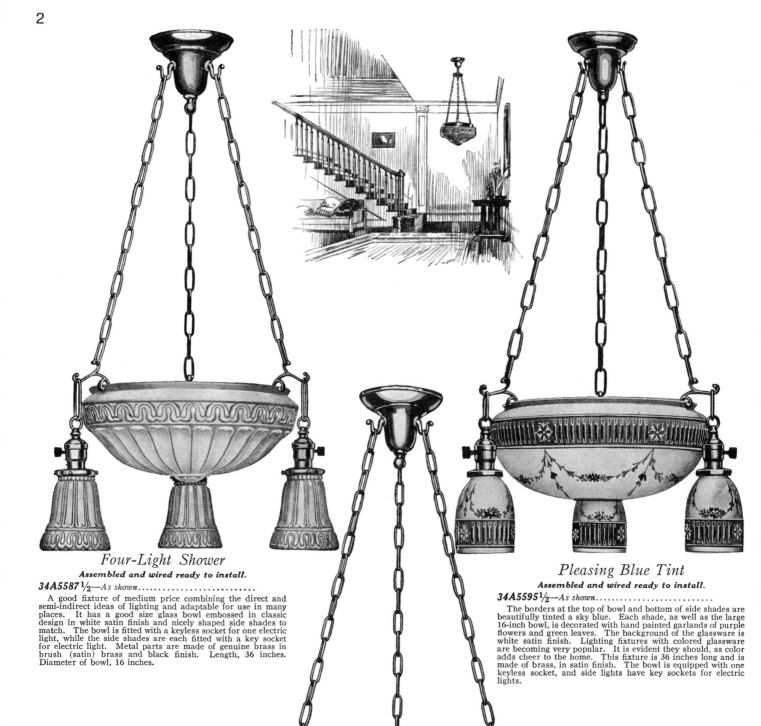

Four-Light Shower
Assembled and wired ready to install.

34A5587½—*As shown*...........................

A good fixture of medium price combining the direct and semi-indirect ideas of lighting and adaptable for use in many places. It has a good size glass bowl embossed in classic design in white satin finish and nicely shaped side shades to match. The bowl is fitted with a keyless socket for one electric light, while the side shades are each fitted with a key socket for electric light. Metal parts are made of genuine brass in brush (satin) brass and black finish. Length, 36 inches. Diameter of bowl, 16 inches.

Pleasing Blue Tint
Assembled and wired ready to install.

34A5595½—*As shown*...........................

The borders at the top of bowl and bottom of side shades are beautifully tinted a sky blue. Each shade, as well as the large 16-inch bowl, is decorated with hand painted garlands of purple flowers and green leaves. The background of the glassware is white satin finish. Lighting fixtures with colored glassware are becoming very popular. It is evident they should, as color adds cheer to the home. This fixture is 36 inches long and is made of brass, in satin finish. The bowl is equipped with one keyless socket, and side lights have key sockets for electric lights.

One-Light Straight Arm Bracket
Assembled and wired ready to install.

34A5017½—*As shown*...................

Made of genuine brass in brush (satin) brass finish. Extends 6 inches from the wall. It has a plain round canopy 4½ inches in diameter and 3½ inches deep. The arm is ¾ inch in diameter with turned end fitting and 2¼-inch plain socket cover. The bracket is wired and fitted with a key socket for one electric light. It is fitted with a plain bell shaped frosted glass shade.

Four-Light Shower
Assembled and wired ready to install.

34A5586½—*As shown*...........................

The embossing on the bowl adds greatly to the general appearance of the entire fixture. The glass bowl is pure white in soft satin finish, closely resembling Italian marble, embossed in ribbed and lotus flower design. Inside of the bowl is fitted a keyless socket for one electric light, and each of the side drop lights is fitted with a key socket for one electric light. Metal parts are made of genuine brass in brush (satin) brass finish. Length, 36 inches. Diameter of bowl, 15½ inches. This is an ideal fixture for the dining room.

Ball Lamp Bracket
Assembled and wired ready to install.

34A5090½—*Without lamp*..............

An unusually attractive bracket with excellent lines and good proportions. Severely plain ball lamp brackets are much in vogue at present and this one meets every requirement. It is made of genuine brass brush (satin) brass finish with round back, 4¼ inches in diameter, and ½-inch tubing arm fitted with attractive ball lamp holder and key socket. Round lamp is not included in the price. We recommend our 34A6878 Lamp shown on page 78.

3

Three-Light Semi-Indirect Fixture
Assembled and wired ready to install.
34A5631½—As shown.....................

Three-light electric fixture of exceptional artistic appearance. The lotus leaf design is carefully carried out on the bowl. The bowl is of white satin finish translucent glass, richly embossed, with a glazed opal surface inside which gives a splendid reflection. This bowl is 15½ inches in diameter and is equipped with keyless sockets for three electric lights. Metal parts of genuine brass in brush (satin) brass and black finish. Length, 36 inches.

Blue and Green Garlands
Assembled and wired ready to install.
34A5676½—As shown.....................

A dainty appearing fixture which will add that little touch of color every room needs. The edge where the ribbing appears is colored a shade darker than sky blue. Six pretty garlands of tiny purple flowers and green leaves seem to hang from the blue border. The background of the entire bowl is satin white. One electric light is provided for by one keyless socket inside of bowl. Metal parts are made of solid brass and are finished in satin brass. Length over all, 36 inches. Diameter of bowl, 16 inches.

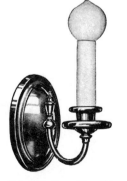

One-Light Candle Fixture
Assembled and wired ready to install.
34A5136½—Without lamp.................

A plain and unobtrusive type of bracket, yet the very simplicity of design makes it attractive. The oval wall plate is 6 inches long and 4 inches wide; the arm is ½ inch in diameter with turned cast brass urn shape ornament. Fitted with white enameled candle, 1¼ inches in diameter, and keyless socket inside of candle. The round frosted lamp shown is not included in the price. We recommend using our 34A6825 Lamp shown on page 78. Made of genuine brass in brush (satin) brass finish. Extends 7 inches from the wall.

Pompeian One-Light Fixture
Assembled and wired ready to install.
34A5624½—As shown.....................

This is a good medium priced fixture. It is made of genuine brass, and is finished in brush brass (satin color). The length is 36 inches. Canopy measures 5½ inches in width. Beautiful glass bowl, which is finished in a soft velvet white paper color on the outside. This bowl is 16 inches in diameter and is equipped with one keyless socket for electric light inside. Lighting fixtures of this type can be used in both living and dining rooms.

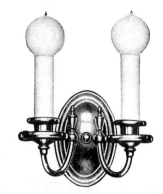

Two-Light Candle Fixture
Assembled and wired ready to install.
34A5137½—Without lamps.................

Frequently it is necessary to use both one and two-light brackets in the same room, and where this is done the brackets should be same pattern. This bracket and 34A5136½ at left are designed for this purpose. Fitted with white enameled candles, 1¼ inches in diameter, and keyless sockets inside of candles. The round frosted lamps shown are not included in the price. We recommend using our 34A6825 Lamp shown on page 78. Made of genuine brass in brush (satin) brass finish. Extends 7 inches from wall. Spread, 5½ inches.

Beautiful Semi-Indirect Fixtures

A Lighting Beauty
Assembled and wired ready to install.

34A5803½—*As shown*...........................

Without a doubt this is one of the most beautiful and effective semi-indirect lighting fixtures as yet designed. It is entirely different from the regular glass bowl semi-indirect, as an electric light is inside of each glass shell shape dish. Each dish is removable for cleaning by simply lifting it out. The color of the glass is slightly iridescent and its reflecting power is wonderful. In the center is a removable plug for attaching an electric toaster, fan, vacuum cleaner, etc. The fixture is also equipped with a tiny switch which turns the light on or off. The body is made of solid cast brass, beautifully finished in the new polychrome finish. The background is antique gold color, ornamented with hand painted flowers in natural colors. It is 28 inches long and about 17 inches wide and is fitted for three electric lights. A fixture you will always admire.

A Lighting Beauty
Assembled and wired ready to install.

34A5804½—*As shown*....................

Although this fixture is similar to 34A5803½, yet it is different. It is gorgeous in appearance with its six lights—five around and one in center. When viewed from below it appears like some gigantic beautiful flower in full bloom. The glass shades are slightly iridescent in color and give a wonderful light. Each shade is easily removed for cleaning by lifting it out. The fixture has six keyless sockets for electric lights. The finish is antique gold color polychrome with hand painted colored flowers. We are sure you will be pleased with this fixture. It is 36 inches long and about 20 inches wide.

Flood Light Bracket
Assembled and wired ready to install.

34A5103½—*As shown*...............

The feature of this bracket is the manner in which the light is distributed. When mounted on the wall the slightly iridescent glass dish is tilted forward and the light is diffused sideways and upward, thereby illuminating a large portion of the wall. An effect similar to invisible cove lighting. Made of solid brass and finished in antique gold color, decorated with hand painted flowers to match other fixtures shown on this page. The light inside of the glass dish is controlled by a tiny switch in the center of the bracket. The bracket is about 12 inches high and 8 inches wide at widest part.

An exact reproduction of the under side of the fixture shown above when viewed from below.

This photograph shows the beautiful appearance of the fixture shown above when viewed from below.

Velvet Brown and Gold Color

Velvet Brown and Gold Color
Assembled and wired ready to install.
34A5750½—As shown.........................

A three-light electric fixture of this type goes very well in small living or dining rooms and is also very appropriate in large reception halls. It is made of solid brass and is finished in velvet brown and gold color, a very pretty finish. Is about 36 inches long and 14 inches wide. The pan is 12 inches wide. It is fitted with key sockets for turning lights on or off. The glassware is in a delicate shade of brown on a background of satin white, to match the color of the fixture.

Velvet Brown and Gold Color
Assembled and wired ready to install.
34A5239½—As shown.....................

This pendant is made of solid brass and is finished in that beautiful finish called velvet brown and gold color. It is 36 inches long and is equipped with key socket and the glass is tinted in brown color around the border, to match color of fixture.

Velvet Brown and Gold Color
Assembled and wired ready to install.
34A5757½—As shown.........................

This fixture is 36 inches long and about 16 inches wide. It is made of solid brass and finished in a beautiful velvet brown and gold color. The ceiling canopy is 5¼ inches wide and the large pan measures 14 inches in diameter. There are four key sockets for turning the lights on or off. The glassware is tinted in delicate brown color around the border to match the color of the fixture.

Velvet Brown and Gold Color
Assembled and wired ready to install.
34A5711½—Without lamps...............

Wherever a short fixture is desired and in homes with low ceilings this fixture is ideal. It is finished in velvet brown and gold color, a very desirable finish. All plain parts are in velvet brown and the embossed parts are in highly polished gold color. The fixture is made of solid brass, is about 10 inches long and 14 inches wide. The round frosted lamps shown are not included in the price. We recommend using our 34A6825 Lamps shown on page 78.

Velvet Brown and Gold Color
Assembled and wired ready to install.
34A5242½—As shown.........................

An ideal fixture for homes with low ceilings or where a short fixture is desired. The fixture, being very low, gives opportunity for everyone to admire its beauty at once. The beautiful contrast of brown tone and gold color in which this fixture is finished is unsurpassed by any finish up to the present time. The entire fixture is made of brass, is 12 inches long and 16 inches wide. The 12-inch bowl shade is tinted around the border in a delicate brown on a background of satin white,

Velvet Brown and Gold Color
Assembled and wired ready to install.
34A5709½—Without lamps...............

A lighting fixture of this type is very ornamental. The ball lamps cluster so nicely and the velvet brown and gold color finish make it a very decorative and desirable fixture. All embossed parts are highly polished and are a beautiful contrast to the rest of the fixture. The fixture is made of solid brass and is about 10 inches long and 15 inches wide. The round frosted lamps shown are not included in the price.

Fancy Two-Light Fixture
Assembled and wired ready to install.

34A4609½—Without lamps........................

A fancy two-light ceiling fixture that can be used in any small room or hall. The finish is velvet brown and gold color. We know you will like the fixture when you see it. The ball lamps are interchangeable to glass shades at any time you so desire. The entire fixture is made of brass and is about 16 inches long and about 14 inches wide, fitted with two key sockets for electric lights. The round frosted lamps are not included in the price. We recommend using our 34A6825 Lamps shown on page 78.

Ball Lamp Fixture
Assembled and wired ready to install.

34A4613½—Without lamps............................

We show this fixture with ball lamps. It is a variation from the fixtures shown with glass shades, yet, should you at any time desire to use glass shades, you simply unscrew the lamps and attach the shades and use the same lamps inside of shades, making a different fixture entirely. It is finished in velvet brown and gold color. The entire fixture is made of brass and is about 16 inches long and about 16 inches wide. Has three key sockets for electric lights. The round frosted lamps are not included in the price. We recommend using our 34A6825 Lamps shown on page 78.

A Fancy Cluster
Assembled and wired ready to install.

34A5796½—*Velvet brown and gold color. Without lamps*..

34A5810½—*Genuine silver plate and black. Without lamps*..

Fixtures with ball lamps are very ornamental as well as economical. The ball lamps serve two purposes. They take the place of glass shades and give you the light as well. Remove ball lamps and attach glass shades and you have a different fixture if you so desire. The fixture is 36 inches long and is made of solid brass, finished in velvet brown and gold color, or **genuine silver plate and black.** Equipped with keys on sockets for turning light on or off. The round frosted lamps are not included in the price. We recommend using our 34A6825 Lamps, shown on page 78.

Velvet Brown and Gold Color Fixtures

Ball Lamp Fixture
Assembled and wired ready to install.

34A5797½—Without lamps..

A three-light electric fixture of this type goes very well in small living or dining rooms and is also very appropriate in large reception halls. It is finished in velvet brown and gold color, a very pretty finish. Made of solid brass and is 36 inches long and about 16 inches wide. It is equipped with keys on sockets for turning lights on or off. Should you at any time care to change the fixture to have glass shades, you can do so by removing ball lamps and attaching the shades. The round frosted lamps are not included in the price. We recommend using our 34A6825 Lamps shown on page 78.

Cut Glass Ball
Assembled and wired ready to install.

34A5765½—Without lamps...

Cut glass has become very popular for lighting fixtures. It is brilliant when lighted and is sure to attract attention and admiration. This fixture is made of solid brass and is 36 inches long and about 16 inches wide. It is finished in that beautiful new finish called velvet brown and gold color. Has one keyless socket inside of the cut glass ball and key sockets on the four side lights. The round frosted lamps are not included in the price. We recommend using our 34A6825 Lamps shown on page 78.

Velvet Brown and Gold Color Pendants

Ball Lamp Bracket
Assembled and wired ready to install.
34A5114½—*Without lamp....*

This bracket is finished in velvet brown and gold color, and will match any of our fixtures in velvet brown and gold color finish. It is made of solid brass. Wall plate measures 6x4 inches and has an applied cast brass arm. Extends 6 inches from the wall and is equipped with a key socket. The round frosted lamp is not included in the price. We recommend using our 34A6825 lamp shown on page 78.

Fancy Ball Light
Assembled and wired ready to install.
34A7041½—*As shown..........*

Finished in velvet brown and gold color. This ceiling light will match any of our fixtures that are in the same finish. It is 8½ inches high and is fitted with one keyless socket and frosted fancy glass ball, tinted a delicate pink color with garlands of green leaves and pink flowers on a white satin background.

A Candle Bracket
Assembled and wired ready to install.
34A5119½—*Without lamp......*

It is not always necessary to have a bracket with glass shades to match a center fixture that is equipped with shades. A candle bracket matches with almost any type fixture. The bracket shown here is finished in velvet brown and gold color and matches all our fixtures shown in that finish. Entire bracket is made of solid brass. Oval wall plate is 6x4 inches. Extends 5 inches. The round frosted lamp is not included in the price. We recommend using our 34A6825 lamp shown on page 78.

Tapering Lantern
Assembled and wired ready to install.
34A5264½—*As shown......*

A very pretty and effective lantern. The metal parts are finished a pleasing shade of brown and ornamented in burnished gold color. The lantern is 12 inches long and 7 inches at widest part, with six crystal pebbled glass panels. It has a hinged top for inserting electric lamp and to clean glass when necessary. Inside of the lantern is a keyless socket for electric light. Length over all is 36 inches.

Hexagonal Lantern
Assembled and wired ready to install.
34A5249½—*As shown......*

This lantern is very effective for lighting halls and enclosed porches. Finished a beautiful velvet brown and burnished gold color. The six glass panels are a beautiful shade of amber and resemble onyx marble. It is ornamented with seven tiny brass tassels which give this lantern just enough decoration to be attractive. It is 36 inches long. Lantern measures 11x7 inches and has one keyless socket for electric light.

Brown Tone and Gold Color
Assembled and wired ready to install.
34A5245½—*As shown.................*

This pendant is made of solid brass and finished in that beautiful finish called brown tone and gold color. It is 36 inches long and is equipped with key socket for one electric light. It is fitted with a fancy frosted glass shade in flower and ribbed design. This pendant matches other fixtures listed in brown tone and gold

Reeded Rod Pendant
Assembled and wired ready to install.
34A5250½—*As shown.....................*

Length to bottom of glass shade, 36 inches. Made of solid brass. Beautiful velvet brown and gold color finish. Has a fancy ceiling canopy and socket cover. The reeded rod is ornamented in the center with a small cast brass husk. Has one key socket for electric light. Frosted fancy glass shade, tinted a delicate pink color, with garlands of green leaves and pink flowers on a white satin background.

Brown and Gold Pendant
Assembled and wired ready to install.
34A5251½—*As shown.................*

This pendant is 36 inches long. It is made of solid brass and finished in a new shade of velvet brown and gold color to match other fixtures shown in this book. Equipped with one key socket for electric light. Has frosted fancy glass shade, tinted a delicate pink color, with garlands of green leaves and pink flowers, on a white satin background.

Hall or Bedroom Ceiling Fixture
Assembled and wired ready to install.

34A4607½—*As shown*...........................

A very appropriate fixture for a hall or bedroom. Finished in velvet brown and gold color, the same as other fixtures shown on this page. It is 16 inches long and about 14 inches wide at widest part. Equipped with two key sockets for electric lights. Has fancy frosted glass shades, tinted in delicate pink color with garlands of green leaves and pink flowers on a white satin background.

Three-Light Fixture
Assembled and wired ready to install.

34A4615½—*As shown*...........................

There are a great many rooms where a four-light fixture is too large, and with this thought in mind we have designed this fixture. It is finished a velvet brown color with all of the cast and embossed parts in highly polished gold color. This fixture is 16 inches long and about 18 inches wide. Made of genuine brass. Has three key sockets for electric lights. Fancy frosted glass shades tinted in delicate pink color with garlands of green leaves and pink flowers on a white satin finish background.

Brown Tone Candle Fixture
Assembled and wired ready to install.

34A5426½—*Without lamps*...........................

A modest fixture, yet pretty enough to be the center of attraction in any living room. It is finished in velvet brown and gold color. The background is a soft velvet brown color and all embossed parts are highly polished in gold color. A finish that you will admire. The fixture is 36 inches long and about 18 inches wide. There are five electric candle lights. The round frosted lamps are not included in the price. We recommend using our 34A6825 Lamps shown on page 78.

Velvet Brown and Gold Color Fixtures

An Effective Design
Assembled and wired ready to install.

34A5780½—*As shown*...........................

The design of this fixture is very novel and attractive. Finished in velvet brown and gold color and is a perfect match for other fixtures finished in velvet brown and gold that are shown in this book. Made of brass and is 36 inches long and about 15 inches wide. There is one keyless socket inside of center bowl and the three outer lights are controlled by key sockets for electric lights. The glassware is frosted and has a slight tint of brown to match the fixture.

Four-Light Fixture
Assembled and wired ready to install.

34A5778½—*Velvet brown and gold color, as shown*...........................
34A5809½—*Genuine silver plate and black, as shown*...........................

Length to bottom of glassware, 36 inches; width, about 18 inches. Made of solid brass and finished in velvet brown, with all embossing and cast ornaments in highly polished gold color or **genuine silver plate and black.** It is fitted with four key sockets for electric lights, and is equipped with fancy frosted glass shades, tinted in delicate pink color with garlands of green leaves and pink flowers on a white satin background.

A Ceiling Ornament
Assembled and wired ready to install.

34A4611½—*Without lamps* . . . .

A lighting fixture of this type is very ornamental. The five ball lamps cluster so nicely, and the velvet brown and gold color makes it a very decorative and desirable fixture. All embossed and cast metal parts are highly polished and are a beautiful contrast to the rest of the fixture. The fixture is made of solid brass and is about 16 inches long and about 17 inches wide. Has five key sockets for electric lights. The round frosted lamps are not included in the price. We recommend using our 34A6825 Lamps shown on page 78.

Two-Light Fixture for Small Rooms
Assembled and wired ready to install.

34A5225½—*As shown* . . . .

A fixture that is appropriate for lighting small rooms. Finished in a pretty background of velvet brown, with all embossed and cast ornaments in highly polished gold color to match other fixtures shown on this page. It is 36 inches long and about 14 inches wide, and is made of solid brass with two key sockets for electric lights. Has fancy frosted glass shades, tinted a delicate pink color with garlands of green leaves and pink flowers on a white satin background.

Velvet Brown and Gold Color Fixtures

A Hall Fixture
Assembled and wired ready to install.

34A5227½—*Without lamps* . . . .

This pretty two-light fixture is finished in velvet brown and gold, a finish you will admire. The plain parts are a light shade of brown and the embossing and cast ornaments are highly polished, gold color. It makes a very neat fixture for halls or bedrooms. Is made of solid brass and is 36 inches long and about 14 inches wide. Has keys on sockets for turning lights on or off. The round frosted lamps are not included in the price. We recommend using our 34A6825 Lamps shown on page 78.

Velvet Brown and Gold Fixture
Assembled and wired ready to install.

34A5278½—*As shown* . . . .

Length to bottom of glassware, 36 inches; width, about 18 inches. Made of solid brass and finished in a pretty background of velvet brown, with all embossing and cast ornaments in highly polished gold color. Has fancy frosted glass shades tinted a delicate pink color with garlands of green leaves and pink flowers on a white satin background. Fitted with three key sockets for electric lights. The finish of this fixture is very striking and attractive.

Velvet Brown and Gold Color Fixtures

10

*You
Cannot Buy as
Good a Fixture
Elsewhere
at This Price*

*The
Most Popular
Fixture
Because It Is
the Best Value*

Four-Light Special Value Fixture
Assembled and wired ready to install.

34A5783½—*As shown*...

Length to bottom of glassware, 36 inches; width, about 18 inches.
Made of solid brass and finished in brown tone and gold, with all
embossing and cast ornaments in highly polished gold color. Fitted
with four key sockets for electric lights, and is equipped with fancy
frosted glass shades. This fixture is very appropriate for living
or dining rooms. The finish of this fixture is very striking and
attractive and matches all of our fixtures finished in brown tone
and gold color.

Complete as Shown
**WIRED READY TO
HANG**

*Brown Tone
and
Gold Color
Finish*

A Pretty Bracket
Assembled and wired ready to install
34A5132½—*Without lamp*........

This bracket is finished in brown tone and gold color and is suitable for most any room. It is made of solid brass. Extends 5½ inches from wall. Back plate is 4x6 inches. Has key socket. The round frosted lamp is not included in the price. We recommend using 34A6825 Lamp

A Classy Bracket
Assembled and wired ready to install.
34A5133½—*Without lamp*.......

A candle bracket will always be in keeping, regardless of other surroundings. This bracket is finished in brown tone and polished gold color and matches all our fixtures shown in this finish. Made of solid brass. Oval back measures 4x6 inches. Has keyless socket. The round frosted lamp is not included in the price. We recommend using 34A6825 Lamp

Velvet Brown and Gold Color
Assembled and wired ready to install.
34A5424½—**5-Light.** *Without lamps*.....................
34A5423½—**4-Light.** *Without lamps*.....................

We are sure that this pleasing candle fixture will become very popular. Modest, yet striking enough to be the center of attraction in any living room. It is finished in velvet brown and gold color. The background is a soft brown color and all embossed and cast ornaments are highly polished gold color, making a finish that everyone cannot help but admire. The entire fixture is made of solid brass, and is 36 inches long and about 17 inches wide. The round frosted lamps are not included in the price. We recommend using our 34A6825 Lamps

These Popular Brown Tone and Gold Color Fixtures Are Priced Exceedingly Low

For Small Rooms
Assembled and wired ready to install.
34A5279½—*As shown*....................

A fixture that is appropriate for lighting small rooms. Finished in a pretty background of brown tone with all embossed and cast ornaments in highly polished gold color to match other fixtures shown on this page. It is 36 inches long, about 15 inches wide, and made of solid brass. Has two key sockets for electric lights, and frosted fancy glass shades.

Brown Tone and Gold Color
Assembled and wired ready to install.
34A5276½—*As shown*....................

Length to bottom of glassware, 36 inches; width, about 18 inches. Made of solid brass and finished in a pretty background of brown tone, with all embossing and cast ornaments in highly polished gold color. Has three key sockets for electric lights, and is equipped with frosted fancy glass shades. The finish of this fixture is very striking and attractive.

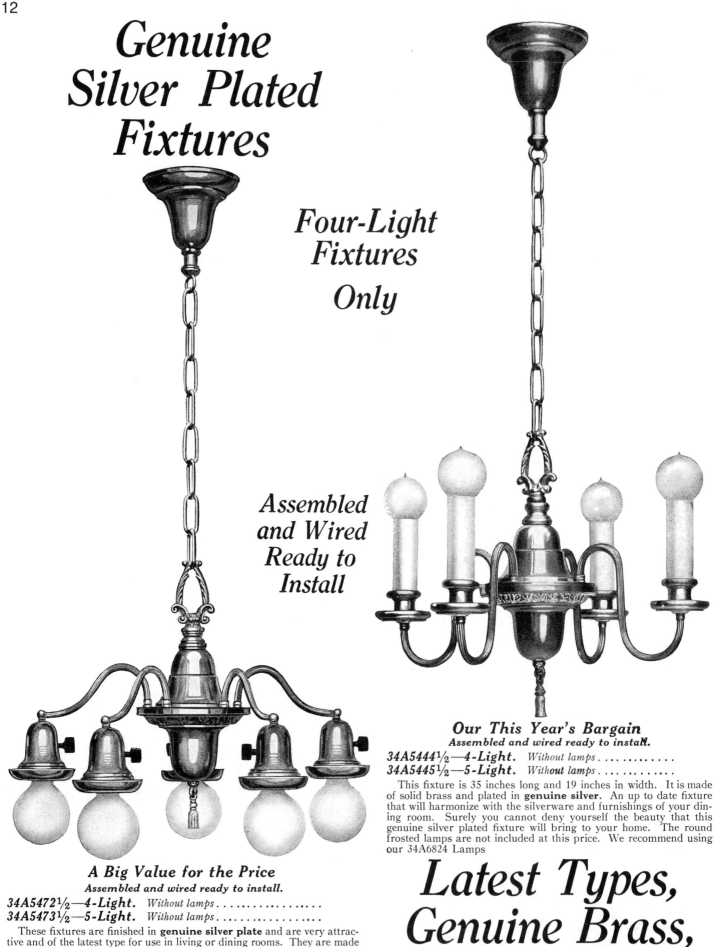

Genuine Silver Plated Fixtures

Four-Light Fixtures Only

Assembled and Wired Ready to Install

Our This Year's Bargain
Assembled and wired ready to install.

34A5444½—4-Light. *Without lamps* . . . .
34A5445½—5-Light. *Without lamps* . . . .

This fixture is 35 inches long and 19 inches in width. It is made of solid brass and plated in **genuine silver.** An up to date fixture that will harmonize with the silverware and furnishings of your dining room. Surely you cannot deny yourself the beauty that this genuine silver plated fixture will bring to your home. The round frosted lamps are not included at this price. We recommend using our 34A6824 Lamps

A Big Value for the Price
Assembled and wired ready to install.

34A5472½—4-Light. *Without lamps* . . . .
34A5473½—5-Light. *Without lamps* . . . .

These fixtures are finished in **genuine silver plate** and are very attractive and of the latest type for use in living or dining rooms. They are made of genuine brass, with an embossed ceiling canopy, bottom body shell and ball lamp covers, and ornamented at bottom with fancy brass ornament and tassel. You can make no mistake in ordering one of these fixtures for your home. The round frosted lamps are not included in the price.

Latest Types, Genuine Brass, Lowest Prices

Velvet Brown and Gold Color Fixtures

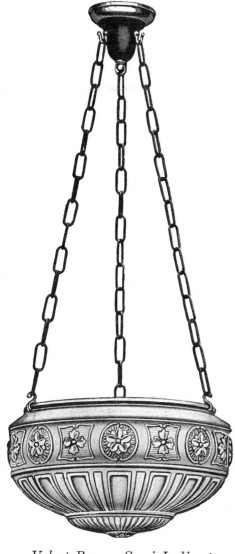

Velvet Brown Semi-Indirect
Assembled and wired ready to install.
34A5596½—As shown......................

The metal parts of this pretty, yet inexpensive semi-indirect fixture are finished in a velvet brown and gold color to match our line of new velvet brown and gold color fixtures shown in this book. The fixture is 36 inches long and made of solid brass. Is fitted with one keyless socket inside of bowl. The bowl is 16 inches in diameter and has a fancy embossed satin finish.

Ball Lamp Side Lights
Assembled and wired ready to install.
34A5592½—As shown.....................

The electric ball lamp fixtures have become very popular. This fixture matches our new line of ball lamp fixtures shown in this book. Length, 36 inches. The finish is a soft velvet brown and gold color. The glass bowl is 15½ inches in diameter, with white satin finish, beautifully etched, and in pale blue wreath and bowknot design. Ball lamps are 3 inches in diameter and are controlled by key sockets. One keyless socket inside of bowl.

Brown Tone and Gold Color
Assembled and wired ready to install.
34A5019½—Without lamps.............

A beautiful bracket with fancy stamped brass back, beautifully embossed in laurel leaf design, finished in brown tone and gold color. From an ornamental center extend two round arms, ⅜ inch in diameter, supporting candle cups and enameled candles fitted with Edison base sockets for electric lamps. The round ball lamps are not included in the price. We recommend our 34A6825 Lamp

For the Dining Room
Assembled and wired ready to install.
34A5781½—As shown................................

You need this fixture for your dining room. The center bowl is 12 inches wide and arranged for one electric light on keyless socket inside. The side lights are controlled by keys on the sockets. The fixture is finished a pretty shade of velvet brown, with all embossed and cast ornaments in highly polished gold color. It is made of solid brass and is 36 inches long; width, about 24 inches at widest part. Fancy frosted glass bowl and side shades tinted a delicate pink color, with garlands of green leaves and pink flowers on a white satin background.

A New and Pretty Light
Assembled and wired ready to install.
34A4810½—As shown..................

Finish is brown tone and gold color. The fancy network band encircles an amber color closed bottom glass shade, with six amber color glass drops hanging below. The amber color light from this fixture has a very pleasing effect. It is about 10 inches long and 7 inches wide and is fitted with one keyless socket.

Silver Plated Colonial Bracket
Assembled and wired ready to install.

34A5038½—*Without lamp*........................

This bracket having very plain lines and without ornamentation is adaptable for many places. It is made of genuine brass and has an oval stamped back, 8 inches long and 4½ inches wide, with cast brass ornament in center. The 7/16-inch gracefully curved arm is fitted with white enamel candle. The round frosted lamps are not included in the price. We recommend our 34A6825 Lamp shown on page 78.

Silver Plated Colonial Bracket
Assembled and wired ready to install.

34A5039½—**2-Light.** *Without lamps*..............

Made of genuine brass in silver plated finish. Extend 6 inches from the wall. Spread, 7½ inches. The stamped oval wall plate is 8 inches long and 4½ inches wide, with a cast ornament in center. Gracefully curved ornamental arms, 7/16 inch in diameter, are fitted with candle holders and white enameled candles, 1¼ inches in diameter. The candles are fitted with Edison base keyless sockets inside of candles. The round frosted lamps shown are not included in the price. We recommend using our 34A6825 Lamp shown on page 78.

Spanish Bronze and Gold Color
Assembled and wired ready to install.

34A5450½—*Without lamps*...........................

Spanish bronze and dull gold color is unlike the finish seen every day. A fixture in this color shows refinement and helps give the room a subdued effect, so much desired in home decorations today. It is 36 inches long and about 20 inches wide. The arms which support the candle lights are made of flat tubing, a distinction that only the highest grade fixtures have. The round lamps shown are not included in the price. We recommend using our 34A6825 Lamp shown on page 78.

Old Ivory and Blue
Assembled and wired ready to install.

34A5212½—*Without lamps*..................

This is a charming fixture which is suitable for the sun parlor, hall or bedroom and is one of the latest types offered. It is finished in old ivory, except the vase shape body and the socket covers which are finished in delicate French blue. The length is 36 inches to bottom of knob and it is about 10 inches wide. The frosted round lamps are not included in the price. We recommend our 34A6825 Lamp shown on page 78.

Old Ivory and Gold Color
Assembled and wired ready to install.

34A5207½—*Without lamps*........

Picture what a charming ceiling piece this is and imagine how it will beautify your home. For the sun parlor, bedroom, hall or living room where center lighting is desired it is ideal. The canopy, urn shape body and top of socket covers are in old ivory finish, while the arms, ball lamp plates and bottom knobs are in gold finish. The length is 12 inches and it is about 10 inches wide. The frosted round lamps are not included in the price. We recommend our 34A6825 Lamp shown on page 78.

Cathedral Glass Hall Lantern
Assembled and wired ready to install.

34A5268½—*As shown*........................

For small sun parlors, dens and halls this lantern is an appropriate piece. It has square link brass chain and fancy cast brass loop. The finish is mahogany color with gilt relief on canopy, fancy loop and tassel at bottom. The lantern measures 8 inches in length, 5½ inches in diameter at widest part and 3¾ inches at bottom and is fitted with amber cathedral glass edges and crackled glass center. Length, about 36 inches.

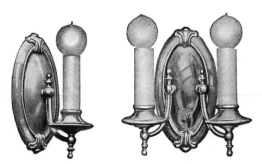

Satin Silver Bracket
Assembled and wired ready to install.

34A5005½—1-Light. *Without lamp* ....
34A5006½—2-Light. *Without lamps* ....

Here is a satin finish silver bracket at a remarkably low price that will attract favorable comment wherever installed. It has a beautifully designed stamped back, spun brass candle cups and turned brass ornaments. The back measures 8½ inches long and 4½ inches wide. Spread, on two-light, about 6 inches. The price does not include lamps. We recommend our 34A6825 Lamps

Silver and Black
Assembled and wired ready to install.

34A5406½—Without lamps ....

This particularly attractive ball lamp piece makes an excellent living room center light. The heavy castings are beautifully embossed and the entire fixture is finished in genuine silver plate with black worked into the embossings. It is 36 inches in length and about 18 inches wide. The frosted round lamps are not included in the price. We recommend our 34A6878 Lamps

Genuine Silver Plated Fixture
Assembled and wired ready to install.
34A5442½—Without lamps ....

You will like this fixture. It is neat and simple, having enough ornamentation to be decorative. It is 36 inches long and about 19 inches wide. The finish is genuine silver in satin effect, called butler silver. It is made of solid brass, and has five lights. The round frosted lamps are not included in the price. We recommend using our 34A6825 Lamps

Tinted Old Ivory Color
Assembled and wired ready to install.

34A4808½—As shown ....

An appropriate and pretty ceiling fixture for hall, sun parlor, vestibule or bedroom. It is 14½ inches long and 7 inches at the widest part. It is made of brass finished in old ivory and decorated with pink, yellow and blue flowers. The color of the shade is slightly iridescent and its lighting effect is wonderful. It is equipped with one keyless socket.

Genuine Silver and Black
Assembled and wired ready to install.

34A5408½—Without lamps ....

We know you will agree with us that a genuine silver plated fixture of such exceptionally good design at this price is a big value. It is 36 inches long and about 19 inches wide. The finish is genuine silver plate with black relief in the castings. This is an exceedingly artistic five-light fixture. The round frosted lamps are not included in the price. We recommend our 34A6825 Lamps

16

Silver and Gold Color
Assembled and wired ready to install.
34A5179½—Without lamp.......

This bracket is rich looking, but not overdone. It matches 34A5177½ and 34A5178½, shown on page 10. It is finished in genuine silver plate and trimmed in gold color, a new style finish that you will like. The 3⅛-inch round frosted lamp shown is not included in the price. We recommend using our 34A6878 Lamp

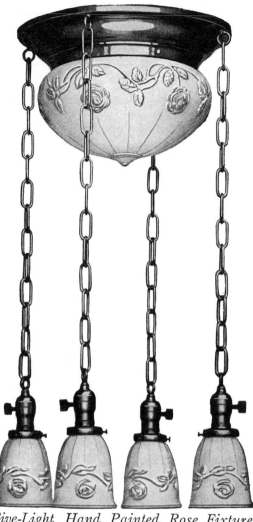

Five-Light Hand Painted Rose Fixture
Assembled and wired ready to install.
34A5728½—As shown................................

The frosted glassware on this fixture has a raised design of hand painted red roses and green leaves, making it a very attractive fixture. Length over all, 36 inches. Large ceiling pan is 14½ inches wide and supports the four outer lights. The fixture is wired with silk covered wire to one keyless socket in glass bowl and four key sockets on side lights. Finish of fixture is satin brass.

Fancy Candle Bracket
Assembled and wired ready to install.
34A5056½—Without lamp......

This is an exceedingly attractive bracket that will look well in any home. We feel sure that you will be more than pleased and agreeably surprised at its appearance. It is made of genuine brass in brush (satin) brass finish and has a round 5-inch back handsomely embossed in bead design. The bracket is wired and fitted with white enameled candle. The price does not include the round lamp. We recommend our 34A6825 Lamp

Three-Light Electric Shower
Assembled and wired ready to install.
34A5771½—As shown......................

Length to bottom of glassware, 36 inches. Diameter of pan, 12 inches. Made of genuine brass in satin brass finish. The ceiling canopy is 5¼ inches wide. From this canopy extend three chains supporting the 12-inch pan. From the edge of the pan hang three lights on link chain connections. Wired with silk cord through the chains to key sockets. The glass shades are fancy and frosted.

Two-Light Electric Candle Bracket
Assembled and wired ready to install.
34A5139½—Without lamps..........

Genuine brass in brush (satin) brass finish. Extends 7½ inches from the wall. Canopy, 6 inches long and 4 inches wide. Has two ⅜-inch gracefully curved arms. Arms are fitted with spun brass bobaches, candle cups and white enameled 1¼-inch candles. Wired and fitted with Edison base keyless sockets inside of candles. The round frosted lamps are not included in the price. We recommend using our 34A6825 Lamps

Four-Light Electric Shower
Assembled and wired ready to install.
34A5775½—As shown......................

Length to bottom of glassware, 36 inches. Diameter of pan, 14 inches. The entire fixture is made of genuine brass and finished in satin brass. Ceiling canopy, 5¼ inches wide, which supports the large pan with the side lights. Wired with silk covered wire and has key sockets. The glassware is fancy and frosted. The plainness of this fixture makes it ideal for most any living or dining room.

Five-Light Electric Ceiling Shower
Assembled and wired ready to install.

34A5755½—*As shown*...........................

Length to bottom of glassware, 10 inches. Made of genuine brass in satin brass finish. Round ceiling pan, 14½ inches in diameter. This pan forms a holder for a 10x12-inch bowl and is fitted for one electric light. There are four lights suspended from the outer edge of the pan. The fixture is wired with silk covered wire to keyless socket. The glassware is satin finish, with raised design of hand colored red roses.

Attractive Ceiling Fixture
Assembled and wired ready to install.

34A5731½—*Without lamps*.....................

A lighting fixture of this type is very ornamental. The five ball lamps cluster so nicely that it really is pleasant to look at. It is made of genuine brass. Length, over all, about 10 inches. The ceiling pan is 14 inches wide. Has five key sockets. Finish of fixture is satin brass. The round frosted lamps shown are not included in the price. We recommend using our 34A6825 Lamps

Three-Light Ceiling Fixture
Assembled and wired ready to install.

34A5759½—*As shown*.....................

The electric fixture is made of solid brass. Length to bottom of glassware, 14 inches. Width of round pan, 12 inches. The fixture is wired with silk covered wire to three key sockets. The glassware is fancy and frosted. Finished in satin brass.

Three-Light Chain Shower
Assembled and wired ready to install.

34A5807½—*As shown*..................

Made of genuine brass. Finished in satin brass. Length to bottom of glassware, 26 inches. Ceiling pan is about 12 inches wide. This pan supports three solid brass chains, to which are attached three key sockets for electric lights. The fixture is wired with silk covered wire and is equipped with fancy frosted design glassware to match other fixtures shown on this page.

Ball Lamp Ceiling Fixture
Assembled and wired ready to install.

34A5219½—*Without lamps*...............

An oval pan with ball lamps makes a very pretty fixture for hallways and bedrooms. This fixture is about 8 inches long, the pan is oval shape and measures 12x6 inches. Entire fixture is made of brass and is finished in satin brass. The round frosted lamps shown are not included in the price. We recommend using our 34A6825 Lamps

Four-Light Electric Ceiling Shower
Assembled and wired ready to install.

34A5741½—*As shown*.....................

Length to bottom of glassware, 10 inches. Made of genuine brass. Round ceiling pan, 14½ inches in diameter. This pan forms a holder for a 10x12-inch glass bowl and is fitted with one electric light. There are three lights suspended from outer edge of the pan. The fixture is wired with silk covered wire to keyless sockets. Finish of the fixture is satin brass. The glassware is satin finish, with raised design of hand painted roses.

Five-Light Ceiling Fixture
Assembled and wired ready to install.

34A5795½—*As shown*........................

An ideal fixture for homes with low ceilings, or wherever a short fixture is desired. The fixture being hung close to the ceiling gives a good distribution of light. It is 16 inches long. The pan is 14 inches wide and is equipped with five key sockets wired with silk covered wire. Glassware is fancy frosted. The entire fixture is made of genuine brass and is finished in satin brass.

Three-Light Ball Lamp Fixture
Assembled and wired ready to install.

34A5724½—*Without lamps*............

A three-light fixture of this type goes very well in small living or dining rooms and is also very appropriate for large reception halls. It is finished in satin brass, made of genuine brass and is about 10 inches long. The pan is 12 inches wide and is fitted with three side lights for round frosted lamps. The electric round lamps are not included in the price. We recommend using our 34A6825 Lamps

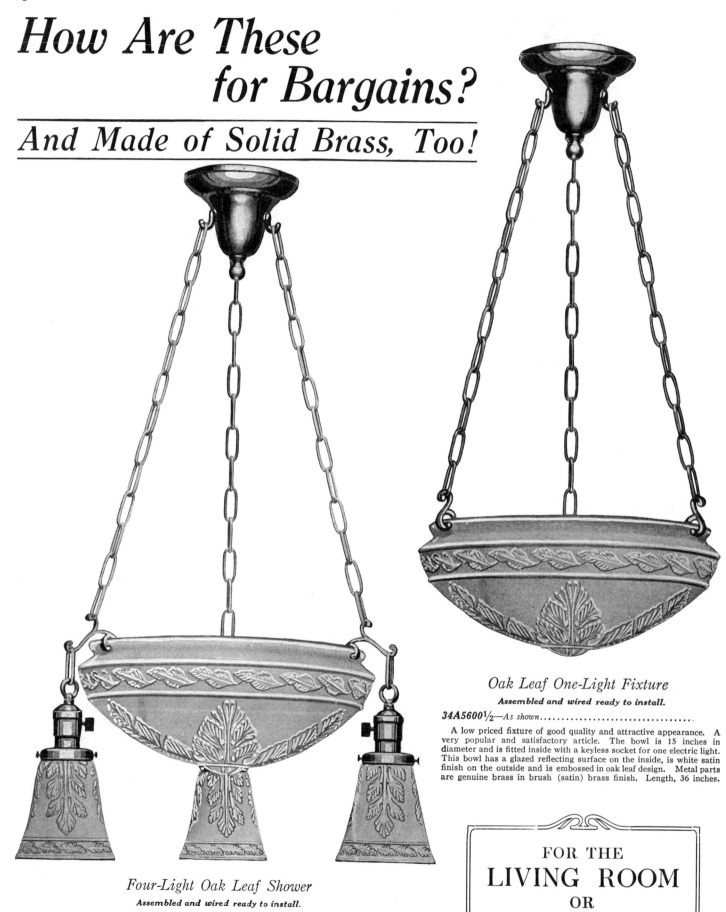

18

How Are These for Bargains?

And Made of Solid Brass, Too!

Four-Light Oak Leaf Shower
Assembled and wired ready to install.

34A5589½—As shown...

This is a low priced fixture of good quality and attractive appearance, very desirable for use in many places where the combination of direct and semi-indirect light is desired. This is an exceedingly popular fixture, and we are sure that it will please you. The glass bowl and side shades are frosted in a soft satin finish and the oak leaf embossing stands out in excellent relief. Inside of the bowl is a keyless socket fitted for one electric light, and each of the side pendants has a key socket for one electric light. Metal parts are made of genuine brass in brush (satin) brass finish. Length, 36 inches. Diameter of bowl, 15 inches.

Oak Leaf One-Light Fixture
Assembled and wired ready to install.

34A5600½—As shown...

A low priced fixture of good quality and attractive appearance. A very popular and satisfactory article. The bowl is 15 inches in diameter and is fitted inside with a keyless socket for one electric light. This bowl has a glazed reflecting surface on the inside, is white satin finish on the outside and is embossed in oak leaf design. Metal parts are genuine brass in brush (satin) brass finish. Length, 36 inches.

FOR THE
LIVING ROOM
OR
DINING ROOM

The Fixtures
on These Two Pages Represent the Best in Their Class at Money Saving Prices

Three-Light Chain Shower
Assembled and wired ready to install.
34A5284½—As shown.........

Large embossed ceiling pan, 12 inches in diameter, supports three electric lights on key sockets. The fixture is 25 inches long and is made of genuine brass, finished in satin brass and shaded with Flemish black on the embossed parts. The glassware is frosted inside and glazed outside and matches other fixtures on this page. The fixture is wired with silk covered wire.

Embossed Oval Shower
Assembled and wired ready to install.
34A5272½—As shown...........

This two-light embossed oval pan fixture is appropriate for halls, bedrooms and all other smaller rooms. It is 36 inches long and has an oval pan measuring 12x6 inches. The canopy is 5¼ inches wide. To the under side of the oval pan are attached two key socket covers for electric lights. Wired with silk covered wire. The glass is semi-fancy and matches other fixtures on this page. Finish is satin brass with Flemish black shading on embossed parts.

An Embossed Shower Fixture
Assembled and wired ready to install.
34A5805½—As shown.........................

Fixture is made of solid brass. It is finished in satin brass and the embossed parts are shaded with Flemish black. It is 36 inches long and about 14 inches across at widest part. The large pan measures 12 inches and supports from the outer edge the three electric lights on key socket covers. Silk covered wire is used to wire the fixture. The glassware is semi-fancy and appropriate.

Four Lights Prettily Arranged
Assembled and wired ready to install.
34A5753½—As shown....................................

The lighting effect of this fixture is prettily arranged, the side lights are suspended from the outer edge and one light in the center of the pan. Length, over all, 36 inches, and about 14 inches wide at widest part. Large pan is 12 inches wide. The entire fixture is made of brass and is finished in satin brass, with the embossed parts in shaded Flemish black. It is wired with silk covered wire to four key socket covers. The glassware is semi-fancy and appropriate.

Oval Pan Fixture
Assembled and wired ready to install.
34A5265½—*As shown* . . . .

This two-light oval pan fixture is adapted for halls, bedrooms and all other smaller rooms. It is 9 inches long and has an oval pan, 12x6 inches. To the under side are attached two key socket covers for electric lights, wired with silk covered wire. The glass matches other fixtures shown on this page. Finish of fixture is satin brass, shaded with Flemish black.

One-Light Embossed Bracket
Assembled and wired ready to install.
34A5013½—*As shown* . . . .

Made of genuine brass and finished in satin brass, shaded with Flemish black. Extends 6 inches from the wall. Is fitted with key socket. Frosted semi-fancy glass shade. Matches all fixtures shown on this and the opposite page, and can be used in any room where a bracket is desired.

Embossed Three-Light Shower
Assembled and wired ready to install.
34A5220½—*As shown* . . . .

Made of genuine brass and finished in satin brass with Flemish black shading on embossed parts. It is 11 inches long and about 14 inches wide at widest part. The ceiling pan is 12 inches wide and supports three side lights with key sockets. Silk covered wire is used. The glass is neat and appropriate.

Round Beam Light
Assembled and wired ready to install.
34A5233½

Without lamp . . . .

Genuine brass in brush (satin) brass and black finish. It has a round canopy, 3¼ inches in diameter, with screw holes for attaching, and a cast brass tulip shape husk and fitted with keyless socket. The round frosted lamp is not included in the price. We recommend using our 34A6825 Lamp shown on page 78.

Square Beam Light
Assembled and wired to install.
34A5234½

Without lamp . . . .

Genuine brass in brush (satin) brass and black finish. The square canopy is 3 inches in diameter, with screw holes for attaching, and has a cast brass tulip shape husk and keyless socket. The round frosted lamp is not included in the price. We recommend using our 34A6825 Lamp shown on page 78.

An Embossed Four-Light Shower
Assembled and wired ready to install.
34A5756½—*As shown* . . . .

The finish of this fixture is satin brass with the embossed parts shaded with Flemish black. Length of fixture is 36 inches. Width, about 15½ inches at widest part. The pan is 14 inches wide. The entire fixture is made of solid brass and is wired to four key socket covers suspended from the outer edge of pan. Silk covered wire.

One-Light Electric Pendant
Assembled and wired ready to install.
34A5246½—*As shown* . . . .

Length to bottom of glassware, 36 inches. Made of genuine brass and finished in satin brass with shaded Flemish black. The canopy is 5¼ inches wide. The fixture is wired with silk covered wire to key socket.

A Neat Four-Light Shower
Assembled and wired ready to install.
34A5723½—*As shown* . . . .

The glassware on this fixture is of a neat design and is snow white in color. Length of fixture is 36 inches and width about 15 inches at widest part. The large pan is 14 inches wide and forms a holder for the 10x11-inch bowl. There are three key socket covers on the side lights and one keyless socket inside of bowl. Entire fixture is made of genuine brass. It is finished in satin brass

Albertive Bronze Color Bracket
Assembled and wired ready to install.
34A5029½—*Without lamp* ....

This bracket resembles in general type and appearance many of the brackets now being offered, but differs in quality and finish. The color of the finish harmonizes with the present day idea of interior decorations and color scheme, and is therefore very popular. The price does not include the ball lamp. We recommend our 34A6825 Lamp

Cream Color Candle Bracket
Assembled and wired ready to install.
34A5040½
Pink tint. *Without lamp* ....
34A5041½
Blue tint. *Without lamp* ....

An unusually attractive bracket with fancy oval stamped back, finished in cream color, with either delicate blue or pink decorations. The back plate measures 8½ inches long and 4½ inches wide, with fancy shaped round tubing arm supporting candle cups and white enameled candle. The round lamp is not included in the price. We recommend our 34A6825 Lamp shown on page 78.

Four-Light Electric Shower
Assembled and wired ready to install.
34A5790½—*As shown*......................

Length to bottom of glassware, 36 inches. Diameter of pan, 14 inches. Made of genuine brass and finished in satin brass. From the edge of the pan extend four electric lights on solid brass chains, wired with silk covered wire to key sockets. The fixture is equipped with four fancy frosted glass shades.

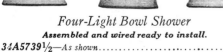

Four-Light Bowl Shower
Assembled and wired ready to install.
34A5739½—*As shown*............................

Made of genuine brass. Finished in satin brass. Length to bottom of glassware, 36 inches. The ceiling canopy is 5¼ inches wide, and supports the large 14½-inch pan which forms a holder for the 10x12-inch glass bowl. There is one keyless socket inside of the glass bowl and three key sockets on the side lights. The glassware is frosted and has a raised design of hand painted red roses and green leaves.

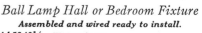

Ball Lamp Hall or Bedroom Fixture
Assembled and wired ready to install.
34A5248½—*Without lamps*...............

A ball lamp fixture of this type looks very appropriate in a hall or bedroom. It is made of genuine brass and is 36 inches long. The canopy is 5¼ inches wide. Oval pan is 12 inches long and 6 inches wide. To the under side of the oval pan are attached two ball lamp key sockets. The fixture is finished in satin brass and is wired with silk covered wire. The round frosted lamps are not included in the price. We recommend using our 34A6825 Lamps shown on page 78.

The Latest Ideas
in
Lighting Equipment

Ivory and Gold Color
Assembled and wired ready to install.

34A5427½—*Without lamps*..........................

This dainty and exceedingly attractive five-light ball lamp ceiling piece is one that you and your friends will admire. Made entirely of brass, finished in gold color, except the vase shape center ornament, which is in ivory color. These colors harmonize with almost any decoration and furnishings. Around the base of the vase shape ornament are five delicately shaped hooks supporting crystal glass drops and at the bottom is a crystal glass bead chain and cut glass ball. Length to bottom of glass ball, 15 inches and width, about 19 inches. The frosted round lamps are not included in the price. We recommend our 34A6878 Lamp

Ivory and Gold Color
Assembled and wired ready to install.

34A5412½—*Without lamps*.............................

This five-light fixture will appeal to the most artistic taste and you will have the satisfaction of knowing that it is the very latest in design. It is an ideal fixture for living room or parlor with high ceiling, where the lights are desired low. It is 36 inches in length and about 20 inches wide. Finished in gold color with vase ornament in ivory finish, ornamented with crystal glass drops and crystal cut glass bottom ball. The frosted round lamps are not included in the price. We recommend our 34A6878 Lamp

HIGH QUALITY GOODS

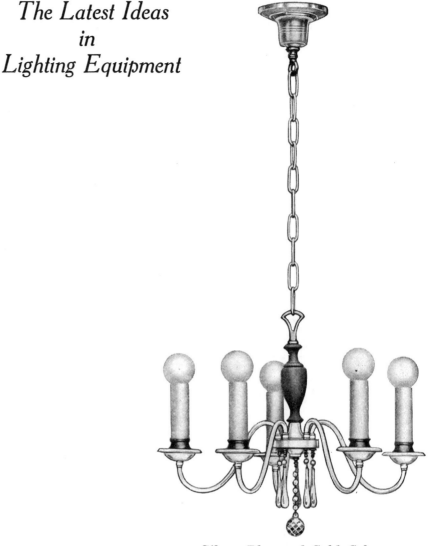

Silver, Blue and Gold Color
Assembled and wired ready to install.

34A5419½—*Without lamps*.............................,

This is an exceedingly attractive ornament and appropriate fixture for the dining room. The simple lines and dainty appearance make it unusually attractive. It is 36 inches in length and about 19½ inches wide. Made of brass in silver plated and gold color with vase shape ornament and five crystal glass drops in turquoise blue, which harmonize beautifully with the silver finish. At the bottom is a crystal cut glass ball on crystal bead chain. The frosted round lamps are not included in the price. We recommend our 34A6825 Lamp

Silver and Blue and Ivory and Gold
Assembled and wired ready to install.

34A5084½—*1-Light.* Ivory and gold color. *Without lamps.*
34A5085½—*2-Light.* Ivory and gold color. *Without lamps.*
34A5088½—*1-Light.* Silver and blue color. *Without lamps.*
34A5089½—*2-Light.* Silver and blue color. *Without lamps.*

These beautiful brackets are finished to match the fixtures on this page. Be particular to select the correct finish. These are high quality goods, the product of a well known factory and are the latest ideas that are being offered this season. The round frosted lamps are not included in the price. We recommend our 34A6825 Lamp

KITCHEN ELECTRIC CEILING FIXTURE

This shapely ceiling fixture for the kitchen produces an even white light and is uniform in performance. The design is along plain lines which enhances the qualities already present in the glass in securing the maximum of good lighting. Wired complete, one light. Fashioned with 4-inch white enameled metal holder with milk colored glass shade. Pull-chain type—cord furnished.

No. 7T/182PC Complete......

THE LEADER LINE

This line presents a real opportunity to refixture your home with a great value. Or you may be considering the installation of electric fixtures in a new home. This line should prove equally as interesting in either instance. Each of the fixtures selected for this offering are well made, of pleasing design and are expertly finished. While they are exceptionally low priced, yet they will render a most satisfactory service and grace the home with charm. All fixtures are wired complete, but, of course, do not include bulbs illustrated. We know that each and every purchaser can effect a most substantial saving if this installation is selected, and that they will be highly pleased with the intrinsic value presented.

FIVE-LIGHT ELECTRIC DROP FIXTURE
For the Dining Room

Here is a most acceptable type of five-light electric drop fixture for the dining room. Note the smartness and general appearance of this pattern, also the exquisite artistry employed in the design. This fixture, like all others from the "Leader Line," maintains high standard in construction, is cleverly executed, masterfully finished and popularly priced. It is modern in every respect and will illuminate the dining room effectively and pleasingly. Length 36 inches. Spread 19½ inches. Wired complete for five drop lights. (Bulbs not included at prices quoted.) Finished attractively in Silver and Black or Bronze Tone. Specify preference when ordering.

No. 7T/6616BS Silver Tone Finish................

No. 7T/6616BB Bronze Tone Finish................

FIVE-CANDLE ELECTRIC FIXTURE
For the Living Room

It is indeed a source of comfort to know that artistry in design can be so cleverly interwoven with a popular price, as it is in the charming living room five-candle electric fixture illustrated above. This pattern is the most popular of all of our "Leader Line" living room fixtures and rightly so, for it embodies first class materials, masterful workmanship, and is nicely finished in the prevailing style. This fixture must really be seen hanging in the living room to be truly appreciated. It is so fashioned that it will illuminate the living room in a most pleasing and correct manner. Length 36 inches. Spread 19½ inches. Wired complete for five-candle lights. (Bulbs not included at price quoted.) Finished artistically in Silver and Black or Bronze Tone. Specify preference when ordering.

No. 7T/6615CS Silver Tone Finish................

No. 7T/6615CB Bronze Tone Finish................

PORCH ELECTRIC CEILING FIXTURE

Everyone knows how convenient it is to press the button and flood the porch with a bright white light so that friends arriving or departing may find their way up and down the stairs without fear of stumbling or falling. Here is an inexpensive fixture that will serve your porch illuminating problem in a most satisfactory way. The metal base which holds the milk colored glass shade is finished in black. Wired complete for one light.

No. 7T/CRI Porch Fixture Complete.......

TWO-LIGHT ELECTRIC CEILING FIXTURE
For the Bed Room

This type fixture is being installed extensively in the bedroom this season. It is especially adapted for this type room and will prove to be a very satisfactory illuminator. It is very cleverly designed and executed as you can very readily see. Only the best of materials and workmanship enter into its construction, assuring you a quality product, regardless of the extremely low price prevailing. Wired complete, two lights. Spread 14 inches. This fixture is pleasingly finished in Ivory Polychrome, the finish which is so popular for bedroom fixtures.

No. 7T/2602 Bedroom Fixture Complete.............

BATHROOM ELECTRIC CEILING FIXTURE

There is no place in the home where proper illumination is more necessary than the bathroom. The master of the house, when taking his morning shave, can appreciate this statement probably more than any other member of the household. It is therefore essential that a satisfactory fixture, such as this one, be installed in the bathroom. The 2¼ inch White Enamel Metal holder suspends the milk colored glass shade furnished. The fixture is the pull chain type and cord is furnished.

No. 7T/784PC Bathroom Fixture
Complete ....

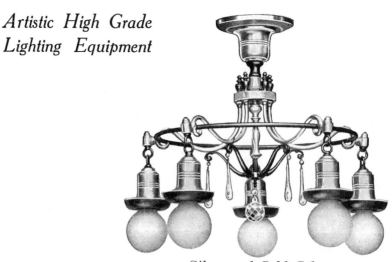

Silver and Gold Color

Assembled and wired ready to install.

34A5421½—*Without lamps*...............................

Made of genuine brass tubing, finished in a beautiful combination of brushed genuine silver and ancient gold color and ornamented with five crystal glass drops and cut glass ball. The length is 16 inches to bottom of lamps and it is about 18 inches in width. The 3⅛-inch frosted round lamps are not included in the price. We recommend our 34A6878 Lamps

Silver and Gold Color

Assembled and wired ready to install.

34A5407½—*Without lamps*..............................

You cannot select a more appropriate candle piece for the dining room than this artistic and exceedingly attractive five-light fixture. The graceful bending of the brass tubing forming the arms and the connecting ring, with delicate center scroll body, forms a most pleasing effect. Finished in genuine brushed silver and antique gold color with six crystal glass drops and cut glass pendant ball. The length is 36 inches to bottom of the glass ball and it is about 18 inches wide. The frosted round lamps are not included in the price. We recommend our 34A6825 Lamps

Silver and Gold Color

Assembled and wired ready to install.

34A5409½—*Without lamps*..............................

There is a touch of refinement and elegance to this fixture which makes it distinctive and compels admiration. It is made of brass tubing finished in a combination of genuine brushed silver and old gold color and trimmed with five crystal glass drops and cut glass ball. The length is 36 inches to bottom of lamps and it is about 18 inches wide. The 3⅛-inch frosted round lamps are not included in the price. We recommend our 34A6878 Lamps

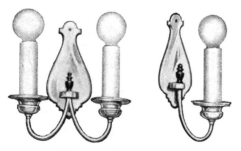

Silver and Gold Color

Assembled and wired ready to install.

34A5080½—*1-Light.* Without lamp..................
34A5081½—*2-Light.* Without lamps..................

These beautiful Georgian period brackets with their simple and delicate design are extremely attractive and unusual. They have a beautifully shaped cast brass wall plate, 3⅜ inches at widest part, with daintily shaped tubing arms and spun candle cups. The entire bracket is finished in dull (satin) silver, except the urn ornament and beading around the candle cups, which are in gold color. The round frosted ball lamps are not included in the price. We recommend our 34A6825 Lamps

ELEGANCE
AND
REFINEMENT

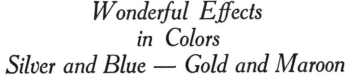

Wonderful Effects
in Colors
Silver and Blue — Gold and Maroon

25

Gold and Maroon Color
Assembled and wired ready to install.

34A5425½—*Without lamps*..............................

A ball lamp fixture hung close to the ceiling is very ornamental and decorative. It is finished entirely in an ancient gold color. In the center is a maroon color vase shape ornament. Slender topaz color glass drops hang gracefully above the arms, and a sparkling crystal glass ball ornaments the bottom. The fixture is about 18 inches long and about 20 inches wide. The 3⅛-inch round frosted lamps shown are not included in the price. We recommend using our 34A6878 Lamps

Silver and Gold Color Fixture
Assembled and wired ready to install.

34A5417½—*Without lamps*..............................

Notice the delicate and graceful makeup of this beautiful electric chandelier. It is made of solid brass, is 36 inches long and about 19 inches wide. It is genuine silver plated and trimmed with gold color. The vase shape ornament in the center is finished in turquoise blue color. Turquoise blue color glass drops and a sparkling glass ball finish the makeup of this beautiful fixture. The round frosted lamps shown are not included in the price. We recommend using our 34A6825 Lamps

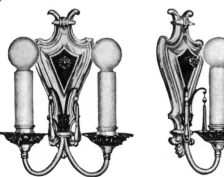

Silver, Blue and Gold Color
Assembled and wired ready to install.

34A5077½—1-Light. *Without lamps*...................
34A5078½—2-Light. *Without lamps*...................

These brackets will command attention and create favorable comment from your friends, and will prove a source of admiration to yourself. The cast brass back is of beautiful design finished in genuine satin silver with center in French blue. The knob, center ornament with holders for the two crystal drops and cast brass candle plates are in ancient gold color. The frosted round lamps are not included in the price. We recommend our 34A6825 Lamps

QUALITY AND BEAUTY

Antique Gold Color
Assembled and wired ready to install.

34A5415½—*Without lamps*..............................

This fixture is very attractive, yet is modest and has that refined appearance that every one looks for in lighting fixtures. It is finished entirely in a color of ancient gold. In the center is a maroon color vase shape ornament. A slender topaz color glass drop hangs gracefully above each arm and a sparkling crystal glass ball ornaments the bottom. Length, about 36 inches. Width, about 20 inches. The 3⅛-inch round frosted lamps shown are not included in the price. We recommend our 34A6878 Lamps

Beautiful Crystal Fixtures

Silver and Blue Fixture
Assembled and wired ready to install.

34A5416½—*Without lamps*.................................

One of the season's most beautiful designs in candle fixtures. From a truly artistic standpoint this fixture is an exception. The graceful contour formed by the dainty metal parts will appeal to the most critical. The entire fixture is finished in genuine satin silver with narrow blue lines on the edges of the shells. Just enough to give it a slight contrast and artistic touch. It is also ornamented with clear crystal glass drops on the candle plates under each candle and on the large center body. The fixture is made of genuine brass and is 36 inches long, with a spread of about 17 inches. Completely wired and fitted with five keyless sockets. The round frosted lamps shown are not included in the price. We recommend using our 34A6825 Lamps

Silver Gray and Gold Color
Assembled and wired ready to install.

34A5452½—*Without lamps*.................................

This is one of the most popular high grade fixtures in our line. Printers' ink can not reproduce the beauty of this beautiful piece of the fixture designers' art. It simply gives you an idea how it will look. It is 36 inches long and is finished in a startling combination of French gray silver, the cast ornaments are in gold color. Gold color glass drops are added to make this a fixture of beauty and refinement. It is about 20 inches wide and is made of solid brass. Completely wired and fitted with five key sockets. The 3⅛-inch round frosted lamps shown are not included in the price. We recommend using our 34A6878 Lamps

Crystal Trimmed Ceiling Light
Assembled and wired ready to install.
34A5241½
Without lamp..........

For the sun parlor, hall or bedroom this is an exceptionally appropriate and beautiful ceiling fixture. The ceiling band measures 5 inches in diameter and the length to bottom of ball lamp is about 8 inches. The finish is antique gold color with touches of red in the indentation around the top. Crystal beads are festooned around the top with crystal drops, at the junction. The 3⅛-inch lamp is not included in the price. We recommend using our 34A6878 lamp

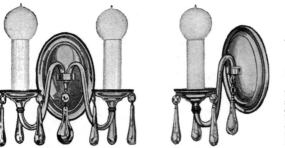

Silver and Blue Candle Brackets
Assembled and wired ready to install.

34A5198½—1-Light. *Without lamp*....................
34A5199½—2-Light. *Without lamps*................

These dainty brackets are finished in genuine silver plate. Decorated with blue around the edges of the shells and ornamented with clear crystal glass drops. These brackets match the large fixture shown above. Extend 6½ inches from the wall. The back plate measures 6x4 inches. The round frosted lamps are not included in the price. We recommend using our 34A6825 Lamps

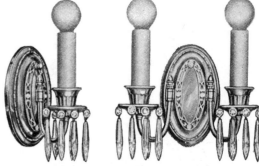

Silver and Black Finish
Assembled and wired ready to install.

34A5168½—1-Light. *Without lamp*....................
34A5169½—2-Light. *Without lamps*....................

These brackets are genuine silver plate, with the embossed parts in black relief. They are made of solid brass and the workmanship is of the highest grade. The back plate is 7½ inches long and 4½ inches wide. Each bracket is equipped with a switch to turn light on or off. The round frosted lamps shown are not included in the price. We recommend our 34A6825 Lamps

Sparkling Effects in Crystal
Silver and Black — Brown and Gold

An Amber Beauty
Assembled and wired ready to install.

34A4806½—*As shown*.......................

One of the daintiest and most appropriate ceiling lights for the hall, sun parlor or small room. It is wonderfully decorative when our 34A6888 Amber Color Lamp is used, giving a beautiful soft light which not only adds materially to the beauty of the surroundings, but is also restful to the eyes. The finish is a rich amber gold color with black relief in the indentations of the 7-inch reflector crown which supports three tiers of 47 amber glass drops and cut glass ball. Length to bottom of glass ball, 13 inches.

Silver and Black
Assembled and wired ready to install.

34A4804½—*As shown*.......................

This beautiful crystal piece will add considerably to the appearance of your hall, sun parlor or any place in the home where used. It fits close to the ceiling and has a reflector crown, 7½ inches in diameter, from which is suspended in three tiers, 75 crystal cut glass prisms and ball. The many colored rays of light reflected by these prisms give a beautiful effect and remarkable diffusion of light. The fixture is finished in silver and black and is 14 inches in length to bottom of glass ball.

A Dining Room Beauty
Assembled and wired ready to install.

34A5462½—*Without lamps*.......................

When as beautiful a fixture as this is installed over the table in your dining room, radiating sparkling light in all directions, cheerfulness is also radiated by the company present. It is finished in silver with black worked into the embossings, making a beautiful contrast and rich appearance. The four side lights are fitted with key sockets and a keyless socket is attached inside of the cut glass bowl. There are 58 cut crystal glass prisms around the edge of bowl. It is 40 inches in length to bottom of lamps and about 22 inches wide. Lamps are not included in the price. We recommend our 34A6825 Lamp shown on page 78.

Amber and Gold Color
Assembled and wired ready to install.

34A4800½—*As shown*.......................

This is a beautiful hall or sun parlor fixture and one with which you will be more than pleased. It is something new and when our 34A6888 amber color lamp is used, produces that much desired soft amber light that is so restful to the eyes. The canopy and body reflector is in amber gold finish and chain and loops in gilt finish. It makes an ideal hall lamp. The fixture is 30 inches long to bottom of glass ball and has a 7-inch body reflector suspending 47 amber glass drops and cut glass ball.

Gold Color and Crystal
Assembled and wired ready to install.

34A5464½—*As shown*.......................

An ideal piece for the reception hall, sun parlor or small living room, or, in case of large rooms, two fixtures, one at each end. The heavy 15-inch cast metal band is beautifully embossed and finished in gold color and from it are suspended about 95 crystal glass prisms and ball. It has a white enameled reflector and two keyless sockets. Length over all is 12 inches.

Amber Glass Lantern
Assembled and wired ready to install.

34A4802½—*As shown*.......................

This type of lantern will look well in any style of a house. It is made of brass and finished in brown tone and gold color. The cylinder is pebbled amber color glass and amber color glass drops hang from the upper edge. It is 28 inches long over all. Lantern is 8½ inches long and 7 inches wide and is equipped for one light on chain pull socket. You will be well pleased, because this really is a beautiful lantern.

Appropriate Fixtures
for
Bedrooms and Halls

One-Light Pendant
**Assembled and wired
ready to install.**

34A5252½—*As shown.*

Made of brass in (satin) brass finish. Length, 36 inches over all. Ceiling canopy, 4½ inches in diameter, with short stem. A solid brass round link chain supports a 4-inch globe holder for one electric light. Wired with silk cord laced through the chain to key socket. Embossed 6x8-inch satin finish glass ball.

One-Light Chain Pendant
Assembled and wired ready to install.
34A4902½—*As shown*..........

Length to bottom of glassware, 36 inches. Genuine brass in brush (satin) brass finish. It has a round ceiling canopy, 4½ inches in diameter, and genuine brass chain and 2¼-inch shade holder. The fancy shaped glass shade measures 6½ inches in diameter and has an open bottom and is embossed at top and around the bottom in classic design. The shade is of white satin finished glass tinted on top and bottom in old ivory color and decorated with scene design on white background. Fitted with key socket.

One-Light Pendant
**Assembled and wired
ready to install.**

34A5253½—*As shown.*

Length to bottom of glassware, 36 inches. Genuine brass in brush (satin) brass finish. Has 4½-inch round ceiling canopy; solid brass round link chain, fitted with 2¼-inch plain socket cover for one electric light. Silk cord laced through the chain to a key socket. Satin finish fancy shade, 6 inches in diameter, embossed in flower and lotus leaf design.

Pink and Old Ivory
Assembled and wired ready to inst~ll
34A4903½—*As shown*..........

Length to bottom of glassware, 36 inches. Made of genuine brass in brush (satin) brass finish. The round ceiling canopy is 4½ inches in diameter which supports the brass chain and 2¼-inch holder for glassware. The open bottom crystal glass shade is very attractive as it is finished in old ivory color with fluted design top and embossed around the bottom in rope, leaf and flower design tinted in pink and green colors. This makes an attractive dresser or bedroom light wired and fitted with key socket for one electric light.

One-Light Chain Pendant
**Assembled and wired
ready to install.**

34A5256½—*As shown*........

Length to bottom of glassware, 36 inches. Made of genuine brass in brush (satin) brass finish. It has a round ceiling canopy, 4½ inches in diameter, with short stem and solid brass link chain for one electric light. Wired with silk cord laced through the chain to a key socket and 2¼-inch shade holder. Fancy frosted glass shade. This pendant can be fitted with special socket with pull chain at an additional charge of 22 cents.

Chain Reflector Pendant
**Assembled and wired
ready to install.**

34A4916½—*As shown*...........,

Length, 36 inches. Genuine brass in brush (satin) brass finish. Ceiling canopy, 4½ inches in diameter, with short stem and solid brass round link chain for one electric light. Wired with silk cord laced through the chain to a key socket and 2¼-inch shade holder. Frosted glass 40 or 60-watt tungsten reflector. This pendant can be equipped with chain pull socket for 22 cents additional.

One-Light Pendant
Assembled and wired ready to install.

34A4904½—*As shown*........

Length to bottom of glassware, 36 inches. Made of genuine brass in brush (satin) brass finish. The round ceiling canopy is 4½ inches in diameter which supports the glass shade, and 2¼-inch shade holder for glassware. It has an open bottom glass shade in crystal white finish ornamented on bottom with embossed flower and leaf design hand tinted pink and green.

Semi-Indirect Ceiling Fixture
Assembled and wired ready to install.
34A4614½—As shown..............

Length to bottom of glassware, 11 inches. Diameter of bowl, 11 inches at widest part. Made of genuine brass in brush (satin) brass finish. Spun brass ceiling canopy, 6 inches in diameter, and three-rod holder. This holder supports a 10x11-inch satin finish glass bowl, hand painted with festoons of pink tea roses and green leaves. The fixture is wired to one keyless socket. It is a pleasing design.

You May Well Be Proud
to Have Your Home
Lighted With Fixtures
Such as These

Semi-Indirect Ceiling Fixture
Assembled and wired ready to install.
34A4612½—As shown.................

Length to bottom of glass bowl, 11 inches. Diameter of bowl, 11 inches at widest part. Made of genuine brass in brush (satin) brass finish. Spun brass ceiling canopy, 6 inches in diameter, and three-rod holder. This holder supports a 10x11-inch frosted glass paneled bowl. The panels are hand decorated with pink rosebuds in their natural colors and latticework design. The fixture is wired to one keyless socket.

One-Light Ceiling Fixture
Assembled and wired ready to install.
34A4608½—As shown................

Length to bottom of glassware, 11 inches. Made of genuine brass in brush (satin) brass and black finish. It has a ceiling band, 7 inches in diameter, embossed in panel and scroll design, with 3¼-inch holder for glassware. The fixture is fitted with porcelain wired separable keyless socket. Frosted glass satin finish fancy paneled ball.

This Bracket Matches the Fixtures Shown on Page 9

A Pretty Bracket
Assembled and wired ready to install.
34A5145½—Silver and blue finish. Without lamps.

A bracket of this type and finish will add the finishing touch to any living, dining or bed room. It comes in two finishes, genuine **silver plate, trimmed in delicate baby blue color** or **velvet brown and gold color,** to match fixtures shown on page 9. It is made of genuine brass. The wall plate measures 8x4 inches and the bracket extends 6 inches from the wall. The ball lamps shown are not included in the price. We recommend our 34A6825 Lamps

34A5142½—Velvet brown and gold color.
Without lamps ....

Either
Velvet Brown and Gold Color
or
Genuine Silver Plate and Blue

One-Light Fancy Ball Ceiling Fixture
Assembled and wired ready to install.
34A4630½—As shown.................

Length to bottom of ball, 8½ inches. Genuine brass in brush (satin) brass and black finish. Ceiling band is 7½ inches in diameter and is beautifully embossed around the edge in laurel wreath design. The fixture is fitted with porcelain wired separable keyless socket. Frosted glass 6-inch ball, Grecian key border, beautifully etched in scroll design.

One-Light Ceiling Fixture
Assembled and wired ready to install.
34A7038½—As shown............

Made of genuine brass in brush (satin) brass finish. Round ceiling band, 10½ inches in diameter at top, with screw holes for attaching to the ceiling. It has a 10-inch removable holder at bottom for glassware which prevents the light showing between the band and the glassware. Wired and fitted with one keyless socket. Frosted glass hemisphere, 10 inches in diameter, decorated with hand painted pink roses and green leaves.

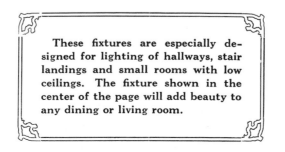

These fixtures are especially designed for lighting of hallways, stair landings and small rooms with low ceilings. The fixture shown in the center of the page will add beauty to any dining or living room.

One-Light Ceiling Fixture
Assembled and wired ready to install.
34A4600½—As shown.............

Length to bottom of glassware, 9 inches. Made of genuine brass in brush (satin) brass finish. It has a spun brass ceiling canopy, 3½ inches in diameter, to which is attached three solid brass round link chains, supporting an 8-inch spun brass band. This band forms a holder for a frosted glass dish, 8 inches in diameter, exquisitely hand painted in rose and pansy design in their natural colors, with sunburst effect at bottom. The fixture is wired to one keyless socket.

Inexpensive Ceiling Showers
Assembled and wired ready to install.

34A5689½—3-Light. *As shown*.......
34A5688½—2-Light..................

Length to bottom of glassware, 13½ inches. Made of genuine brass in brush (satin) brass finish. Round 12-inch pan with a large round beaded center ornament and solid brass short link chains. The design is simple, very artistic and of pleasing appearance. The fixture is wired with silk cord laced through the chains to keyless sockets, fitted with 2¼-inch shade holders. Frosted glass shades with Grecian key border design.

Two-Light Square Ceiling Fixture
Assembled and wired ready to install.

34A5216½—*As shown*..................

Length to bottom of glassware, 14½ inches. Spread, 10 inches. Made of genuine brass in brush (satin) brass finish. It has a square ceiling canopy, 4½ inches in diameter, and square stem, ¾ inch in diameter, with square cast body, from which extend two square arms for electric lights. The fixture is wired with keyless sockets and 2¼-inch brass shade rings. Frosted glass square shades.

Five-Light Ceiling Fixture
Assembled and wired ready to install.

34A5232½—*As shown*..................

Length to bottom of center ball, 13½ inches. Diameter of pan, 15½ inches. Made of genuine brass in brush (satin) brass finish. The large ceiling plate, 15½ inches in diameter, has a plain spun edge with large spun tapered center ornament. Around the edge of pan are attached four 2¼-inch keyless socket covers, and the center ornament is fitted with a 3¼-inch socket cover for electric lights. The fixture is wired with rubber covered wire connecting the keyless sockets.

A Pleasing Design Shower
Assembled and wired ready to install.

34A5761½—*As shown*.........................

Made of genuine brass. Length to bottom of center glassware, 22 inches. The ceiling pan is 14 inches wide. There are three lights suspended from the outer edge of this pan and one in the center which hangs 7 inches lower than the outside lights. This arrangement makes this a very attractive fixture. Glassware is fancy frosted. The fixture is wired with silk covered wire to four key sockets and is finished in satin brass.

Two-Light Spindle Ceiling Fixture
Assembled and wired ready to install.

34A5280½—*As shown*.......................

Length to bottom of glassware, 20 inches. Dimensions of ceiling pan, 14 inches long and 8 inches wide. Made of genuine brass in brush (satin) brass and black finish. The oval ceiling pan is beautifully embossed around the edge in beaded design, with plain oval convex center and cast brass acorn knob. From the ends of the pan are suspended two ornamental spindles supporting 2¼-inch embossed socket covers on solid brass link chain connections for electric lights.

Sheffield Ceiling Showers
Assembled and wired ready to install.

34A5715½—3-Light. *As shown*......
34A5714½—2-Light..................

Length to bottom of glassware, 13½ inches. Made of genuine brass in brush (satin) brass and black finish. Round 12-inch pan with an embossed Sheffield ornament measuring 6½ inches to bottom of knob and embossed Sheffield 2¼-inch keyless socket covers, on solid brass link chains. The fixture is wired with silk cord laced through the chains to keyless sockets for electric lights. Frosted fancy shape floral design glass shades.

Two-Light Round Ceiling Fixture
Assembled and wired ready to install.

34A5215½—*As shown*................

Length to bottom of glassware, 14 inches. Spread, 10 inches. Made of genuine brass in brush (satin) brass finish. Has 4-inch round spun brass canopy with round stem, ⅞ inch in diameter, with a round body ball from which extend two round arms for electric lights. The fixture is wired and fitted with keyless sockets and 2¼-inch brass shade rings. Frosted crystal stripe melon shape glass shades.

Three-Light Electric Ceiling Fixture
Assembled and wired ready to install.

34A4636½—*As shown*..................

Length to bottom of glassware, 12 inches. Spread, 13 inches. Made of genuine brass in brush (satin) brass finish. Spun brass ceiling canopy, 4½ inches in diameter, with short stem, to which is attached an ornamental spindle shape body, 6½ inches long and 5½ inches wide at widest part. From the upper part of this body extend three round tubing arms, ⁷⁄₁₆ inch in diameter, with 2¼-inch keyless socket covers.

Blue and Pink Enameled and Silver Plated Fixtures

Ivory and Crystal
Assembled and wired ready to install.
34A4818½—Without lamps.........................

There are many places in the home where a center ceiling light is required in addition to the side lights and floor lighting. This is an attractive fixture for such purposes. The pan is 12 inches in diameter, fitted with three keyless sockets and finished in ivory color with leaf design applied ornaments. Crystal glass bead chain is draped from three corners with a crystal glass drop at bottom. The ball lamps are not included in the price. We recommend using our 34A6878 Lamps

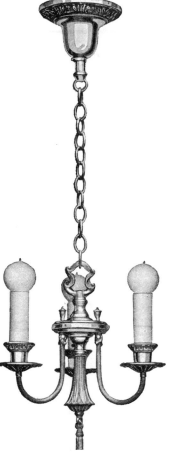

A Little Beauty
Assembled and wired ready to install.
34A5226½—Velvet brown and
gold color...............
34A5214½—Genuine silver
plate with baby blue trim...

This fixture comes in either velvet brown and gold color or genuine **silver plate** tinted in baby blue, to match those two beautiful fixtures shown on page 9. It is made of genuine brass. The fixture is 33 inches long and about 17 inches wide. This is one of the daintiest fixtures in this catalog. The ball lamps shown are not included in the price. We recommend using our 34A6825 Lamps

A Pretty Bracket
Assembled and wired ready to install.
34A5144½—Silver and blue
finish. Without lamp.........
34A5141½—Velvet brown and
gold color. Without lamp.....

A bracket of this type and finish will add the finishing touch to any living, dining or bedroom. It comes in two finishes, genuine **silver plate** trimmed in delicate baby blue color, and velvet brown and gold color, to match fixtures shown on page 9. It is made of genuine brass. The wall plate measures 8x4 inches and the bracket extends 6 inches from the wall. The ball lamp shown is not included in the price. We recommend our 34A6825 Lamps

A Dainty Fixture
Assembled and wired ready to install.
34A5230½— Velvet brown and
gold color................
34A5224½— Genuine silver
plate with baby blue trim...

This fixture comes in either velvet brown and gold color or genuine **silver plate** tinted in baby blue, to match the two beautiful fixtures shown on page 9. It is made of genuine brass. The fixture is 33 inches long and about 17 inches wide. Really this is one of the neatest fixtures in this catalog. The ball lamps are not included in the price. We recommend using our 34A6825 Lamps

Ivory and Blue Enamel
Assembled and wired ready to install.

34A4814½—Without lamps...

You will like this ceiling light, because it is so striking and different. It is made of brass and finished in old ivory and trimmed in a deep blue in a most pleasing combination. It measures at widest part about 12 inches and is about 6 inches long. The round frosted lamps shown are not included in the price. We recommend our 34A6825 Lamps

Ivory and Blue Enamel
Assembled and wired ready to install.
34A4816½

Without lamps............
For cottages, bungalows and small rooms this is an ideal fixture. It is made of brass and finished in old ivory and trimmed with deep blue in such a way that you cannot help but like it at the first glance. It measures in extreme width about 9 inches and is about 5 inches long. The round frosted lamps shown are not included in the price. We recommend our 34A6825 Lamps shown on page 78.

Ornamental Pendant
Assembled and wired ready to install.
34A4962½—As shown.........
Entire length, 26 inches. Genuine brass in brush (satin) brass and black finish. 5-inch ceiling canopy. A ⅜-inch reeded rod supports a 4-inch socket cover for one electric light. Wired with silk cord to a keyless socket. 6x8-inch glass ball, beautifully embossed in old ivory tint with panels in white relief.

One-Light Electric Hall Pendant
Assembled and wired ready to install.
34A4700½—As shown.........
Length, 23 inches; 5-inch canopy. Genuine brass in satin brass finish. Has 8½x9½-inch satin finish glass bowl richly embossed in paneled and floral design, tinted a delicate blue with hand painted sprays of blue and pink forget-me-nots. The fixture is wired to a keyless socket inside of bowl.

Old Ivory and Flowers
Assembled and wired ready to install.
34A4812½—Without lamps..
The entire fixture is in old ivory color and decorated with pink, yellow and blue flowers. You can use this pretty piece in most any room and it is especially adapted for low ceilings. The ceiling pan measures 10 inches in diameter. The 3⅛-inch round lamps shown are not included in the price. We recommend using our 34A6878 Lamps

Ivory Color Glass
Assembled and wired ready to install.

34A7048½—*As shown......*

The illustration cannot do this ceiling piece justice. The ceiling band is 5½ inches in diameter with a 2¼-inch holder for glass. Made of genuine brass in brush (satin) brass finish. The beautifully shaped open bottom glass shade is in ivory color glass in fluted design ornamented around the bottom in embossed design of green leaves and pink flowers. Fitted with a porcelain keyless socket. Height, 8¾ inches.

Etched Ball Ceiling Fixture
Assembled and wired ready to install.

34A4975½—*As shown....................*
Length, 18 inches. Genuine brass in brush (satin) brass finish. Ceiling canopy is 5 inches in diameter. Three solid brass chains, supporting a 4-inch brass holder. Fixture has one keyless socket for electric light. Frosted glass satin finish 8-inch ball, beautifully etched on bottom in lotus flower and panel design.

Decorated Glass
Assembled and wired ready to install.

34A7052½—*As shown......*

A very attractive ceiling piece at a low price. The ceiling band is made of genuine brass in brush (satin) brass finish and measures 5½ inches in diameter at top with a 2¼-inch holder for glass shade. The shade is made of crystal glass in ribbed effect around center with embossed bottom edge of flowers and leaves in pink and green tints between green tint edging. Fitted with porcelain keyless socket. Height, 8 inches.

One-Light Chain Pendant
Assembled and wired ready to install.

34A5283½—*As shown............*

Length to bottom of glassware, 36 inches. Made of genuine brass in brush (satin) brass finish. It has a round ceiling canopy, 4½ inches in diameter, with short stem and solid brass link chain for one electric light. The fixture is wired with silk cord laced through the chain to key socket and has 2¼-inch shade holder. Fancy 5-inch frosted glass ball with beaded crystal ribs. This pendant can be fitted with special socket with pull chain at an additional charge of 17 cents.

Blue Tinted Shade
Assembled and wired ready to install.

34A5255½—*As shown............*

This pendant is very pretty and effective for halls and bedrooms. It has a 6-inch satin finish glass shade, lower part being tinted a sky blue. The upper part is decorated with garlands of purple flowers and green leaves. Made of solid brass, is 36 inches over all, and is finished in satin brass. Has one key socket for electric light.

This pendant can be equipped with a chain pull socket, for turning light on or off by pulling the chain, for an additional 17 cents.

Blue Wreath and Ribbon
Assembled and wired ready to install.

34A5259½—*As shown..............*

This pendant is equipped with an acorn shape shade, decorated with light blue ribbons and wreaths. This fixture blends very nicely with most any surroundings. It is made of solid brass, 36 inches long, and finished in satin brass. Has one key socket for electric light.

This pendant can be equipped with a chain pull socket, for turning light on or off by pulling the chain, for an additional 17 cents.

A New Idea for Dining Rooms
Assembled and wired ready to install.

34A5269½—*As shown....................*

This fixture is made of brass and plated in genuine silver and a slight black relief. It is 46 inches long and is fitted with one chain pull socket. For the average table having a diameter of 52 inches, the distance from the table to the bottom of the glass shade should be 23 inches. A 100-watt lamp gives the desired results. The glass shade is 16 inches wide and beautifully decorated in hand colored leaves on a pretty background of ecru.

Cut Glass Acorn Shape
Assembled and wired ready to install.

34A5257½—*As shown..............*

Just what you want for the reception hall. When lighted the genuine cut glass bowl is very effective. You are attracted by the sharply reflected rays of light that come through the beautiful cutting on the glass bowl. Pendant is made of solid brass, is 36 inches long, and is finished in satin brass. Has one key socket for electric light.

This pendant can be equipped with a chain pull socket, for turning light on or off by pulling the chain, for an additional 17 cents.

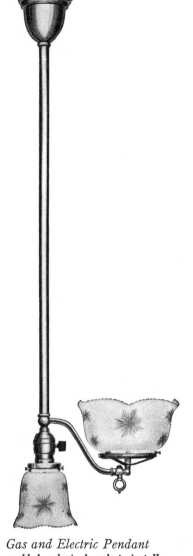

One-Light Electric Hall Fixture
Assembled and wired ready to install.
34A4960½—*As shown*.....................·

Made of brass in brush (satin) brass and black finish. Length, 36 inches. Has 4½-inch round ceiling canopy, and solid brass chains. Glass bowl, 12 inches long and 9 inches in diameter. Is beautifully embossed in artistic panel design with fancy rosette at bottom in an old ivory tint and panels in white relief. The fixture is wired with silk cord to one keyless socket inside of bowl.

Gas and Electric Pendant
Assembled and wired ready to install.
34A3205½—*As shown*...................

One electric light and one gas light. Length, over all, 36 inches. Genuine brass in brush (satin) brass finish. 4½-inch ceiling canopy and ¾-inch stem. Has 2¼-inch electric ring, 4-inch gas ring and pillar gas burner. Fancy pressed crystal glass shades in fancy design.

Art Glass Lantern
Assembled and wired ready to install.
34A5291½—*As shown*...................

Length to bottom of glassware, 36 inches. Made of genuine brass in brush (satin) brass finish. It has a 4½-inch ceiling canopy with short stem. From this stem is suspended a solid brass chain supporting a square cut-out brass frame, 7 inches high and 5¼ inches at bottom, with green art glass sides. The fixture is wired with silk cord to a chain pull socket.

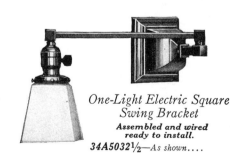

One-Light Electric Round Swing Bracket
Assembled and wired ready to install.
34A5030½—*As shown*....

This bracket has an arm that can be swung to either side, making it possible to direct the light in any position desired. It is very handy above beds for reading, above medicine cabinets, for shaving, etc. It is also very useful in places where there is not much room, as in back of a door. Made of genuine brass in brush (satin) brass finish. Extends 16 inches. It has a plain round wall canopy, 4½ inches in diameter and 2½ inches deep, from which extends a ⅝-inch stem and ball swing fitting. From this fitting extends a ⅜-inch tubing arm with ball knob at end for electric light. The bracket is wired with a key socket and 2¼-inch shade holder. Frosted glass bell shape shade.

Two-Light Straight Arm Bracket
Assembled and wired ready to install.
34A5018½—*As shown*...................

Genuine brass in brush (satin) brass finish. Extends 6 inches from the wall. Spread, 7½ inches. It has a plain round wall canopy, 4½ inches in diameter and 3½ inches deep, and arms ¾ inch in diameter with turned center and end fittings for two electric lights. The bracket is wired to key sockets and has 2¼-inch shade holders. Frosted glass plain shades. Can be hung with lights up or down.

One-Light Electric Square Swing Bracket
Assembled and wired ready to install.
34A5032½—*As shown*....

The light on this bracket is movable from side to side and is a great help in the sewing room, above the work bench and wherever it is not desirable to have the light stationary. When the light is not in use it can be pushed back against the wall and out of the way. Is made of genuine brass in brush (satin) brass finish. Extends 16 inches from the wall. It has a plain square wall canopy, 3 inches in diameter and 1¼ inches deep, from which extends a square stem ⅝ inch in diameter with square swing fitting. From this fitting extends a square tubing arm ⅜ inch in diameter with square cast arm and nipple for electric light. The bracket is wired, with key socket and 2¼-inch shade holder. Frosted glass square shade.

One-Light Angle Bracket
Assembled and wired ready to install.
34A5015½—As shown..........

Made of genuine brass in brush (satin) brass finish. Extends 12 inches from the wall. It has a plain round canopy, 4½ inches in diameter and 3¼ inches deep. The arm is ¾ inch in diameter with turned end ball and angle nipple. The bracket is wired and fitted with a key socket for one electric light, and has 2¼-inch shade holder. Frosted glass shade.

One-Light Straight Arm Bracket
Assembled and wired ready to install.
34A5016½

As shown............

Genuine brass in brush (satin) brass finish. Extends 6 inches. It has a plain round wall canopy, 4½ inches in diameter and 3½ inches deep, with arm ¾ inch in diameter with turned end fitting for one electric light. The wired bracket has a key socket and 2¼-inch shade holder. Frosted glass plain shade. Can be used with light up or down.

Electric Candle Bracket
Assembled and wired ready to install.
34A5138½

Without lamp..........

Genuine brass in (satin) brass finish. Extends 7½ inches. Wall canopy, 6 inches long and 4 inches wide. White enameled candle, 1¼ inches in diameter. Wired and fitted with Edison base keyless socket inside of candle. The round frosted lamp is not included in the price. Use our 34A6825 Lamp

Select a Dome for the Dining Room

Two-Light Art Glass Dome Light
Assembled and wired ready to install.
34A8577½—As shown...

Length to bottom of dome, 54 inches. Shade, 21 inches in diameter across corners. Genuine brass ceiling canopy, 4½ inches in diameter, and solid brass round link chain in brush (satin) brass finish. Six-panel metal overlaid dome, 21 inches in diameter across corners, fitted with amber color art glass and border panels with sunset color glass, overlaid with metal in scroll and leaf design. Wired with silk cord laced through the chain, fitted for two electric lights with chain pull sockets inside of dome.

One-Light Wicker Dome Fixture
Assembled and wired ready to install.
34A8567½—As shown...

Length to bottom of shade, 54 inches. Diameter of shade, 25 inches. This fixture is made of wicker in fumed oak finish. It has a round wicker ceiling canopy, 8½ inches in diameter, with cast brass loop at bottom. To this loop is attached a fancy reed link chain supporting a 25-inch wicker dome. This dome is lined with flowered cretonne in red rose and leaf design. The fixture is wired with cord laced through the reed chain to one key socket for one electric light inside of dome.

One-Light Square Mission Bracket
Assembled and wired ready to install.
34A5050½—As shown..........

Genuine brass in brush (satin) brass finish. Extends 6 inches from the wall. It has a square wall canopy, 4½ inches in diameter, from which extends a square arm, ¾ inch in diameter, fitted for one electric light. The wired bracket has key socket and 2¼-inch shade holder. Frosted glass square shade. Can be used with light up or down.

One-Light Electric Bracket
Assembled and wired ready to install.
34A5001½—As shown..........

Made of genuine brass in brush (satin) brass finish. Extends 12 inches. Canopy, 3 inches in diameter and 1¼ inches deep, from which extends a ⅜-inch tubing arm for electric light. Has key socket and 2¼-inch shade holder. Crystal glass fancy design shade.

One-Light Electric Bracket
Assembled and wired ready to install.
34A5004½—As shown..........

Made of genuine brass in brush (satin) brass finish. Extends 14 inches from the wall. It has a wall canopy, 4½ inches in diameter and 3½ inches deep, with ⅜-inch arm for electric light. The bracket is wired to key socket and has 2¼-inch shade holder. Crystal glass fancy design shade.

One-Light Curved Arm Bracket
Assembled and wired ready to install.
34A5002½—As shown..........

Genuine brass in brush (satin) brass finish. Extends 6 inches. It has a wall canopy, 4 inches in diameter and 3 inches deep, with ⅜-inch arm fitted with a key socket and 2¼-inch shade holder for one electric light. Crystal glass shade in fancy design.

Cut Glass Ceiling Fixture
**Assembled and wired
ready to install.**

34A4982½—*As shown*......

Length over all, 8¼ inches. Genuine brass in brush (satin) brass and black finish. Ceiling pan is 6½ inches in diameter, embossed in reed and ribbon design, and forms a 3¼-inch holder for glassware. Has one porcelain separable keyless socket wired for one electric light. Frosted genuine cut glass 8-inch ball in sunburst design.

One-Light Ceiling Fixture
**Assembled and wired
ready to install.**

34A7020½—*As shown*......

Length to bottom of glassware, 6½ inches. Made of genuine brass in brush (satin) brass finish. Has 5¼-inch ceiling band and 2¼-inch holder for glassware. The fixture is fitted with a porcelain separable keyless socket and is wired for one electric light. Frosted glass tungsten reflector, 6 inches in diameter, for 25-watt lamp.

One-Light Ball Ceiling Light
**Assembled and wired
ready to install.**

34A7011½—*As shown*......

Length to bottom of glass ball, 7 inches. Metal parts made of genuine brass in brush (satin) brass finish. It has a ceiling band which measures 6¼ inches across the top and extending at bottom to form a 3¼-inch holder for glassware. The fixture is fitted complete with porcelain base keyless socket and has frosted glass 6-inch ball.

Fancy Ball Ceiling Light
**Assembled and wired
ready to install.**

34A7023½—*As shown*........

Length to bottom of glassware, 10¾ inches. Made of genuine brass in brush (satin) brass finish. The ceiling band measures 5¼ inches in diameter at top, with a 3¼-inch holder at bottom for glassware. Fitted with wired porcelain separable keyless socket for one electric light. Frosted glass 8-inch ball artistically ornamented with clear beaded ribs.

Chain Pull Light
**Assembled and wired
ready to install.**

34A7043½—*As shown*......

Length to bottom of glassware, 9 inches. Made of genuine brass in brush (satin) brass finish. Has round plain design ceiling band, 5¼ inches in diameter at top, with a 3¼-inch holder for glassware. Wired and fitted with brass chain pull socket for one electric light. Frosted glass 6-inch ball.

Fancy Ceiling Light
**Assembled and wired
ready to install.**

34A7021½—*As shown*......

Length to bottom of glassware, 7½ inches. Made of genuine brass in brush (satin) brass finish. The ceiling band is 5¼ inches at top, with a 2¼-inch holder for glassware. Fixture is equipped with porcelain separable keyless socket wired for one electric light. Frosted prismatic shade with deep crystal mitered ribs.

Chain Pull Light
**Assembled and wired
ready to install.**

34A7045½—*As shown*........

Length to bottom of glassware, 7¼ inches. Made of genuine brass in brush (satin) brass finish. It has a round ceiling band, 5¼ inches in diameter at top, with a 2¼-inch holder for glassware. The fixture is wired and fitted with brass chain pull socket for one electric light. Frosted glass reflector for 25-watt lamp.

Ball Ceiling Light
**Assembled and wired
ready to install.**

34A7022½—*As shown*......

Length to bottom of glassware, 9 inches. Made of genuine brass in brush (satin) brass finish. It has a round ceiling band, 5¼ inches in diameter at top, with a 3¼-inch holder for glassware. Fitted with porcelain separable keyless socket and wired for one electric light. Frosted glass 6-inch ball.

Fluted Design Ceiling Fixture
**Assembled and wired
ready to install.**

34A4980½—*As shown*......

Length over all, 11¼ inches. Genuine brass in brush (satin) brass and black finish. Ceiling band is 7½ inches in diameter. It is beautifully embossed around the edge and it extends to form a 3¼-inch holder for glassware. Has porcelain wired separable keyless socket for one electric light. Frosted glass, satin finish, fancy paneled ball.

Two-Light Art Glass Electric Dome Light
Assembled and wired ready to install.

34A8580½—*As shown*...................

Length to bottom of dome, 54 inches. Shade, 20 inches in diameter across corners. Genuine brass ceiling canopy, 4½ inches in diameter, and solid brass round link chain in brush (satin) brass finish. Six-panel metal overlaid dome, 20 inches in diameter, fitted with amber color art glass and border panels with sunset color glass, making a beautiful glass color combination. The dome is overlaid with cut-out metal in landscape design. The fixture is wired with silk cord laced through the chain and is fitted for two electric lights with chain pull sockets inside of dome.

Plain Ball Ceiling Light
**Assembled and wired
ready to install.**

34A7024½—*As shown*.....

Length to bottom of glassware, 13 inches. Made of genuine brass in brush (satin) brass finish. The ceiling band is extra large and deep and is of plain design. It measures 7 inches in diameter at top, with a 4-inch holder at bottom for glassware. Fitted with wired porcelain separable keyless socket for one electric light. Frosted 8-inch ball.

One-Light Ceiling Fixture
Assembled and wired ready to install.

34A7034½—*As shown*...........

Length to bottom of glassware, 6¾ inches. Genuine brass in brush (satin) brass finish. Ceiling band measures 5¼ inches in diameter at top and forms a 2¼-inch holder at bottom for glassware. Fixture is fitted with a wired porcelain separable keyless socket for one electric light. Pressed clear glass, light radiating, prismatic reflector for 60-watt lamp.

Two-Light Oval Ceiling Fixture
Assembled and wired ready to install.

34A5499½—*Without lamps*.....

Length, 6 inches. Dimensions of oval pan, 8 inches long and 4¾ inches wide. Genuine brass in brush (satin) brass finish. Two Colonial spun brass husks are attached to outer edge. Wired and fitted with two keyless sockets. The round frosted lamps are not included in the price. We recommend using our 34A6825 Lamps

One-Light Pendant

Assembled and wired ready to install.

34A4913½

As shown . . . .

Length to bottom of glassware, 16 inches. Made of genuine brass in brush (satin) brass finish. The round ceiling canopy is 4½ inches in diameter with ¾-inch stem which supports the glass shade. This open bottom shade is of crystal glass of old ivory color with fluted pattern top and embossed around bottom rope, flower and leaf design tinted in pink and green colors. The fixture is wired and fitted with keyless socket.

One-Light Ceiling Pendant

Assembled and wired ready to install.

34A4910½

As shown . . . .

Length to bottom of glassware, 17 inches. Made of genuine brass in brush (satin) brass finish. It has a round ceiling canopy, 4½ inches in diameter with ¾-inch stem, link chain connection and 2¼-inch brass shade holder. The fixture is wired with silk cord and fitted with a keyless socket for one electric light. Frosted glass, open bottom, 5-inch electric shade.

One-Light Ceiling Pendant

Assembled and wired ready to install.

34A4909½

As shown . . . .

Length to bottom of glassware, 17¼ inches. Made of genuine brass in brush (satin) brass finish. It has a round ceiling canopy, 4½ inches in diameter, and ¾-inch stem, link chain connection and 2¼-inch brass shade ring. The fixture is wired with silk cord and fitted with a keyless socket for one electric light. Frosted glass tungsten reflector for 25-watt lamp.

One-Light Pendant

Assembled and wired ready to install.

34A4911½

As shown . . . .

Length to bottom of glassware, 18 inches. Made of genuine brass in brush (satin) brass finish. It has a round canopy, 4½ inches in diameter, and ¾-inch stem. It has an open bottom glass shade of unusually pretty design in crystal white finish ornamented on bottom, with embossed flower and leaf design hand tinted in pink and green. The fixture is wired and fitted with keyless socket.

One-Light Pendant

Assembled and wired ready to install.

34A4908½

As shown . . . .

Length to bottom of glassware, 16¼ inches. Made of genuine brass in brush (satin) brass finish. It has a round ceiling canopy, 4½ inches in diameter and short stem ¾ inch in diameter. The fixture is wired with silk cord to keyless socket and has 2¼-inch brass shade holder. Frosted glass clear crystal ribbed shade.

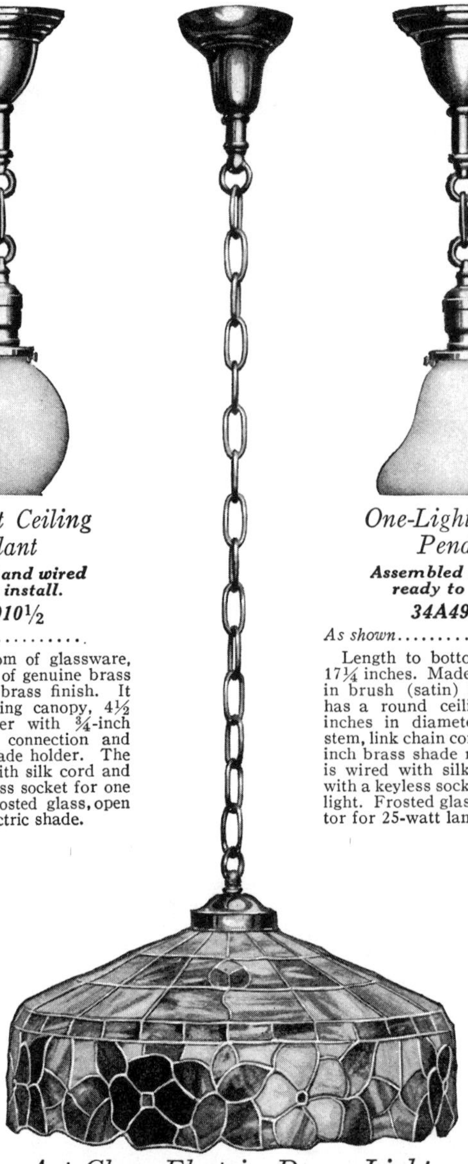

Art Glass Electric Dome Light
Assembled and wired ready to install.

34A8552½—*As shown* . . . .

Length, 48 inches. Shade, 18 inches in diameter. Solid brass chain, ceiling canopy and dome cap in brush (satin) brass finish. The leaded mosaic art glass shade is composed of approximately 195 pieces of amber-green, pink and ruby color art glass in wild rose and leaf design. The leading between the individual pieces of art glass is gilded. Fitted for two electric lights with key sockets inside dome.

Round Tungsten Ceiling Pendant

Assembled and wired ready to install.

34A7554½

As shown . . . .

Length to bottom of glassware, 15½ inches. Made of genuine brass in brush (satin) brass finish. It has a ceiling canopy, 5 inches in diameter, and ⅞-inch round stem. This stem supports a 2¼-inch plain round socket cover on link connection. The fixture is wired with silk cord and fitted with a keyless socket for one electric light. Frosted glass 40 to 60-watt tungsten reflector.

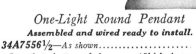

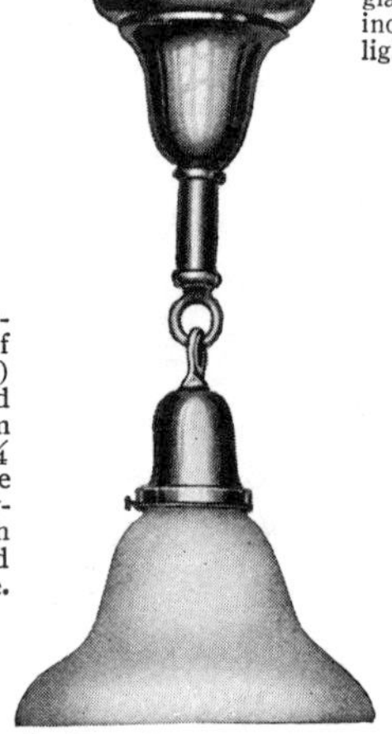

One-Light Round Pendant
Assembled and wired ready to install.

34A7556½—*As shown* . . . .

Length to bottom of glassware, 15½ inches. Made of genuine brass in brush (satin) brass finish. It has a ceiling canopy, 5 inches in diameter and 4 inches deep, with stem ⅞ inch in diameter. This stem supports a 2¼-inch plain round socket cover on link connection for one electric light. The fixture is wired with silk cord to keyless socket. Frosted glass 100-watt tungsten reflector.

One-Light Ceiling Fixture
Assembled and wired ready to install.

34A4625½—*As shown* . . . .

Length to bottom of glassware, 13½ inches. Genuine brass in brush (satin) brass finish. Has 5-inch ceiling canopy beautifully embossed in fancy design and fitted with short stem. From this stem is suspended a 2¼-inch socket cover, embossed in fancy design, on solid brass loop connection. The fixture is wired and fitted with a keyless socket for one electric light. Satin finish fancy fluted shade.

One-Light Ceiling Pendant
Assembled and wired ready to install.

34A4905½—*As shown* . . . .

Length to bottom of glassware, 16½ inches. Made of genuine brass in brush (satin) brass finish. It has a ceiling canopy, 5 inches in diameter, and ⅞-inch stem. From the stem is suspended a 2¼-inch socket cover on link chain connection. The fixture is wired with silk cord laced through the links and fitted with a keyless socket for one electric light. Furnished complete with light radiating prismatic tungsten reflector for 60-watt lamp.

One-Light Electric Ceiling Fixture
Assembled and wired ready to install.

34A4628½—*As shown* ....

Length, 8½ inches. Made of genuine brass in brush (satin) brass finish. Round spun brass ceiling pan, 15½ inches in diameter, which forms a 12-inch holder for glassware and is fitted for one electric light with keyless socket. Satin finish glass bowl, 14 inches in diameter at widest part, embossed in panel and classic fluted design.

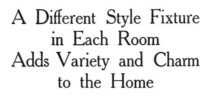

A Different Style Fixture
in Each Room
Adds Variety and Charm
to the Home

One-Light Electric Ceiling Fixture
Assembled and wired ready to install.
34A4626½—*As shown* ....

Length to bottom of glass bowl, 7 inches. Made of genuine brass in brush (satin) brass finish. Spun brass ceiling pan, 13½ inches in diameter, which forms a 10-inch holder for glassware and is fitted for one electric light with keyless socket. Frosted Colonial glass bowl, 12 inches in diameter at widest part, etched in grape and vine design.

One-Light Ceiling Fixture
Assembled and wired ready to install.
34A7040½—*As shown* ....

Length to bottom of glassware, 9 inches. Made of genuine brass in brush (satin) brass finish. It has a large ceiling canopy, measuring 7¼ inches in diameter, with plain spun extended center which forms a 4-inch holder for glassware. A very appropriate fixture for halls, etc. Design is simple and artistic, and it is a very efficient lighting unit. The fixture is fitted with a porcelain separable keyless socket and an 8-inch frosted glass squat ball.

A Beautiful Bracket
Assembled and wired ready to install.

34A5143½—*Silver and blue finish. Without lamp.*

This bracket comes either in *velvet brown and gold color,* or genuine **silver plate, tinted in baby blue,** to match the two beautiful fixtures shown on page 9. It is made of genuine brass. The wall plate measures 8x4 inches and the bracket extends 5 inches from the wall. The ball lamp shown is not included in the price. We recommend using our 34A6825 Lamp shown on page 78.

34A5140½—*Velvet brown and gold color.*
Without lamp ....

**Either
Velvet Brown and Gold Color
or
Genuine Silver Plate and Blue**

One-Light Ceiling Fixture
Assembled and wired ready to install.
34A5244½—*As shown* ....

Length to bottom of glassware, 10 inches. Genuine brass in brush (satin) brass and black finish. It has a brass ceiling pan, 6½ inches in diameter, with edge embossed in reed and ribbon design and plain spun extended center that forms a 3¼-inch holder for glassware. Complete fixture is fitted with porcelain separable keyless socket and 6-inch fancy Grecian border design frosted glass ball with clear crystal stripes.

A Ceiling Beauty
Assembled and wired ready to install.
34A4977½—*Complete as shown* ......

This is undoubtedly one of the most attractive ceiling fixtures that are being offered. It makes an ideal hall or bedroom light, but can be used in other places as well. Genuine brass ceiling band and finished in old ivory, 7 inches at top with 4-inch holder for glassware. The 9-inch glass ball is finished in mottled old ivory color with the side band in opal, handsomely hand decorated in orange and pink flowers with green leaves. Length, over all, 10¼ inches.

We can equip the ceiling fixtures shown on this page with a pull chain switch, which will operate the light on or off inside of glass bowl, for 75 cents additional to the price of each fixture.

One-Light Ceiling Fixture
Assembled and wired ready to install.
34A4610½—*As shown* ....

Length to bottom of glassware, 16 inches. Made of genuine brass in brush (satin) brass and black finish. It has a round ceiling canopy, 5 inches in diameter, with applied cast ornaments. To this canopy is attached a cast socket cover (husk) for one electric light. Wired and fitted with keyless socket and 3¼-inch shade holder. Satin finish fluted glass ball, 8 inches deep, embossed in lotus leaf and floral design.

We Recommend These Two *Attractive Companion Fixtures*

For Your

Living Room *and* Dining Room

Genuine Silver and Blue Finish

Velvet Brown and Gold Color

Genuine Silver and Blue Finish

Velvet Brown and Gold Color

A Magnificent Candle Fixture
Assembled and wired ready to install.

34A5438½—Silver and blue finish. *Without lamps*....................

If you have any desire to install new lighting fixtures, or are building your new home, don't hesitate to purchase this fixture for your dining room and its companion at the left for the living room. They are two of the prettiest fixtures we show in this catalog. This fixture, like its companion, is finished in genuine **silver plate** and the embossed parts are slightly tinted in a faint tracing of baby blue, a combination of colors that you will admire. The fixture is 36 inches long and about 17 inches wide. The ball lamps shown are not included in the price. We recommend using our 34A6825 Lamps

34A5439½—Velvet brown and gold color. *Without lamps*................

A Beautiful Cluster of Lights
Assembled and wired ready to install.

34A5440½—Silver and blue finish. *Without lamps*.........................

It is almost impossible in this small space to tell you of the beauty of this fixture. You can see the design from the picture, but to admire its wonderful finish you should see the fixture itself. It is finished in genuine **silver plate,** and the embossed parts are slightly tinted in a faint tracing of baby blue, a combination of colors that you will admire. The fixture is 36 inches long and about 17 inches wide. The ball lamps shown are not included in the price. We recommend using our 34A6825 Lamps

34A5764½—Velvet brown and gold color. *Without lamps*...................

Silver and Gold Color
Assembled and wired ready to install.

34A5177½—1-Light. Without lamp.......................
34A5178½—2-Light. Without lamps.......................

It is really surprising what a beautiful and striking finish is obtained with genuine silver plate trimmed in gold color. These brackets are rich looking, yet not so fancy as to be overdone. The back plate measures about 4½ inches wide and 9 inches long. Width between lamps, 7 inches. Extends from wall, about 6 inches. The ball lamp shown is not included in the price. We recommend using our 34A6825 Lamps

Mahogany and Gold Finish Fixture
Assembled and wired ready to install.

34A5802½—Without lamps...................................
This is truly a magnificent fixture. All of the plain parts are finished in a color closely resembling mahogany. The massive cast arms and ornaments are in burnished gold finish. The contrast of these two beautiful finishes makes this a fixture worthy of admiration. It is 36 inches long, with a spread of about 18 inches. Made of genuine brass. All ornaments are massive cast brass and are skillfully chased. Fixture is wired complete to five keyless sockets. Ball lamps not included. We recommend our 34A6878 Lamp

Hexagonal Hall Lantern
Assembled and wired ready to install.

34A5270½—As shown.
Nearly every home needs a light in the front hall and a lantern is exceptionally appropriate. This type will look well and is appropriate for any style of house. The lantern measures 15 inches in length and is 8 inches in diameter at widest part. It is fitted with clear crackled glass, ornamented at the top with spun brass crown and fancy loop and at bottom with leaf design plate and tassel. The fixture is finished in mahogany and gilt color, and is equipped with keyless socket. Length, about 36 inches.

Spanish Bronze and Bright Gold Color
Assembled and wired ready to install.

34A5460½—Without lamps.........................,
Spanish bronze and bright gold color is a finish that will appeal to those who desire refinement and subdued effect such as are so popular today. The fixture is 36 inches long and about 17 inches wide. It is made of solid brass. It has a beautiful vase shaped brass ornament mounted in between the arms. This vase is made from a flat piece of sheet brass and hand shaped in a swiftly revolving machine. The round frosted lamps shown are not included in the price. We recommend our 34A6878 Lamp

Ball Lamp Ceiling Cluster
Assembled and wired ready to install.

34A5243½—Without lamps...................................
An exceedingly attractive centerpiece for living room, dining room or large sun parlor. The ceiling plate is 5½ inches in diameter and has an embossed beaded edge. The cast brass bottom plate is beautifully chased in lattice, leaf and lotus flower design, with fancy metal tassel at bottom. The fixture is finished in ancient gold color, with lotus flowers and tassel in ancient polychrome colors. Round frosted 3⅛-inch lamps are recommended, but are not included in the price. We recommend our 34A6878 Lamp

Weatherproof Iron Porch and Outdoor Fixtures

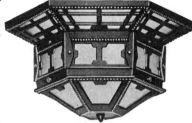

One-Light Electric Ceiling Lantern
Assembled and wired ready to install.

34A7069½—*As shown* . . . .

Made of iron in dead black finish. Ornamental hexagon lantern, 7½ inches long and 13½ inches in diameter across top, with closed bottom. Cut-out metal sides form the lantern frame, which is fitted with frosted pebbled glass panels. The fixture is wired to a porcelain keyless socket for one electric light.

One-Light Square Electric Bracket
Assembled and wired ready to install.

34A7076½—*As shown* . . . . .

Extends 7 inches. Made of wrought iron in dead black finish. It has a 5-inch square canopy and arm, ¾ inch in diameter, with fancy ornamental cast bottom and 3¼-inch globe holder at top with fitting for one electric light. The fixture is wired to a porcelain keyless socket. Frosted glass 6-inch ball.

One-Light Electric Lantern Bracket
Assembled and wired ready to install.
34A7079½

As shown . . . .

Made of cast iron in dead black finish. Extends 11 inches. It has a square wall canopy, 5 inches in diameter, and square arm, 1¼ inches in diameter, with square end terminating in a round bottom ball. This arm supports a cast iron ornamental hexagon lantern, 10 inches long and 6 inches wide, with cast iron closed top and knob. Fitted with frosted cathedral glass panels under a cast metal open framework in artistic design. The fixture is wired to a porcelain keyless socket.

One-Light Electric Ceiling Fixture
Assembled and wired ready to install.

34A7081½—*As shown* . . . .

Length to bottom of fixture, 8 inches. Made of cast iron in dead black finish. It has a hexagon ceiling plate, 13 inches across corners, with extended hexagon ornamental paneled body with closed bottom. The panels in the body are fitted with frosted cathedral glass under a cast metal open framework in artistic design. The fixture is wired to a porcelain keyless socket for one electric light.

One-Light Electric Bracket
Assembled and wired ready to install.

34A7013½—*As shown* . . . .

Extends 9 inches. Made of wrought iron in dead black finish. It has a wall plate, 4⅞x9⅛ inches, with egg and dart border. From this plate extends a massive cast arm with 3¼-inch globe holder with fitting for one electric light. The fixture is wired to a porcelain keyless socket. Frosted glass 6-inch ball.

Iron Porch Lantern
Assembled and wired ready to install.

34A7061½—*As shown* . . . ,

This bracket is to be attached to the side wall, most generally alongside of the entrance door. Lantern swings on hinges, so that electric bulb can easily be inserted. Height, 12 inches. Extends 4½ inches. Made of sheet iron and finished in black. Fitted with frosted cathedral glass panels under a cast metal open framework in window design. The fixture is wired to a porcelain keyless socket.

One-Light Electric Lantern Pendant
Assembled and wired ready to install.

34A7083½—*As shown* . . . .

Length to bottom of lantern, 30 inches. Made of cast iron in dead black finish. It has a hexagon ceiling canopy, 5½ inches in diameter, with short stem and iron chain. The chain supports a cast iron ornamental paneled hexagon lantern, 8½x6 inches, fitted with frosted cathedral glass, under a cast iron open framework in artistic design. The fixture has porcelain keyless socket for one electric light.

One-Light Electric Wall Lantern
Assembled and wired to install.
34A7067½

As shown . . . .

Made of iron in dead black finish. Extends 5 inches from the wall. Ornamental wall lantern, 12 inches in length over all and 8 inches wide, with cut-out metal sides fitted with frosted pebbled glass panels. The fixture is wired to a porcelain keyless socket for one electric light.

One-Light Electric Fancy Ceiling Light
Assembled and wired ready to install.

34A7018½—*As shown* . . .

Length to bottom of glassware, 7¼ inches. Cast iron ceiling band in dead black finish. Diameter at ceiling, 6 inches with 3¼-inch fitter for glassware. Complete with porcelain keyless socket. Frosted glass ball with panels outlined in black. Mission style.

One-Light Electric Wall Lantern
Assembled and wired ready to install.
34A7093½

As shown . . . .

Made of iron in dead black finish. Extends 7¾ inches from the wall. Wall plate, 13 inches long and 4½ inches wide, closed top and bottom. This lantern measures 13 inches in length and 6 inches in diameter across the top. Has frosted pebbled glass panels. The fixture is wired to a porcelain keyless socket for one electric light.

Pantry, Closet and Outdoor Electric Fixtures

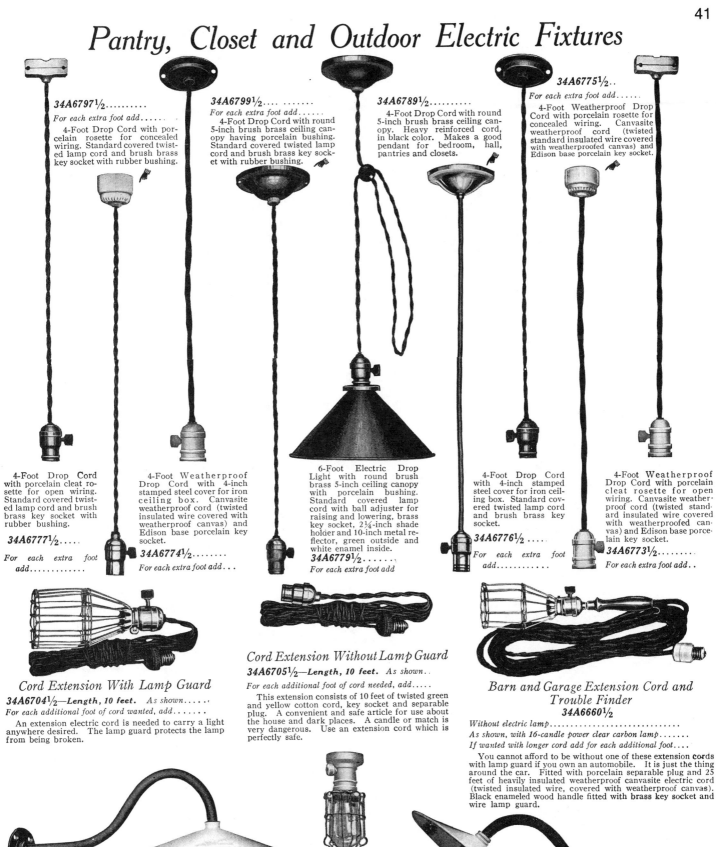

34A6797½..........
For each extra foot add......
4-Foot Drop Cord with porcelain rosette for concealed wiring. Standard covered twisted lamp cord and brush brass key socket with rubber bushing.

34A6799½.... ....
For each extra foot add......
4-Foot Drop Cord with round 5-inch brush brass ceiling canopy having porcelain bushing. Standard covered twisted lamp cord and brush brass key socket with rubber bushing.

34A6789½..........
4-Foot Drop Cord with round 5-inch brush brass ceiling canopy. Heavy reinforced cord, in black color. Makes a good pendant for bedroom, hall, pantries and closets.

34A6775½..
For each extra foot add.....
4-Foot Weatherproof Drop Cord with porcelain rosette for concealed wiring. Canvasite weatherproof cord (twisted standard insulated wire covered with weatherproofed canvas) and Edison base porcelain key socket.

4-Foot Drop Cord with porcelain cleat rosette for open wiring. Standard covered twisted lamp cord and brush brass key socket with rubber bushing.
34A6777½.....
For each extra foot add............

4-Foot Weatherproof Drop Cord with 4-inch stamped steel cover for iron ceiling box. Canvasite weatherproof cord (twisted insulated wire covered with weatherproof canvas) and Edison base porcelain key socket.
34A6774½........
For each extra foot add...

6-Foot Electric Drop Light with round brush brass 5-inch ceiling canopy with porcelain bushing. Standard covered lamp cord with ball adjuster for raising and lowering, brass key socket, 2¼-inch shade holder and 10-inch metal reflector, green outside and white enamel inside.
34A6779½......
For each extra foot add

4-Foot Drop Cord with 4-inch stamped steel cover for iron ceiling box. Standard covered twisted lamp cord and brush brass key socket.
34A6776½.....
For each extra foot add............

4-Foot Weatherproof Drop Cord with porcelain cleat rosette for open wiring. Canvasite weatherproof cord (twisted standard insulated wire covered with canvas) and Edison base porcelain key socket.
34A6773½........
For each extra foot add..

Cord Extension With Lamp Guard
34A6704½—Length, 10 feet. *As shown.....*
For each additional foot of cord wanted, add.......
   An extension electric cord is needed to carry a light anywhere desired. The lamp guard protects the lamp from being broken.

Cord Extension Without Lamp Guard
34A6705½—Length, 10 feet. *As shown..*
For each additional foot of cord needed, add.....
   This extension consists of 10 feet of twisted green and yellow cotton cord, key socket and separable plug. A convenient and safe article for use about the house and dark places. A candle or match is very dangerous. Use an extension cord which is perfectly safe.

Barn and Garage Extension Cord and Trouble Finder
34A6660½
Without electric lamp..............................
As shown, with 16-candle power clear carbon lamp.......
If wanted with longer cord add for each additional foot....
   You cannot afford to be without one of these extension cords with lamp guard if you own an automobile. It is just the thing around the car. Fitted with porcelain separable plug and 25 feet of heavily insulated weatherproof canvasite electric cord (twisted insulated wire, covered with weatherproof canvas). Black enameled wood handle fitted with brass key socket and wire lamp guard.

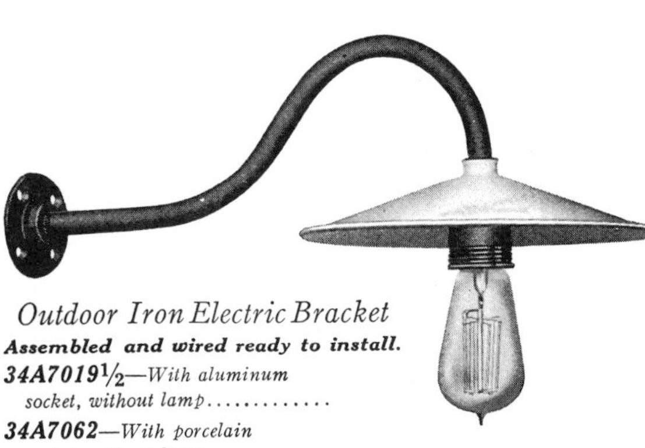

Outdoor Iron Electric Bracket
Assembled and wired ready to install.
34A7019½—With aluminum socket, without lamp............
34A7062—With porcelain socket, without lamp.............
   For street lighting, entrances to barns, garages and outbuildings, and homes where the entrance to the cellar is from the outside. Made of iron in dead black finish. Extends 20¾ inches. Has ⅝-inch round arm, 16 inches long. Light is directly downward. Fitted with 10-inch enameled steel reflector. Fixture is equipped with weatherproof socket, either aluminum or porcelain. The lamp shown is not included in the price.

Porcelain Key Ceiling Light
Assembled ready to install.
34A6751½
Less lamp...........
   Made of porcelain. Can be used as a bracket or ceiling light in the garage, cellar or in damp places, etc., to be used with concealed knob and tube wiring. Porcelain key wall socket fitted with wire lamp guard, but without tungsten lamp.

Outdoor Iron Electric Bracket
Assembled and wired ready to install.
34A7085½—With aluminum socket, without lamp..................
34A7059—With porcelain socket, without lamp...................
   Put this weatherproof bracket above the entrance to the garage, barn or on any post or tree for yard lighting. The light is thrown at an angle, giving light to a large area. Made of iron in dead black finish. Extends 22½ inches. Has ⅝-inch round arm. Has 10-inch enameled steel reflector. Fixture is equipped with weatherproof socket, either aluminum or porcelain. The lamp is not included in the price.

Lighting for Stores, Halls and Public Buildings

One-Light Ceiling Fixture
Assembled and wired ready to install.

34A4535½—*As shown*.....................

Length to bottom of glass bowl, 13 inches. Ceiling band made of genuine brass in brush (satin) brass finish. This band measures 5¼ inches in diameter at top and forms a 2¼-inch holder at bottom for glassware. Fitted with a wired porcelain separable keyless socket for one electric light. Opal glass ribbed reflector, 11 inches in diameter and 4¼ inches deep, with lower bowl, 6 inches in diameter and 5 inches deep.

Store Lighting Fixture
Assembled and wired ready to install.

34A5261½—*As shown*.....................

Length to bottom of glass ball, 36 inches. Metal parts are finished satin brass. It has a spun brass ceiling canopy, 5 inches in diameter. The ventilated holder supporting the glass ball is 6 inches in diameter. This glass ball is fitted with one porcelain keyless socket for electric light. It is frosted inside and glazed outside. This gives it a very strong reflecting power. The glass ball is 14 inches wide and is adapted to the use of nitrogen lamps up to 200 watts.

34A5260½—*As shown*.....................

Same as above, except that glass ball measures 11 inches in width and takes up to 150-watt lamp.

Notice!
The Most Popular Store Lighting Fixtures are shown on this page

---

Store Lighting Fixture
Assembled and wired ready to install.

34A4927½—*As shown*.....................

Length to bottom of glass bowl, 36 inches. Metal parts are finished satin brass. It has a spun brass ceiling canopy, 5 inches in diameter. The ventilated holder supporting the glass ball is 6 inches in diameter. This glass ball is fitted with one porcelain keyless socket for electric light. It is glazed both inside and outside. This gives it a very strong reflecting power. The glass ball is 14 inches wide and is adapted to the use of nitrogen lamps up to 200 watts.

One-Light Electric Ceiling Fixture
Assembled and wired ready to install.

34A4626½—*As shown*.....................

Length to bottom of glass bowl, 7 inches. Made of genuine brass in brush (satin) brass finish. Spun brass ceiling pan, 13½ inches in diameter, which forms a 10-inch holder for glassware and is fitted for one electric light with keyless socket. Frosted Colonial glass bowl, 11¾ inches in diameter at widest part, etched in grape and vine design.

Ceiling Light
Assembled and wired ready to install.

34A4623½—*As shown*.....................

Length to bottom of glass bowl, 10 inches. Width of glass, 12 inches. The fixture is finished in satin brass and measures 7¼ inches at top and is equipped with one keyless socket. The glass ball is glazed both inside and outside. This gives it a very strong reflecting power.

Genuine Brascolite Fixture
Assembled and wired ready to install.

Catalog No.	Size Lamp to Be Used, Watts	Pan, Inches	Bowl, Inches	Without Lamp
34A4563½	100-200	14	8¼	....

The ceiling pan (or reflector) is made of steel, heavily coated with white enamel. From this pan extend three hooks and adjustable rods. These rods support a heavy pressed light radiating glass bowl, which can easily be regulated to give the correct reflection according to size of lamp used; also allows the bowl to be detached for cleaning or inserting new lamp.

Adjustable Lamps

Electric Adjustable Desk Lamp

34A8029 —*As shown*........

Made of metal in statuary bronze finish. Fancy metal base, 5½ inches wide and 7 inches long, embossed in flower and leaf design. Flexible arm which permits placing the light in any position and at any angle. Wired complete, with key socket, 6 feet of cord, plug and metal shade, aluminum lined. Shipping weight, 7 pounds.

Electric Adjustable Desk Lamp

34A8409½ —*Without lamp*..................

Height as illustrated, 15 inches. Genuine brass in brush (satin) brass finish. At the top of the stem is a cast adjustable ball. Adjustable brass shade lined with white enamel. Fitted with chain pull socket and 6 feet of cord. For round frosted lamp see 34A6825
Shipping weight, 10 pounds.

Electric Adjustable Desk Lamp

34A8412½ —*As shown*..........

Genuine brass in brush (satin) brass finish. Base, 5½ inches in diameter, is weighted to prevent upsetting. Stem, ¾ inch in diameter, fitted with flexible brass arm which permits placing the light in any position and at any angle. Wired complete, with key socket, 6 feet of cord and revolving sleeve plug. Metal shade, aluminum lined. Shipping weight, 10 pounds.

Reading Lamps

Electric Adjustable Desk Lamp

34A8025 —*As shown*...........

Made of metal in statuary bronze finish. Base, 5 inches in diameter, embossed in lotus leaf design. Stem, ¾ inch in diameter and 4 inches long, with adjustable fitting at top for raising and lowering lights to position desired. Wired complete, with 6 feet of cord, plug, key socket and metal shade, aluminum lined. Shipping weight, 6 pounds.

Electric Adjustable Desk Lamp

34A8415½ —*As shown*..........

Height from bottom of base to top of rod when upright, 16 inches. Made of genuine brass in brush (satin) brass finish. Stem is ⅜ inch in diameter and 13 inches long. At each end is an adjustment and thumbscrew for regulating to any position. Wired complete, with 6 feet of cord, plug, key socket and metal shade, aluminum lined. Shipping weight, 8 pounds.

Electric Reading Lamp

34A8441 —*As shown*..

Height to top of shade as shown, 50 inches. Statuary bronze and green relief. Ornamental base, 8 inches in diameter. Stem, 1 inch in diameter, with flexible arm which permits the light to be thrown at any angle desired. Wired complete, with 7 feet of cord, plug, key socket and 6¾-inch shade, aluminum lined. Shipping weight, 25 pounds.

Electric Reading Lamp

34A8435 —*As shown*...

Genuine brass in brush (satin) brass finish. Height, 50 inches. Can be raised 11 inches. Cast iron base, 9½ inches, and ¾-inch telescoping brass stem with flexible brass arm, which permits the light to be thrown at any angle desired. Spun brass 12-inch adjustable tray and smoking set. Complete with 6 feet of cord and plug. Shipping weight, 25 pounds.

Expertly constructed of extra weight and richly finished in the new attractive finishes, so popular at the present day. Enhance surroundings in your home by refixturing this season with these up-to-date artistic designs, which are priced extremely low in this display.

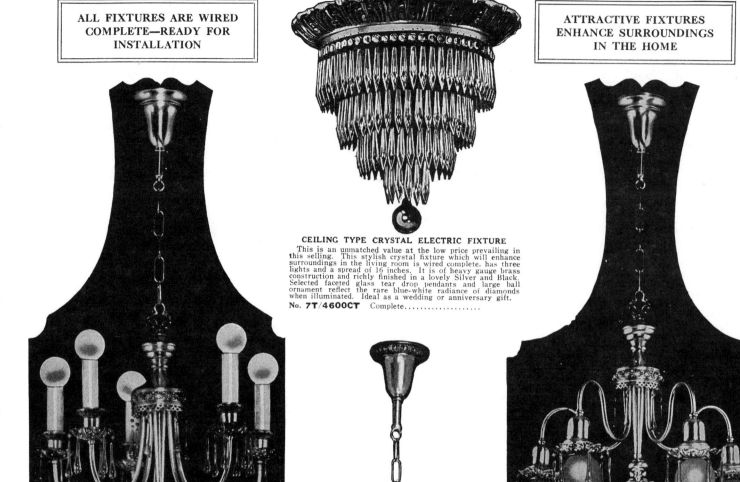

CEILING TYPE CRYSTAL ELECTRIC FIXTURE

This is an unmatched value at the low price prevailing in this selling. This stylish crystal fixture which will enhance surroundings in the living room is wired complete, has three lights and a spread of 16 inches. It is of heavy gauge brass construction and richly finished in a lovely Silver and Black. Selected faceted glass tear drop pendants and large ball ornament reflect the rare blue-white radiance of diamonds when illuminated. Ideal as a wedding or anniversary gift.

No. **7T/4600CT** Complete...................

"SHERWOOD DE LUXE" FIVE-CANDLE ELECTRIC FIXTURE

The masterful artistry manifested in the magnificent creation portrayed above is of such an unsurpassed degree that this splendid fixture is suitable for the finest of homes, even though the price is very moderate in this display. Length, 36 inches. Spread 20 inches. Wired complete and has five-candle lights which are very effective. Exquisitely finished in your choice of Silver and Black or Gold and Black, which specify when ordering. The fixture is delicate in character, yet sufficiently large to suit the average room.

No. **7T/7800C** Complete (Specify Finish)..............

"SHERWOOD DE LUXE" FIVE LIGHT DROP FIXTURE

For richness and beauty of design this clever five-light fixture one of this season's superb creations. Exclusive and unusual striking in appearance, made by skilled hands with infinite ca it will radiate its splendor in the well appointed home in a m gratifying manner. Note the graceful faceted glass tear drops wh are used so effectively and the smart lines and delicate colo spinnings, each of which are so pleasing to the eye. Length inches. Spread 21½ inches. Finished in Silver and Black or G and Black.

No. **7T/7800B** Complete (Specify Finish)............

TWO LIGHT ELECTRIC WALL BRACKET

These electric wall brackets provide a lighting scheme and a decorative theme which is considered vogue in every well appointed home. This bracket covers a 4-inch box. It is richly finished with choice of Silver Tone or Bronze Tone. Priced low and nicely finished throughout.

No.	Finish
7T/2402/S	Silver Tone
7T/2402/B	Bronze Tone

CRYSTAL ELECTRIC FIXTURE

Especially designed for the dining room. A sturdily constructed three-light fixture, measuring 36 inches long. Spread 16 inches. Wired complete. Exquisitely finished in a lovely Silver and Black. Attractively embossed frame. Complete with selected faceted glass tear drop pendants and large ball ornament. The factory price is remarkably low in this selling.

No. **7T/4600D** Complete...................

TWO LIGHT ELECTRIC WALL BRACKET

This is a very high quality wall bracket of attracti design which is nicely made and finished throughout. Fe tured with a MIRROR center which enhances its appearan Richly finished in Silver and Black. Covers a 4-inch b Drilled for crystals (requiring six crystals for each cand stick, which can be furnished at a nominal expense). Pri very moderately.

No. **7T/7205** Complete...................

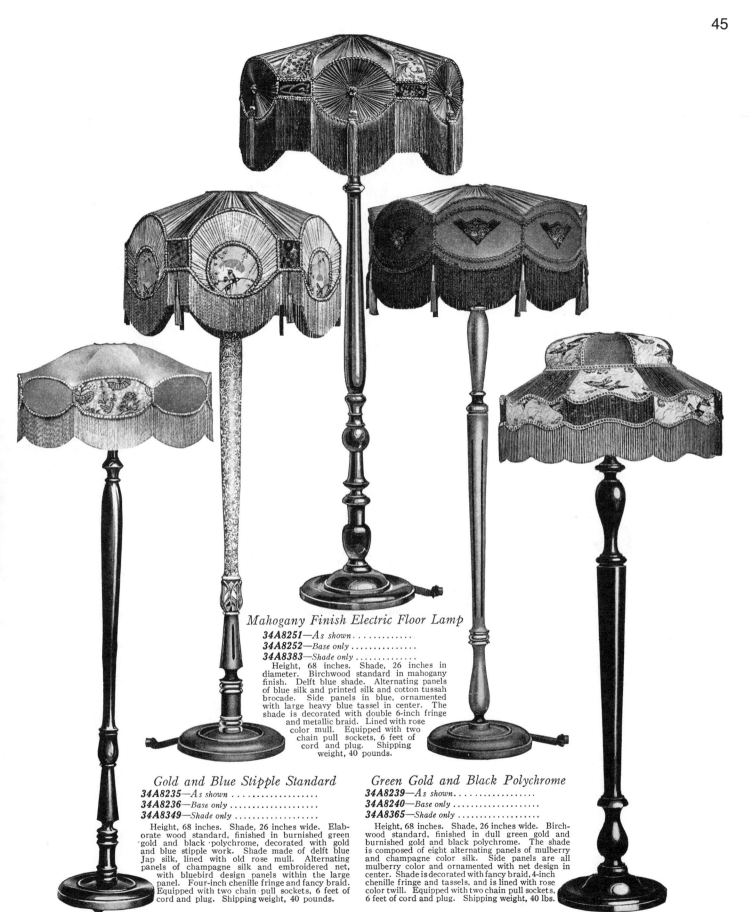

Mahogany Finish Electric Floor Lamp

34A8251—*As shown* . . . .
34A8252—*Base only* . . . .
34A8383—*Shade only* . . . .
Height, 68 inches. Shade, 26 inches in diameter. Birchwood standard in mahogany finish. Delft blue shade. Alternating panels of blue silk and printed silk and cotton tussah brocade. Side panels in blue, ornamented with large heavy blue tassel in center. The shade is decorated with double 6-inch fringe and metallic braid. Lined with rose color mull. Equipped with two chain pull sockets, 6 feet of cord and plug. Shipping weight, 40 pounds.

Gold and Blue Stipple Standard

34A8235—*As shown* . . . .
34A8236—*Base only* . . . .
34A8365—*Shade only* . . . .
Height, 68 inches. Shade, 26 inches wide. Elaborate wood standard, finished in burnished green gold and black polychrome, decorated with gold and blue stipple work. Shade made of delft blue Jap silk, lined with old rose mull. Alternating panels of champagne silk and embroidered net, with bluebird design panels within the large panel. Four-inch chenille fringe and fancy braid. Equipped with two chain pull sockets, 6 feet of cord and plug. Shipping weight, 40 pounds.

Green Gold and Black Polychrome

34A8239—*As shown* . . . .
34A8240—*Base only* . . . .
34A8365—*Shade only* . . . .
Height, 68 inches. Shade, 26 inches wide. Birchwood standard, finished in dull green gold and burnished gold and black polychrome. The shade is composed of eight alternating panels of mulberry and champagne color silk. Side panels are all mulberry color and ornamented with net design in center. Shade is decorated with fancy braid, 4-inch chenille fringe and tassels, and is lined with rose color twill. Equipped with two chain pull sockets, 6 feet of cord and plug. Shipping weight, 40 lbs.

Mahogany Finish Floor Lamp

34A8710—*As shown* . . . .
34A8711—*Base only* . . . .
34A8328—*Shade only* . . . .
Height, 68 inches. Width of shade, 24 inches. Birchwood standard, mahogany finish. Top of shade, delft blue Japanese silk with rose colored lining of sateen. Alternating curtain panels of delft blue Japanese silk and figured silk and cotton tussah brocade. Fancy metallic braid and 4-inch blue chenille fringe. Equipped with two chain pull sockets, 6-foot cord and plug. Shipping weight, complete, 35 pounds.

Mahogany Finish Floor Lamp

34A8706—*As shown* . . . .
34A8707—*Base only* . . . .
34A8325—*Shade only* . . . .
Height, 67 inches. Fancy round shade, 27 inches wide. Birchwood standard in mahogany finish. The top and sides of the shade are made of alternating panels of rose color Jap silk and printed brocaded silk and cotton tussah in bluebird design. Inside lining is silk and cotton rose color mull. Fringe is artificial silk chenille, 3½ inches long. The braid is cotton yarn with heavy metallic thread. Equipped with 6-foot cord and plug and two chain pull sockets. Shipping weight, complete, 40 pounds.

46

Wicker Electric Portable

34A8068—As shown . . . .
Fumed oak, mahogany or old ivory finish. (*State finish desired.*) Height, 18 inches. 13½-inch shade with fancy figured cretonne lining. Has pull socket for one electric light, 6 feet of cord and plug. Shipping weight, 8 pounds.

Three-Light Wicker Fixture
Assembled and wired ready to install.

34A5650½—As shown . . . .
Semi-indirect wicker fixture in fumed oak finish. 7-inch ceiling canopy. Has fancy reed link chains supporting a 19-inch wicker basket, fitted with a frosted glass bowl at the bottom. Wicker portion is lined with flowered cretonne. The light coming through the cretonne produces a very pleasing effect in a living room or sun parlor. The fixture is wired to three keyless sockets for electric lights inside of bowl. Length over all, 32 inches.

Handmade Wicker Fixtures

Wicker fixtures are particularly suitable for lighting and furnishing sun parlors, porches and summer cottages. One of the most pleasant spots about the home is the sun parlor or screened-in porch, furnished with wicker lighting fixtures.

Wicker Electric Floor Lamp

34A8405—As shown . . . .
Made of wicker, in fumed oak, mahogany or old ivory finish. (*State finish desired.*) Height, 5 feet 7 inches. Base, 15 inches. Diameter of shade, 26 inches; lined with flowered cretonne in rose design. Fitted for two electric lights with chain pull sockets, 6 feet of cord and plug. Shipping weight, 50 pounds.

Wicker Electric Portable

34A8069—As shown . . . .
Made of wicker in fumed oak finish. Height, 23 inches. Wicker standard and 20-inch wicker shade with open latticework lined with beautiful figured floral cretonne in red rose and green leaf design. Fitted for two electric lights, with chain pull socket, 6 feet of cord and plug. Shipping weight, 12 pounds.

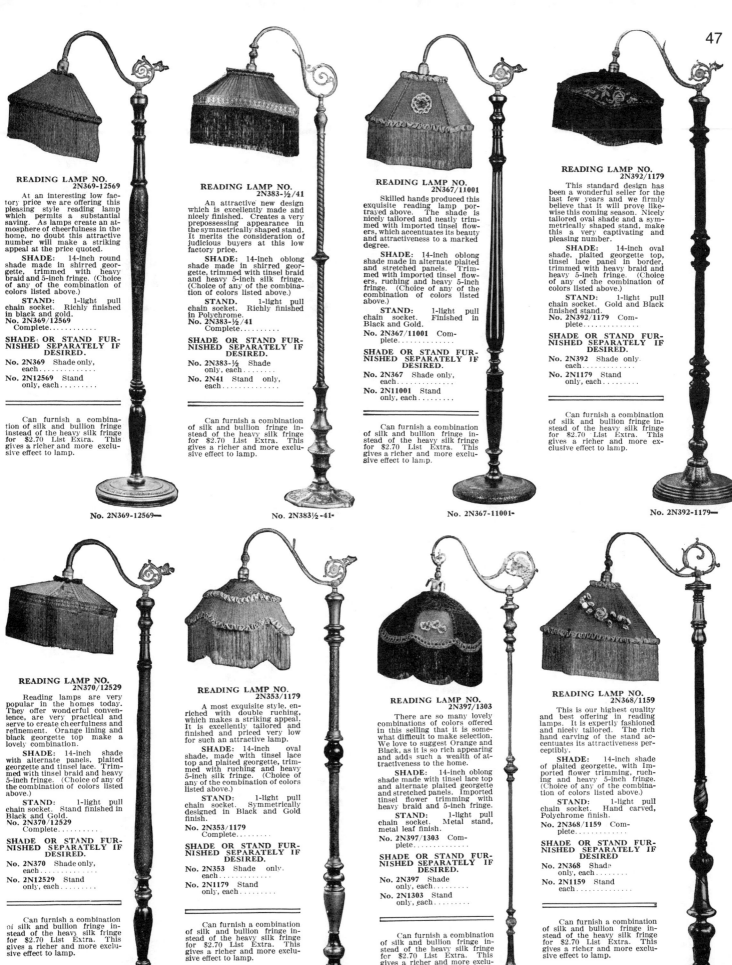

READING LAMP NO. 2N369-12569

At an interesting low factory price we are offering this pleasing style reading lamp which permits a substantial saving. As lamps create an atmosphere of cheerfulness in the home, no doubt this attractive number will make a striking appeal at the price quoted.

SHADE: 14-inch round shade made in shirred georgette, trimmed with heavy braid and 5-inch fringe. (Choice of any of the combination of colors listed above.)

STAND: 1-light pull chain socket. Richly finished in black and gold.
No. 2N369/12569 Complete..........

SHADE OR STAND FURNISHED SEPARATELY IF DESIRED.

No. 2N369 Shade only, each.......

No. 2N12569 Stand only, each........

Can furnish a combination of silk and bullion fringe instead of the heavy silk fringe for $2.70 List Extra. This gives a richer and more exclusive effect to lamp.

No. 2N369-12569—

READING LAMP NO. 2N383-½/41

An attractive new design which is excellently made and nicely finished. Creates a very prepossessing appearance in the symmetrically shaped stand. It merits the consideration of judicious buyers at this low factory price.

SHADE: 14-inch oblong shade made in shirred georgette, trimmed with tinsel braid and heavy 5-inch silk fringe. (Choice of any of the combination of colors listed above.)

STAND: 1-light pull chain socket. Richly finished in Polychrome.
No. 2N383-½/41 Complete........

SHADE OR STAND FURNISHED SEPARATELY IF DESIRED.

No. 2N383-½ Shade only, each.......

No. 2N41 Stand only, each.......

Can furnish a combination of silk and bullion fringe instead of the heavy silk fringe for $2.70 List Extra. This gives a richer and more exclusive effect to lamp.

No. 2N383½ -41-

READING LAMP NO. 2N367/11001

Skilled hands produced this exquisite reading lamp portrayed above. The shade is nicely tailored and neatly trimmed with imported tinsel flowers, which accentuates its beauty and attractiveness to a marked degree.

SHADE: 14-inch oblong shade made in alternate plaited and stretched panels. Trimmed with imported tinsel flowers, ruching and heavy 5-inch fringe. (Choice of any of the combination of colors listed above.)

STAND: 1-light pull chain socket. Finished in Black and Gold.
No. 2N367/11001 Complete.........

SHADE OR STAND FURNISHED SEPARATELY IF DESIRED.

No. 2N367 Shade only, each.......

No. 2N11001 Stand only, each........

Can furnish a combination of silk and bullion fringe instead of the heavy silk fringe for $2.70 List Extra. This gives a richer and more exclusive effect to lamp.

No. 2N367-11001-

READING LAMP NO. 2N392/1179

This standard design has been a wonderful seller for the last few years and we firmly believe that it will prove likewise this coming season. Nicely tailored oval shade and a symmetrically shaped stand, make this a very captivating and pleasing number.

SHADE: 14-inch oval shade, plaited georgette top, tinsel lace panel in border, trimmed with heavy braid and heavy 5-inch fringe. (Choice of any of the combination of colors listed above.)

STAND: 1-light pull chain socket. Gold and Black finished stand.
No. 2N392/1179 Complete.........

SHADE OR STAND FURNISHED SEPARATELY IF DESIRED.

No. 2N392 Shade only each.......

No. 2N1179 Stand only, each........

Can furnish a combination of silk and bullion fringe instead of the heavy silk fringe for $2.70 List Extra. This gives a richer and more exclusive effect to lamp.

No. 2N392-1179—

READING LAMP NO. 2N370/12529

Reading lamps are very popular in the homes today. They offer wonderful convenience, are very practical and serve to create cheerfulness and refinement. Orange lining and black georgette top make a lovely combination.

SHADE: 14-inch shade with alternate panels, plaited georgette and tinsel lace. Trimmed with heavy braid and heavy 5-inch fringe. (Choice of any of the combination of colors listed above.)

STAND: 1-light pull chain socket. Stand finished in Black and Gold.
No. 2N370/12529 Complete..........

SHADE OR STAND FURNISHED SEPARATELY IF DESIRED.

No. 2N370 Shade only, each...........

No. 2N12529 Stand only, each........

Can furnish a combination of silk and bullion fringe instead of the heavy silk fringe for $2.70 List Extra. This gives a richer and more exclusive effect to lamp.

No. 2N370-12529—

READING LAMP NO. 2N353/1179

A most exquisite style, enriched with double ruching, which makes a striking appeal. It is excellently tailored and finished and priced very low for such an attractive lamp.

SHADE: 14-inch oval shade, made with tinsel lace top and plaited georgette, trimmed with ruching and heavy 5-inch fringe. (Choice of any of the combination of colors listed above.)

STAND: 1-light pull chain socket. Symmetrically designed in Black and Gold finish.
No. 2N353/1179 Complete........

SHADE OR STAND FURNISHED SEPARATELY IF DESIRED.

No. 2N353 Shade only, each...........

No. 2N1179 Stand only, each........

Can furnish a combination of silk and bullion fringe instead of the heavy silk fringe for $2.70 List Extra. This gives a richer and more exclusive effect to lamp.

No. 2N353-1179-

READING LAMP NO. 2N397/1303

There are so many lovely combinations of colors offered in this selling that it is somewhat difficult to make selection. We love to suggest Orange and Black, as it is so rich appearing and adds such a wealth of attractiveness to the home.

SHADE: 14-inch oblong shade made with tinsel lace top and alternate plaited georgette and stretched panels. Imported tinsel flower trimming with heavy braid and 5-inch fringe.

STAND: 1-light pull chain socket. Metal stand, metal leaf finish.
No. 2N397/1303 Complete.............

SHADE OR STAND FURNISHED SEPARATELY IF DESIRED.

No. 2N397 Shade only, each.......

No. 2N1303 Stand only, each........

Can furnish a combination of silk and bullion fringe instead of the heavy silk fringe for $2.70 List Extra. This gives a richer and more exclusive effect to lamp.

No. 2N397-1303—

READING LAMP NO. 2N368/1159

This is our highest quality and best offering in reading lamps. It is expertly fashioned and nicely tailored. The rich hand carving of the stand accentuates its attractiveness perceptibly.

SHADE: 14-inch shade of plaited georgette, with imported flower trimming, ruching and heavy 5-inch fringe. (Choice of any of the combination of colors listed above.)

STAND: 1-light pull chain socket. Hand carved, Polychrome finish.
No. 2N368/1159 Complete...........

SHADE OR STAND FURNISHED SEPARATELY IF DESIRED

No. 2N368 Shade only, each.......

No. 2N1159 Stand each.............

Can furnish a combination of silk and bullion fringe instead of the heavy silk fringe for $2.70 List Extra. This gives a richer and more exclusive effect to lamp.

No. 2N368-1159—

Walnut Finish Bridge Lamp

34A8628—*As shown*..............

Height, 58 inches. Oval shade, 12x9 inches. Standard made of birchwood in walnut finish, with gray and gold color decoration. Top of shade and flounce are made of rose colored Jap silk. Lining is gold color Jap silk. Double artificial silk tan color fringe, 5 inches long. Heavy rose and tan color Jap silk ruching. Equipped with key socket, 6 feet of cord and plug. Shipping weight, 25 pounds.

Mahogany Finish Junior Lamp

34A8702—*As shown*..........
34A8703—*Base only*..........
34A8323—*Shade only*..........

Height, 56 inches. Round shade, 24 inches in diameter. Birchwood standard in mahogany finish. Top of shade is gold color Jap silk. Lining is rose color silk and cotton mull. Side panels in blue and gray color brocaded silk and cotton tussah. Gold color chenille fringe, 3½ inches long. Fancy black and gold color mercerized cotton and metallic braid. Has two chain pull sockets, 6 feet of cord and plug. Shipping weight, complete, 30 pounds.

Oval Shade Junior Lamp

34A8217—*As shown*..............
34A8218—*Base only*..............
34A8387—*Shade only*.............

Height, 60 inches. Shade, 27 inches long and 17 inches wide. Beautiful wood standard finished in burnished green gold and black, decorated with black and gold stipple work, on base and standard. Oval shade made of black silk and Georgette shirred top; lining, interlining and flounce is orange colored silk. Decorated with 5½-inch black fringe, and heavy fancy black and gold ruching. Has two sockets, 6 feet of cord and plug. Shipping weight, complete, 30 pounds.

Gold and Gray Floor Lamp

34A8714—*As shown*..
34A8715—*Base*..
34A8330—*Shade*...

Height, 62 inches. Width of shade, 24 inches. Hand carved wood base in the popular piano size. Gold metal leaf antique finish with gray and black relief. Fancy scalloped square shade with gold colored Japanese silk top covered with gold colored metal net. Inside lining and flounce of gold colored Japanese silk. Edge trimmed with gold colored metallic braid and 6-inch black and gold artificial silk fringe. Equipped with two chain pull sockets, 6 feet of cord and plug. Shipping weight, complete, 30 pounds.

Hand Carved Gold Finished Floor Lamp

34A8718—*As shown*..
34A8719—*Base only*...
34A8332—*Shade only*..

Height, 67 inches. Width of shade, 26 inches. Hand carved and fluted standard finished in Tiffany gold finish and black. Shade has gold colored silk and cotton tussah top covered with silk chiffon; inner lining and flounce rose colored Japanese silk. Trimmed with gold colored metallic fancy braid and 6-inch black and gold colored artificial silk fringe. Equipped with two chain pull sockets, 6 feet of cord and plug. Shipping weight, complete, 35 pounds.

49

Electric Candlestick

34A8209—*As shown*...........

Just picture a pair of these beautiful hand painted candlesticks on your mantel shelf or above the fireplace! You surely will agree they will help beautify your home. The composition base is finished in polychrome (background in antique gold, decorated with blue, green and red colors). The candle is fitted with a candelabra keyless socket and electric lamp, 6 feet of cord and plug. The shield is made of glassine cloth and hand painted in bird design. Height, 17½ inches. Shipping weight, 5 pounds.

Massive Candle-stick

34A8118—*As shown*...............

A candlestick made from pressed composition. The base has the appearance of antique iron and polychrome, prettily decorated with hand painted raised flowers in red, blue, green and gold. The candle is in antique ivory color, encircled with a festoon of colored flowers. Old rose color silk shield with a gilt braid around the edge. Height, 24 inches. Fitted with candelabra socket and electric bulb, 6 feet of cord and plug. Shipping wt., 6 lbs.

Electric Torchere

34A8120—*Canary*.....................
34A8123—*Ruby*.......................

A torchere at either end of a fireplace, mantel shelf, long library table, piano or a buffet adds greatly to the beauty of any home. They are very attractive and showy. The top and base are made of composition in antique gold color. The cylinder is made of paper parchment. Height, 20 inches. Width of cylinder, 3 inches. Complete with one keyless socket, 6 feet of cord and plug. Shipping weight, 6 pounds.

Iron Polychrome Bridge Lamp

34A8259—*As shown*..................,

Height, 60 inches. Width of shade, 14 inches. Made of wrought iron in natural iron and polychrome finish (red, green, blue and bronze decorations). The arm and shade are adjustable to any height or angle. Scalloped shade made of delft blue Japanese silk. Lining and flounce, gold color silk. The shade is trimmed with two-tone braid and blue 5-inch fringe. Equipped with one key socket, 6 feet of cord and plug. Shipping weight, 35 pounds.

Mahogany Finish Bridge Lamp

34A8626—*As shown*................

Height, 58 inches. Round shade, 12 inches wide. Standard made of birchwood in beautiful mahogany finish with adjustable metal arm. Top of shade is made of delft blue Jap silk. Flounce is rose color Jap silk. Lining is rose color mull. Blue artificial silk braid and 5-inch fringe. Equipped with key socket, 6 feet of cord and plug. Shipping wt., 30 lbs.

Wrought Iron Bridge Lamp

34A8111—*As shown*...................................

Height, 62 inches. Width of shade, 12 inches. Made of wrought iron in natural iron and bronze relief finish. The arm is made of strap iron and is adjustable to any height. Shade is made of paper parchment and hand painted in large red and blue flower design. Is equipped with a key socket, 6 feet of cord and plug. Shipping weight, 15 pounds.

Gold and Gray Stipple Bridge Lamp

34A8624—*As shown*.............

Height, 58 inches. Width of shade, 13 inches. Wood standard with weighted base in dull gold and black finish with center shaft in gray and gold color stipple work. Fancy scalloped shade with blue silk Georgette top, inner lining and flounce of orange color silk mull, lined with gold colored silk mull. Crown and edge is trimmed with blue and orange color Japanese silk ruching and 5-inch blue artificial silk fringe. Fitted with one key socket, 6 feet of cord and plug. Shipping weight, 25 pounds.

49

BRIDGE OR READING LAMP
Height 56 Inches
HAND PAINTED
VELVETEEN SHADE

Illuminated, these Hand Painted Velveteen Shade Lamps produce a dazzling brightness of the Oriental effect and a color harmony hitherto unknown. Expressive, beautiful and very charming in the home. It is a very popular accepted style.

SHADE: 13-inch fancy round shape shade made of Velveteen and coated with imported fine glass beads. Decoration consists of beautiful flower pattern with artfully contrasted background. Trimmed effectively with fancy braid, silk and glass fringe. When illuminated, the beads give a rich frosted effect that is typical of this type decoration —very attractive.

STAND: 12-inch fancy round base of iron in open work pattern. Fancy column and brass stem. Richly finished in Polychrome. Wired complete with pull chain socket for one light on adjustable bridge arm. Complete with silk cord and plug.

No. K6N/0126/1385
Complete ....
SHADE OR STAND
FURNISHED SEPARATE
No. K6N/0126
Shade Only, each..............
No. K6N/1385
Stand Only, each..............

BRIDGE OR READING LAMP
Height 56 Inches
HAND PAINTED
VELVETEEN SHADE

Illuminated, these Hand Painted Velveteen Shade Lamps produce a dazzling brightness of the Oriental effect and a color harmony hitherto unknown. Expressive, beautiful and very charming in the home. It is a very popular accepted style.

SHADE: A magnificent oblong 14-inch velveteen shade, coated with fine imported glass beads, giving shade a rich frosted effect. Beautiful floral and scenic design, richly hand painted in striking colors with harmonizing background. Neatly trimmed with fancy braid and six inch heavy colored glass fringe.

STAND: Iron stand, 12-inch hexagonal artistic base, in open work design, enhanced with brass braided stem. Richly finished in Polychrome. One light pull chain socket on adjustable arm. Wired complete, silk cord and plug.

No. K6N/0106/1350½
Complete ....
SHADE OR STAND
FURNISHED SEPARATE
No. K6N/0106
Shade only, each..............
No. K6N/1350½
Stand only, each..............

BRIDGE OR READING LAMP
Height 56 Inches
HAND PAINTED
VELVETEEN SHADE

Illuminated, these Hand Painted Velveteen Shade Lamps produce a dazzling brightness of the Oriental effect and a color harmony hitherto unknown. Expressive, beautiful and very charming in the home. It is a very popular accepted style.

SHADE: 13-inch attractive velveteen shade in Floral and Water scene design, masterly hand painted, embellished with an exquisite background. Coated with fine imported glass beads, giving shade a rich frosted effect. Neatly trimmed with ruching and colored glass fringe. Very effective.

STAND: Iron stand, 12-inch artistic oblong iron base, richly finished in Polychrome. Attractive fancy brass stem. One light pull chain socket on adjustable arm. Wired complete, silk cord and plug.

No. K6N/0112/1354
Complete ....
SHADE OR STAND
FURNISHED SEPARATE
No. K6N/0112
Shade only, each..............
No. K6N/1354
Stand only, each..............

F. O. B. CHICAGO

JUNIOR LAMP No. K6N/0120/1390
Height 60 inches
(Pictured to left)

SHADE: A fancy 18-inch round shade with scalloped bottom. Decorated with beautiful flower pattern with contrasting background. Trimmed with ruching and silk and glass fringe. Coated with fine imported glass beads. Measures 14 inches in depth. A very attractive velveteen shade.

STAND: Has 10-inch fancy iron base with legs. Attractive column and brass stem. Pleasingly finished in rich Polychrome. Wired complete for two lights with adjustable pull chain sockets. Complete with silk cord and plug.

No. K6N/0120/1390
Complete ....

JUNIOR LAMP No. K6N/051/1354
Height 60 inches
(Pictured to right)

SHADE: 20x13-inch oblong hand painted velveteen shade, beautifully decorated in the Parrot and Rose design. Truly a work of art. Coated with fine glass beads, giving shade a rich frosted effect. Trimmed with tinsel braid and six-inch silk and fancy colored glass fringe combination. Background colors are beautiful, in lovely contrast and harmony.

STAND: Attractive iron base, oblong design, length 14 inches. Finished in rich Polychrome. Fancy brass tubing. Tear-drop pendants. Wired complete, two lights, adjustable sockets, silk cord pull chain tassels. Silk cord and plug.

No. K6N/051/
Complete..............

JUNIOR LAMP No. K6N/0100/1353
Height 60 inches
(Pictured to left)

SHADE: Exquisitely designed velveteen shade with four artistic oval panels. Hand painted Parrot and scenic design with contrasting background, masterly executed. Coated with fine Imported beads, giving shade a rich frosted effect. Neatly trimmed with fancy braid and six-inch silk and Imported colored glass fringe. Width 15 inches; depth 22 inches.

STAND: Iron stand, fancy 12-inch iron open work design base, square shape. Attractive column, brass tubed stem. Richly finished in Polychrome. Wired complete, two-light pull chain sockets. Silk Cord and Plug.

No. K6N/0100/1353
Complete ....

JUNIOR LAMP No. K6N/059/1350
Height 60 inches
(Pictured to right)

SHADE: Four wheel hand painted velveteen 19x12-inch oblong shade. Flower and Bird design with attractive color combination background. Coated with fine Imported glass beads, giving shade a rich frosted effect. Neatly trimmed with heavy braid and six-inch silk and fancy colored glass fringe.

STAND: Iron stand with 13-inch embossed round base. Wrought iron ornamentation on column, fancy brass tubing, finished in rich Polychrome. Wired complete, two lights, silk cord pull chain tassels. Silk Cord and Plug.

No. K6N/059/1350
Complete ....

No. K6N/0120/1390 Complete.   No. K6N/051/1354 Complete.   No. K6N/0100/1353 Complete.   No. K6N/059/1350 Complete.

BRIDGE OR READING LAMP
Height 56 Inches
HAND PAINTED PARCHMENT SHADE

Illuminated, this Hand Painted Parchment Shade Lamp provides the proper light for reading and is truly invaluable. As a decorative household furnishing it is unsurpassed. Consequently it serves a two-fold purpose in the home being both utilitarian and decorative.

SHADE: A unique 12-inch hexagon shaped shade made of heavy Parchment. Presents a hand painted water scene with a ship under full sail depicted on front panel in natural colors and with background of contrasting yet harmonizing colors. Depth 8 inches. The leather lacings at top and bottom are most effective and add a finishing touch which reveals high artistry. This is a very popular priced lamp, suitable for gift purposes.

STAND: Fashioned with a fancy round base supported by legs. The center break is fashioned in the manner of a ball and is genuine Vidrio Onyx. Plated finish, gold lacquered and wired complete for one light on an adjustable bridge arm. Pull chain socket, silk cord and plug.

No. **K6N/0709/V102**
Complete

SHADE OR STAND FURNISHED SEPARATE
No. **K6N/0709** Shade only
Each ....
No. **K6N/V102** Stand only.
Each ....

BRIDGE OR READING LAMP
Height 56 Inches
HAND PAINTED PARCHMENT SHADE

Illuminated, this Hand Painted Parchment Shade Lamp provides the proper light for reading and is truly invaluable. As a decorative household furnishing it is unsurpassed. Consequently it serves a two-fold purpose in the home being both utilitarian and decorative.

SHADE: An outstanding design, six panelled and oblong in shape. Fashioned from heavy Parchment and cleverly decorated, the hand painted floral design is in natural colors with contrasting colors, and is especially attractive. Width 12 inches. Depth 8 inches. Leather lacing top and bottom proves most effective in the completion of this well tailored shade. You will find this popular priced number to be excellent for gift purposes.

STAND: The stand is very cleverly designed and has a decorative round base supported by four legs. Fancy twist tubing and the center break a ball of genuine Vidrio Onyx, are very delightful to the eye. Plated finish, gold lacquered. Wired complete for one light on adjustable bridge arm.

No. **K6N/0708/V103**
Complete

SHADE OR STAND FURNISHED SEPARATE
No. **K6N/0708** Shade only.
Each ....
No. **K6N/V103** Stand only.
Each ....

BRIDGE OR READING LAMP
Height 56 Inches
HAND PAINTED PARCHMENT SHADE

Illuminated, this Hand Painted Parchment Shade Lamp provides the proper light for reading and is truly invaluable. As a decorative household furnishing it is unsurpassed. Consequently it serves a two-fold purpose in the home being both utilitarian and decorative.

SHADE: Truly an outstanding design is this 11-inch octagon shaped shade with its alternating concave and straight panels. Fashioned from heavy Parchment and beautifully hand painted in contrasting colors. Has leather lacing top and bottom and readily reveals the high artistry employed in its construction. Depth 8 inches. If you are searching for a unique shade this one will please you in a most satisfactory manner.

STAND: Fashioned with a fancy round base supported by legs. The center break is fashioned in the manner of a ball of genuine Vidrio Onyx. Plated finish, gold lacquered and wired complete for one light on adjustable bridge arm. Pull chain socket, silk cord and plug.

No. **K6N/0705/V103**
Complete

SHADE OR STAND FURNISHED SEPARATE
No. **K6N/0705** Shade only
Each ....
No. **K6N/V103** Stand only.
Each ....

BRIDGE OR READING LAMP
Height 56 Inches
HAND PAINTED PARCHMENT SHADE

Illuminated, this Hand Painted Parchment Shade Lamp provides the proper light for reading and is truly invaluable. As a decorative household furnishing it is unsurpassed. Consequently it serves a two-fold purpose in the home being both utilitarian and decorative.

SHADE: This 12-inch round shade is very shapely and ideal for the bridge or reading lamp. Fashioned from heavy Parchment and artistically hand painted in floral design of beautiful harmonizing colors over a rich amber background. Depth 8 inches. The design presented on shade as illustrated is very pleasing and is truly artistic in nature and different in appearance than most popular priced shades.

STAND: This stand is very cleverly designed and has a decorative square metal base. The column is of fancy twisted tubing and has center break, a ball of genuine Vidrio Onyx, each of which are very delightful to the eye. Plated finish, gold lacquered. Wired complete for one light with pull chain socket on adjustable bridge arm. Silk cord and plug furnished.

No. **K6N/0700/V101**
Complete

SHADE OR STAND FURNISHED SEPARATE
No. **K6N/0700** Shade only.
Each ....
No. **K6N/V101** Stand only.
Each ....

FOUR POPULAR PARCHMENT SHADE JUNIOR LAMPS
OF CLEVER DESIGN

JUNIOR LAMP
No. 6N/0610/V101CP
Height 60 inches
☞(*Pictured to Left*)

SHADE: Another delightfully attractive creation which is very unique. Shade measures 18 inches in diameter and is fashioned from heavy Parchment. Is artistically hand painted in a conventional design at both top and bottom. Shade has leather banding, giving it a rich and well finished effect. Depth 10 inches.

STAND: Has fancy base executed in open work pattern. The column is of twisted tubing with Vidrio Onyx ball in center. Fitted with three candle light fixture on brass plate. Operated by canopy switch. Wired complete and is furnished with silk cord and plug. Equipped with adjustable stem so that shade can be raised to suit the individual need. Plated finish, gold lacquered.

No. **K6N/0610/V101CP**
Complete ....

JUNIOR LAMP
No. 6N/0611/V108
Height 60 inches
(*Pictured to Right*) ☞

SHADE: You will be very much enthused with this clever 18-inch round shade which is made from heavy Parchment, for it is truly a very remarkable number. It is artistically hand painted with floral design in striking colors. Has leather binding at top and bottom. High artistry and superb tailoring are manifest throughout. Depth 10 inches.

STAND: The fancy iron base is a splendid example of open work pattern. Is mounted on four legs and has twisted tubing with Vidrio Onyx ball in center. The plated finish, gold lacquer adds a pleasing final touch. Wired complete for two lights with pull chain sockets. Furnished with silk cord and plug.

No. **K6N/0611/V108**
Complete ....

JUNIOR LAMP
No. 6N/0613/V104
Height 60 inches
 (*Pictured to Left*)

SHADE: This is a most attractive 18-inch round shade of heavy Parchment. Is expertly and cleverly hand painted in floral design of natural colors. Is neatly tailored throughout and has leather binding at both top and bottom. The color scheme is very new and appeals to those who give particular care to the selection of their lamps.

STAND: Attractive iron base with column and center break to harmonize. The column is fashioned from fancy tubing which enhances the general appearance in a most gratifying manner. Wired complete for two lights with pull chain sockets. Has plated finish which is gold lacquered. Furnished with silk cord and plug. This lamp while popular in price is nicely finished throughout, being the product of experienced craftsmen. Makes the ideal Wedding, Anniversary or Holiday gift.

No. **K6N/0613/V104** Complete...

JUNIOR LAMP
No. 6N/0612/2307
Height 60 inches
(*Pictured to Right*) ☞

SHADE: All who have seen this attractive shade have realized that it is truly a work of art. It is fashioned from very heavy Parchment, measures 18 inches in diameter and is decorated with a hand painted bird and floral study in attractive colors. Patterned after the art subject entitled "The return of the Swallows." Bound with leather at top and bottom. Depth 10 inches.

STAND: A fancy iron base on legs fashioned in the modern manner. Has iron column and center break with artistic decoration at bottom. Plated finish, gold lacquered and wired complete for two lights with pull chain sockets. Furnished with silk cord and plug.

No. **K6N/0612/2307** Complete..

THREE CANDLE JUNIOR LAMP
(Pictured at left)

Shade: Size 20 inches; cone shape. This shapely Parchment shade is attractively decorated with conventional band design, the color combination of which is Red, Brown, Green and Gold, harmoniously blended.

Stand: Junior style, height 58 inches with 6-inch shade stem extension. Has circular footed metal base with urn shaped column, finished in French Bronze. Wired complete for three candle lights with canopy turn switch.

No. K5H/3051 Junior Lamp, Complete.

THREE CANDLE TABLE LAMP

Shade: Size 14 inches; round shape. Masterfully fashioned from durable Parchment which is decorated with attractive design at top and band around bottom. Black and Gold is the effective color scheme used.

Stand: Height, 18½ inches with 6-inch shade stem extension. The triangular shaped metal base and column is finished most pleasingly in Black and Gold. Wired complete for three candle lights with canopy turn swich.

No. K5H/5055 Table Lamp, Complete ....

THREE CANDLE TABLE LAMP

Shade: Size 14 inches; round shape. Tastefully fashioned from artistically decorated parchment with Bronze festoons on Tan, trimmed with gold bands. A very pleasing design and color combination at a popular price.

Stand: Height, 18½ inches with 6-inch shade stem extension. Fashioned from metal with attractive footed base and well proportioned column, finished in French Bronze. Wired complete for three candle lights with canopy turn switch.

No. K5H/5054 Table Lamp, Complete ....

BRIDGE LAMP

Shade: Size 12 inches; round shape. This very clever Parchment shade is artistically decorated with banded design in French Bronze. It is a very pleasing model which shows up exceptionally well when illuminated.

Stand: Bridge style, adjustable. Height, 57 inches. Constructed with round fancy metal base and urn shaped column, finished in French Bronze. Wired complete with one pull chain adjustable swivel socket.

No. K5H/1050 Bridge Lamp, Complete ....

CHAIR LAMP

Shade: Size 20 inches; cone shape. An attractively treated Parchment shade which is neatly decorated in Maroon and Gold. Just the lamp for reading when you are seated in your comfy chair.

Stand: Chair style, height 55 inches with 6-inch shade stem extension. Has fancy footed metal base and graceful column, finished in Maroon and Gold. Wired complete for three candle lights with canopy turn switch.

No. K5H/2014-2 Chair Lamp, Complete ....

BRIDGE LAMP
(Pictured at right)

Shade: Size 12 inches; round shaped. A neatly tailored shade which is made from plaited Rosewood Celanese and trimmed effectively with Rosewood and Green braid. Silk lined. Furnished in all colors listed at top of page.

Stand: Bridge style, adjustable, Height, 56 inches. Constructed with circular metal footed base and well proportioned column, finished in Maroon and Gold. Wired complete with one pull chain adjustable swivel socket.

No. K5H/1044 Bridge Lamp, Complete ....

TABLE LAMP

Shade: Size 12 inches; round shape. A shapely Parchment shade with banded and panelled design, decorated with festoons. Black, Gold and Brown are the well blended colors used in completing the attractive color scheme.

Stand: Height, 18½ inches. The massive triangular shaped base is made from metal and is surmounted with an embossed urn shaped column, finished in Black and Gold. Wired complete for one light with push button switch.

No. K5H/5077 Table Lamp, Complete ....

THREE CANDLE REFLECTOR LAMP

Shade: Size 20 inches; 8-panel scalloped shape. Fashioned from Rosewood Celanese, plaited and decorated with Gold Metal piping. Silk lined. Furnished in all of the optional colors listed at top of page.

Stand: Reflector style, height 64 inches. Constructed with round fancy metal base and shapely column, finished in Maroon and Gold. Wired complete with metal reflector and three candle light fixture with canopy turn switch. These two fixtures operated independently.

No. K5H/4053 Reflector Lamp, Each ....

BRIDGE LAMP
(Pictured at righ)

Shade: Size 12 inches; round shape. A well proportioned bridge lamp shade which is made from durable Parchment and neatly decorated in Green and Gold. Together with the graceful base it forms a most artistic ensemble.

Stand: Bridge style, adjustable. Height, 57 inches. Fashioned with circular footed metal base with urn shaped column, finished in Pea-Green and Gold. Wired complete with one pull chain adjustable swivel socket.

No. K5H/1051 Bridge Lamp, Complete ....

THREE CANDLE REFLECTOR LAMP

Shade: Size 20 inches; round shape. Parchment is the durable material used in fashioning this lovely shade which is most interestingly decorated with a Black and Gold decoration of conventional design.

Stand: Reflector style, height 64 inches. Fashioned with fancy metal base and embossed urn shaped column, massive in appearance yet graceful, and finished in Black and Gold. Wired complete with metal reflector and three candle lights with canopy turn switch. Fixtures operate independently.

No. K5H/4052 Reflector Lamp, Each ....

BRIDGE LAMP
(Height 56 inches)

The value is truly extraordinary at this ridiculously low factory price this lovely number is offered in this selling. It is well tailored and nicely finished.

STAND:— Magnificently designed and turned and finished in beautiful contrasting colors of black and gold stipple. One-light pull chain socket. Adjustable arm.

SHADE:—14x10-inch oval in shirred silk top, gold tinsel trimmed and double silk fringe. (Choice of any of the solid colors or the exquisite combination of new colors, which specify when ordering.)

No. 2M2569BR
Complete, each.....
STAND OR SHADE FURNISHED SEPARATE IF DESIRED
No. 2M2569BRA
Stand only, each....
No. 2M2569BRB
Shade only, each....
If a Silk Cord Pull Chain Tassel is wanted for this lamp in a harmonizing color, the same can be furnished at an extra cost of $0.85 List.

No. 2M2569BR

BRIDGE LAMP
(Height 56 inches)

For reading purposes this style lamp is convenient and very serviceable. It is offered at a very low factory price in this selling which permits more than a mere substantial saving.

STAND:—A distinctive and beautiful polychrome stand in the popular Walnut Tiffany finish over burnished gold. This combination gives a dark lustrous and rich finish. One-light pull chain socket. Adjustable arm.

SHADE:— The shade measures 14 inches in diameter, and is made of pleated georgette with metal cloth ruching top and bottom. (Choice of any of the solid colors or the exquisite combination of new colors listed above, which specify when ordering.)

No. 2M2678BR
Complete, each.....
STAND OR SHADE FURNISHED SEPARATE IF DESIRED
No. 2M2678BRA
Stand only, each....
No. 2M2678BRB
Shade only, each....
If a Silk Cord Pull Chain Tassel is wanted for this lamp in a harmonizing color, the same can be furnished at an extra cost of $0.85 List.

No. 2M2678BR

BRIDGE LAMP
(Height 56 inches)

This standard lamp was so popular last season we deemed it necessary to again illustrate with these attractive new creations. It is excellently made and finished.

STAND:—Of graceful solid appearing polychromed wood. Finished in gold with black two-toning and black enamel bands. The shaft and base are finished in a new and beautiful mottled clay finish called stipple. One light pull chain socket, silk cord and plug. Adjustable arm.

SHADE:—The 14x10-inch shade is made of finest grade pleated Georgette with a fancy panel of gold mesh. Lined and interlined with high grade genuine silk. Six-inch fibre silk fringe and silk skirt. May be had in any solid or combination of colors listed above. Makes up beautifully in Taupe over Rose.

No. 2M2879BR
Complete, each.....
STAND OR SHADE FURNISHED SEPARATE IF DESIRED
No. 2M2879BRA
Stand only, each....
No. 2M2879BRB
Shade only, each....
If a Silk Cord Pull Chain Tassel is wanted for this lamp in a harmonizing color, the same can be furnished at an extra cost of $0.85 List.

No. 2M2879BR

BRIDGE LAMP
(Height 56 inches)

A design that is very attractive and prepossessing in appearance. It is priced exceptionally low and represents wonderful value. The tailoring and excellent finish are accomplished by skilled hands at factory.

STAND:—A very captivating slender design that is magnificently hand carved and finished in beautiful contrasting colors of black and gold stipple. One light pull chain socket, silk cord and plug. Adjustable arm.

SHADE:—14-inch scalloped frame, stretched georgette top and ruching trimmed, with 6-inch heavy fibre silk fringe. (Choice of any of the solid or combination of new colors listed above, which specify when ordering.)

No. 2M2539G
Complete, each.....
STAND OR SHADE FURNISHED SEPARATE IF DESIRED
No. 2M2539GA
Stand only, each....
No. 2M2539GB
Shade only, each....
If a Silk Cord Pull Chain Tassel is wanted for this lamp in a harmonizing color, the same can be furnished at an extra cost of $0.85 List.

No. 2M2539G

BRIDGE LAMP
(Height 56 inches)

The presence of lamps in the home lends charm and character to surroundings and radiates that subtle atmosphere of refinement that quickly pleases the most critical eye. In our showing, we offer an attractive design to suit most any purse.

STAND:—Stand turned from four-inch stock beautifully designed with fluted shaft, burnished gold finish, heavily antiqued. Pretty fancy adjustable arm. Solid and Massive in appearance. One-light pull chain socket, silk cord and plug.

SHADE:—Is of oblong hexagonal shape, measuring 14x10 inches, covered in georgette, and lined and interlined with silk. Double silk fringe and skirt. (Choice of any of the solid colors or the new and most exquisite combination of colors listed above, which specify when ordering.)

No. 2M111BR
Complete, each.....
STAND OR SHADE FURNISHED SEPARATE IF DESIRED
No. 2M111BRA
Stand only, each....
No. 2M111BRB
Shade only, each....
If a Silk Cord Pull Chain Tassel is wanted for this lamp in a harmonizing color, the same can be furnished at an extra cost of $0.85 List.

No. 2M111BR

BRIDGE LAMP
(Height 56 inches)

A design of unusual beauty and attractiveness that makes a striking appeal in the slender appearance of the stand and the expert tailoring and finish of the shade.

STAND:—Slender fluted gold polychrome base of beautiful design. Lower portion of imitation marble finish. Base weighted and piped. Artistic adjustable arm. One-light pull chain socket, silk cord and plug.

SHADE:— 14x10-inch shade is made of pleated georgette with imported lace panels. The very latest oval pattern with gold bullion fringe. Black and Gold makes up very pretty. However, you have the choice of any of the solid colors or most exquisite combination of colors listed above, which specify when ordering.

No. 2M96F
Complete, each.....
STAND OR SHADE FURNISHED SEPARATE IF DESIRED
No. 2M96FA
Stand only, each....
No. 2M96FB
Shade only, each....
If a Silk Cord Pull Chain Tassel is wanted for this lamp in a harmonizing color, the same can be furnished at an extra cost of $0.85 List.

No. 2M96F

BRIDGE LAMP
(Height 56 inches)

A distinctive new creation that is exquisitely beautiful, tailored with infinite care and utmost precision as to detail. Would add grace and charm to the living room quarters.

STAND:—Artistically hand carved and finished in antique gold and shaded antique green and brown enamel—a truly gorgeous color combination. Adjustable arm. One light pull chain socket, silk cord and plug.

SHADE:—Pleated Georgette, 12-inch shade, gold tinsel trimming, and double silk fringe. (Choice of any of the solid colors or the most exquisite combination of colors listed above, which specify when ordering.)

No. 2M80H
Complete, each.....
STAND OR SHADE FURNISHED SEPARATE IF DESIRED
No. 2M80HA
Stand only, each....
No. 2M80HB
Shade only, each....
If a Silk Cord Pull Chain Tassel is wanted for the above lamp in a harmonizing color, the same can be furnished at an extra cost of $0.85 List.

No. 2M80H

BRIDGE LAMP
(Height 56 inches)

An exclusive new creation, masterly designed and exceptionally well tailored, to suit those of a fastidious taste, who appreciate original and distinctive designs. Very charming and captivating in appearance.

STAND:—A slender and very artistic shaft. Expertly hand carved and finished in genuine metal leaf, heavily antiqued and decorated with exquisite touches of color on the carved portions which enhance its character to a marked degree. Fancy adjustable arm. One light pull chain socket, silk cord and plug.

SHADE:—12-inch shade of the very latest design and covered with gorgeous imported lace over metal cloth. Lined with peach colored silk of the finest texture. (Your choice of any of the solid or most exquisite combination of colors listed above, which please specify when ordering.)

No. 2M114BR
Complete, each.....
STAND OR SHADE FURNISHED SEPARATE IF DESIRED
No. 2M114BRA
Stand only, each.......
No. 2M114BRB
Shade only, each.......

No. 2M114BR

ALL METAL BRIDGE LAMP
🖐(*Pictured at left*)

SHADE: 12-inch Octagon metal mesh shade with attractive conventional design in a pleasing five-color combination which harmonizes with base. Trimmed with brass channel.

STAND: Square base with rounded corners, urn shaped column and brass tubing. Plated finish, gold lacquered and wired complete for one light with pull chain socket. Has adjustable swivel. Neatly fashioned from metal. Height, 54 inches.

No. K6N/1008-2382 All Metal Bridge Lamp, Complete ..

ALL METAL BRIDGE LAMP
🖐(*Pictured at left*)

SHADE: 12-inch Round metal mesh shade with all-over pattern design in an attractive and harmonizing five-color combination which matches base finish. Trimmed with gold colored tape at top and bottom.

STAND: All metal construction with fancy round base, attractive column and brass tubing. Plated finish, gold lacquered and wired complete with one pull chain socket. Equipped with adjustable ball swivel. Height, 54 inches.

No. K6N/1011-2384 All Metal Bridge Lamp, Complete ..

METAL SHADES

In this day and age where practicability and attractiveness go hand in hand, we find many articles whose intrinsic value is very pronounced. The shades illustrated in this display, being made from finely woven metal mesh, will certainly prove durable, and with their attractive decorations will add just the type of beauty you wish from your lamps. Considering their quality and the service they will render they are extremely low priced.

ALL METAL BRIDGE LAMP
🖐(*Pictured at left*)

SHADE: 12-inch six panelled metal mesh shade with flower design painted in five-color combination. Heavy brass channel between each panel and also around top and bottom rim.

STAND: Attractively fashioned from metal with fancy round base. Has attractive column and center break. Brass tubing. Plated finish, Gold lacquered and wired complete with pull chain socket. Adjustable ball swivel. Height, 54 inches.

No. K6N/1000-2381 All Metal Bridge Lamp, Complete ..

ALL METAL BRIDGE LAMP
🖐(*Pictured at left*)

SHADE: Finely woven metal mesh shade, square with cut corners and slightly curved panels. Decorated with Tapestry design in five-color combination—extremely attractive. Trimmed with brass channel.

STAND: Of metal construction with fancy round base and neat column. Brass tubing. Plated finish. Gold lacquered and wired complete with one pull chain socket. Has adjustable ball swivel. Height, 54 inches.

No. K6N/1005-2383 All Metal Bridge Lamp, Complete ..

ALL METAL REFLECTOR LAMP
(*Pictured above*)

SHADE: 18-inch eight panelled metal mesh shade with conventional design in pleasing five-color combination which harmonizes with base color. Heavy brass channel joins each panel and trims top and bottom rim.
STAND: Reflector style. Height 64 inches. All metal, with fancy round base and heavy column. Finished in black and gold, green and gold or red and gold. (State preference.) Wired complete with 3-lt. candle fixture and metal reflector. A 300 watt bulb is required for the reflector for general room-wide illumination. Candle lights are on separate switch to illuminate shade
No. K6N/1001/2392R All Metal Reflector Lamp, Complete...............
Note: Can furnish 300 watt bulb for $2.65 List additional.
SAME AS ABOVE EXCEPT DOES NOT HAVE REFLECTOR
No. K6N/1001/2392J All Metal 3-lt. Candle Junior Lamp, Complete.....

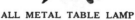

ALL METAL JUNIOR LAMP
🖐
(*Pictured at left*)

SHADE: Eight panelled, 18-inch metal mesh shade with attractive design painted in a combination of five harmonizing colors. Panels are slightly curved to make semi-closed top. Trimmed with brass channel.

STAND: All metal with fancy base and column. Brass tubing. Plated finish. Gold lacquered and wired complete with three-light candle fixture and canopy switch. Has 5-inch adjustable stem holding shade. Height, 60 inches.

No. K6N/1006-2390 All Metal Junior Lamp, Complete......

ALL METAL JUNIOR LAMP
(*Pictured at right*)

SHADE: 18-inch square with cut corners. Metal mesh shade. Decorated attractively in Renaissance design in six-color combination. Very attractive and harmonious. Trimmed with brass channel.

STAND: All metal with fancy octagon shaped base, attractive column and brass tubing. Plated finish, Gold lacquered and wired complete with three-light candle fixture and canopy switch. Has 5-inch adjustable stem holding shade. Height 60 inches.

No. K6N/1002-2393 All Metal Junior Lamp, Complete.....

ALL METAL TABLE LAMP

SHADE: 14-inch metal mesh shade. Square shape with cut corners and slightly curved panels. Decorated in Tapestry design which is developed with a harmonious five-color combination. Trimmed with brass channel.

STAND: All metal with attractively modeled base and column. Has plated finish, Gold lacquered. Wired complete with three-light candle fixture and canopy switch. Height, 24 inches. Equipped with 5-inch adjustable stem holding shade.

No. K6N/1005-V219 All Metal Table Lamp, Complete.......

ALL METAL JUNIOR LAMP
🖐
(*Pictured at left*)

SHADE: 18-inch round metal mesh shade with all-over design painted in harmonizing five-color combination. Trimmed effectively with gold colored tape at top and bottom. A very durable and inexpensive shade.

STAND: All metal, with fancy round base, attractive column and center break. Brass tubing. Plated finish, gold lacquered and wired complete with three-light candle fixture and canopy switch. Has 5-inch adjustable stem holding shade. Height 60 inches.

No. K6N/1011-2381 All Metal Junior Lamp, Complete......

ALL METAL JUNIOR LAMP
🖐
(*Pictured at right*)

SHADE: 18-inch metal mesh shade. An octagon shape with conventional design painted in five harmonious delicate colors. Trimmed with heavy brass channel, which also joins the panels. A very lovely and attractive shade.

STAND: All metal, with square, rounded corner base, fancy urn shaped column and brass tubing. Plated finish, gold lacquered. Wired complete with three-light candle fixture and canopy switch. Equipped with 5-inch adjustable stem holding shade. Height, 60 inches.

No. K6N/1008-2382 All Metal Junior Lamp, Each.........

54

BRIDGE OR READING LAMP
No. 6N/736/V101
Height, 56 Inches

This is a very artistic lamp which is not only excellently designed, but exquisitely tailored and faultlessly finished throughout. It is featured with an ADJUSTABLE ARM—an aid and great convenience when reading. The stand is especially attractive and, quality workmanship considered, it is an unmatched value at the low price prevailing.

SHADE: Lovely 14-inch Oblong shade, made of fine quality shirred Georgette. Charmingly trimmed with fancy braid and pastel flower. The scalloped effect presented is very unique and attractive.

STAND: Made with fancy square base of iron with twisted tubing and Vidrio Onyx center break. Wired complete for one pull chain light on adjustable bridge arm. Plated finish, gold lacquered.

No. 6N/736/V10¹
Complete ....

SHADE OR STAND FURNISHED SEPARATE
No. 6N/736
Shade Only. Each.......
No. 6N/V101
Stand Only. Each......

BRIDGE OR READING LAMP
No. 6N/741/1390
Height, 56 Inches

A very artistic and outstanding design of pleasing proportions in which both shade and stand possess the characteristics of present day styles. The stand especially is very delightfully designed while the shade is so fashioned and tailored that absolute continuity is maintained. Stand is fitted with ADJUSTABLE ARM which adds materially to your comfort when reading.

SHADE: Rich appearing 14-inch fancy oblong shaped shade of plaited crepe, trimmed with attractive braid. Shade is silk lined, artistically designed and faultlessly tailored. For colors available see top of page.

STAND: Fashioned with fancy iron base on legs with attractive column and center break. Has plated finish, gold lacquered. Wired complete with one pull chain socket on adjustable bridge arm.

No. 6N/741/1390
Complete ....

SHADE OR STAND FURNISHED SEPARATE
No. 6N/741
Shade Only. Each........
No. 6N/1390
Stand Only. Each......

BRIDGE OR READING LAMP
No. 6N/776/2324
Height, 56 Inches

Here is a newly designed Modern Art pattern which is captivating in its lovely appearance. The low price quoted is indeed interesting. Fitted with the ADJUSTABLE ARM—a real comfort when reading. The very presence of this lamp in the home radiates cheery charm.

SHADE: Fancy oblong shade made of stretched silk crepe and lined and interlined with silk. Is pleasingly trimmed with harmonizing decorative braid. Shade measures 14 inches in length and 8 inches in depth. Shade is nicely tailored throughout.

STAND: Has Modernistic base mounted on legs. The iron column with center break is very handsome and effective as is the attractive arm and stem head. Plated finish, heavily gold lacquered. Wired complete for one light on adjustable arm with pull chain socket. Silk cord and plug furnished.

No. K6N/776/2324
Complete ....

SHADE OR STAND FURNISHED SEPARATE
No. K6N/776
Shade Only. Each........
No. K6N/2324
Stand Only. Each...

BRIDGE OR READING LAMP
No. 726½/V101
Height, 56 Inches

At an interesting low factory price, we are featuring this exquisite silk shade lamp. It is a graceful style, of expert construction and finish, irrespective of this low price.

SHADE: A beautiful fancy round shaped shade of a high quality shirred georgette. Nicely trimmed with artistic braid and beautiful head fringe. The pattern is very rich and prepossessing.

STAND: Iron stand with fancy square base done in an open work pattern. Has Vidrio Onyx Ball in center. Plated finish neatly gold lacquered. Wired complete for one light with pull chain socket on an ADJUSTABLE BRIDGE ARM. Silk cord and plug are standard equipment.

No. 6N/726½/V101
Complete ....

SHADE OR STAND FURNISHED SEPARATELY
No. 6N/726½
Shade Only. Each.......
No. 6N/V101
Stand Only. Each.......

BRIDGE OR READING LAMP
No. 6N/725/1383
Height, 56 Inches

This new design possesses all the attributes of present day designing, coupled with excellent workmanship and exacting finish. The shade is a very pleasing design and the stand with its ADJUSTABLE ARM feature is very practical.

SHADE: A charming and fancy 13-inch oblong shaped shade of plaited crepe. Center panel is trimmed most effectively with decorative braid. Has fancy braid trimming at top and bottom. Can be furnished in a wide range of lovely colors as listed at top of page. Careful workmanship and finish is featured throughout.

STAND: Has cleverly treated inch iron base with attractive column and center break. The plated finish is heavily gold lacquered. Wired complete with one pull chain socket on adjustable bridge arm.

No. K6N/725/1383
Complete ....

SHADE OR STAND FURNISHED SEPARATE
No. K6N/725
Shade Only. Each.......
No. K6N/1383
Stand Only. Each.......

BRIDGE OR READING LAMP
No. 6N/729/1390
Height, 56 Inches

From this illustration you can no doubt perceive the elegance in design of both the shade and the stand. This lamp is an outstanding value in a popular priced lamp, which combines high artistry with first class materials. A very decorative and practical household illuminator.

SHADE: A clever and charming 12-inch, six panel shade which is fashioned from stretched, washable Celanese. Shade is artistically trimmed with fancy braid at top and bottom. Furnished in various colors listed at top of this page.

STAND: Fashioned with fancy iron base which is mounted on legs. Has attractive column with center break. The plated finish is heavily gold lacquered. Wired complete for one light with pull chain socket on adjustable bridge arm.

No. K6N/729/1390
Complete ....

SHADE OR STAND FURNISHED SEPARATE
No. K6N/729
Shade Only. Each.......
No. K6N/1390
Stand Only. Each.......

BRIDGE OR READING LAMP
No. 6N/736½/2307
Height, 56 Inches.

Completing this most interesting display of bridge lamps is the prepossessing number portrayed above. Of Modernistic design it is most striking and while very low in price it will appeal to even the most exacting.

SHADE: 14-inch oblong shaped shade made of shirred georgette of a good quality. Trimmed with fancy braid, pastel flower and Italian bead fringe, all of which give it a rich appearance. It is nicely tailored and expertly finished throughout.

STAND: The fancy open work patterned base with column and metal breaks to match is very artistic and pleasing. Carefully plated finish, neatly gold lacquered. Wired complete for one light with pull chain socket on adjustable bridge arm. Silk cord and plug also furnished.

No. K6N/736½/2307
Complete ....

SHADE OR STAND FURNISHED SEPARATELY
No. K6N/736½
Shade Only. Each.......
No. K6N/2307
Stand Only. Each.......

BRIDGE OR READING LAMP
No. 6N/726/1393
Height, 56 Inches

When reading this round shade bridge lamp will certainly prove a great convenience. The shade is neatly tailored throughout and the noteworthy stand has an attractive column, enriched with an exquisite center break. A bridge lamp of this type is a highly acceptable gift item.

SHADE: A fine quality of pleated Crepe is used in fashioning this artistic 14-inch round shade. It is most pleasingly trimmed with fancy braid and beautiful pastel flower. Shade can be furnished in any of the lovely colors mentioned at top of page, which specify when ordering.

STAND: Fashioned with fancy iron base which is mounted on legs. Has attractive column with center break. The plated finish used is heavily gold lacquered. Wired complete for one light with pull chain socket on adjustable bridge arm.

No. K6N/726/1393
Complete ....

SHADE OR STAND FURNISHED SEPARATE
No. K6N/726
Shade Only. Each.......
No. K6N/1393
Stand Only. Each..

DECORATIVE RADIO LAMP

A very clever and artistic lamp which is fashioned with oblong Black and Gold Marble base, size 4x12 inches. Fitted with two gold plated kneeling figures and one 5-inch crackled glass, illuminated ball. Height, 7½ inches.

No. 8W/367 Each..........................

DECORATIVE RADIO LAMP

This decorative radio lamp is ideal as a gift item. It is very rich in appearance and has Black and Gold Marble base, size 4x12 inches. Fitted with two cast metal gold plated figures and 5-inch illuminated crackle glass ball. Height, 7½ inches.

No. 8W/347 Each..........................

FLOORETTE BRIDGE LAMP No. 8W/F581/F1001

(Illustrated to left)

Fashioned from artistically designed metal, richly finished in Spanish Brass. Shade is raised and lowered by a slight touch on the patented counterbalanced heavy silk rope which eliminates thumb screws and other adjustment devices. Simple to operate—distinctive and graceful in design. Cone shaped 12-inch shade covered and lined with silk in colors of rose, gold, tan, green or rust. Height, 61 inches. This lamp is so convenient in operation that it will find its way into the majority of homes this season—our price is so low practically every home can afford this convenience. Wired complete with one pull chain socket.

No. K8W/F581/F1001 Floorette Bridge Lamp, each ....

REFLECTORETTE JUNIOR LAMP
No. 8W/R636/R6063

(Illustrated to right)

The Reflectorette Junior Lamp shown to the right is the modern type of illumination for the home. Authorities on interior decoration as well as noted eye specialists recommend this type illumination in the home.

The stand is artistically designed metal which is finished most pleasingly with rich English Bronze and French Gold. Wired complete with three-candle light fixture, also equipped with reflectorette feature which is fully described at bottom center of page. Complete with silk cord and plug. The 20-inch, hand decorated parchment shade is decorated in the popular Empire design. Height of lamp, overall, 64 inches.

No. K8W/R636/R6063 Reflectorette Junior Lamp, each ....

DECORATIVE RADIO LAMP

This lovely radio lamp is truly an illuminated art object. It is fashioned with an artistically designed metal base, 9x5 inches. Finished exquisitely in French Gold. Fitted with 5-inch Amber colored bubble glass electric lighted ball which appears as the firmament when illuminated. Height overall, 11 inches.

No. K8W/660 Each......................

TABLE LAMP
No. 8W/T554/5252

(Illustrated to left)

Genuine Chinese Cloisonne Vase on French Gold metal mounting fitted with two pull-chain sockets. Cone designed stretched silk 14-inch shade which is furnished in the following colors: Tan, Rose, Peach, Gold, Green or Rust. Height 23 inches. Wired complete and furnished with silk cord and plug.

No. K8W/T554/5252 Table Lamp, each...

TABLE LAMP
No. 8W/T596/T6001

(Illustrated to right)

The clever table lamp illustrated to the right is a very unique design which is being offered at a popular price. It is fashioned with a cast bronze base, artistically designed, and finished in a pleasing combination of French Gold and Black. Equipped with a well proportioned 15-inch empire designed, hand painted parchment shade on adjustable stem. Wired complete for three-candle lights, canopy switch, silk cord and plug. Height 26 inches.

No. K8W/T596/T6001 Table Lamp, each.

REFLECTORETTE JUNIOR LAMP
No. 8W/R622/R4391

(Illustrated to left)

The charming Junior Lamp, illustrated to the left, from all appearances is an ordinary three-candle lamp, however it is equipped with the reflectorette feature which is fully illustrated and described to the right.

The metal base is well proportioned and is richly finished in Black Enamel and is trimmed effectively with French Gold. Stand is wired complete for three-candle fixture, reflectorette and canopy switch. Silk cord and plug furnished. The 20-inch pleated silk shade is lined, with two color self trimming. Choice of Rose, Gold, Tan, Green or Rust colors. Overall lamp height, 63 inches.

No. K8W/R622/R4391 Each ....

LIGHT CEILING

IDEAL LIGHT FOR READING

PERFECT LIGHT FOR CARDS

PROPER LIGHT FOR PIANO

REFLECTORETTE JUNIOR LAMP
No. 8W/R109/4310

(Illustrated to right)

Seldom do you find such artistic designing and extreme practicability so closely interwoven as you do in the Reflectorette Junior Lamp illustrated to the right. As you can see from the diagram at the left its utility purposes are unlimited.

The stand is fashioned with a hexagonal shaped base of metal and the entire stand is finished in English Bronze and Pewter. Wired complete with three-candle fixture, reflectorette feature and canopy switch. Silk cord and plug furnished. Has 20-inch Hexagon shaped silk shade, covered and lined with stretched silk. Rose, Gold, Tan, Green or Rust colors available. Overall height, 63 inches.

No. K8W/R109/4310 Each ....

ONE REFLECTORETTE LIGHTS AN ENTIRE ROOM

Possesses all the artistry and utility of high grade lamps combined with a patented construction providing not only soft, decorative illumination, but powerful, glareless room-wide lighting. One lamp will furnish perfect illumination for card playing, music, reading, sewing and general lighting. Pronounced the ideal lighting unit by Stylists, Lighting Experts, Doctors and Home Specialists. A trial in a dark room with all other lights out will quickly demonstrate the superiority of Reflectorette lighting. The large center bulb (300 Watt size all frosted) is used for general room-wide illumination; the candle lights for decorative lighting. U. S. Pat. No. 1164720.

Clever lamp with 17-inch parchment paper shade and decorated with painted band with conventional design in colors to match stand. Ornamental metal base with brass tubing. Wired complete with 3-light candle fixture—equipped with canopy switch. Has adjustable rod and ball swivel on top so that shade may be adjusted to any height or angle. Furnished with cigarette jar, ash receiver and match box holder. These are finished to match stand which is finished in Black and Gold, Green and Gold or Red and Gold. (Specify preference.) Height 49 inches.
No. K6N/2362 Each........

A practical lamp that serves a dual purpose equally well. Equipped with 12-inch round Parchment paper shade with wide band painted in color to match stand. The metal stand has ornamental base with brass tubing. Wired complete with pull chain socket for one light on ball swivel. Furnished with handled glass tray. Finished in Red and Gold, Green and Gold or Black and Gold. (Specify preference.)
No. 6N/2364 Each........

Davenport-Smoker Lamp No. 6N/2362

DAVENPORT-SMOKER LAMP No. 6N/2361
(Illustrated to Left)

Has round, 17-inch diameter Parchment paper shade, decorated with band and gold applique, in colors to harmonize with finish of stand selected. Stand fashioned with ornamental base and brass tubing. Wired complete for three-candle lights with canopy switch. Has adjustable rod and ball swivel on top—adjustable to any height or angle. Removable tray, cigarette jar, ash receiver and match box holder, finished to match stand which comes in Black and Gold, Green and Gold, or Red and Gold. (Specify preference.)
No. K6N/2361 Each ....

DAVENPORT-SMOKER Lamp No. 6N/2360
(Illustrated to Right)

The 17-inch Parchment paper shade is decorated with wide band and gold applique to harmonize with finish of stand. The metal stand has ornamental base and brass tubing. Wired complete for three candle lights with canopy switch. Equipped with ball swivel and adjustable shade rod—adjustable to any height or angle. Handled glass tray furnished. Finished in Black and Gold, Green and Gold, or Red and Gold. (Specify preference.) An inexpensive lamp of dual purpose.
No. 6N/2360 Each ....

Davenport-Smoker Lamp No. 6N/2361

Bridge-Smoker Lamp No. 6N/2364

OUR SPECIAL DAVENPORT-SMOKER LAMP
The convenience of this practical dual purpose Davenport-Smoker lamp is made available to all homes through our special offering. The 17-inch Parchment paper shade is decorated with gold leaf and the banding harmonizes with finish of stand. Stand wired complete for three candle lights with canopy switch. Fixtures include cigarette jar, ash tray, and match box holder finished to match stand which is furnished in Green and Gold, Black and Gold, or Red and Gold. Shade adjustable to any height or angle.
No. K6N/203 Each.....................................

Davenport-Smoker Lamp No. 6N/2360

FLOOR TORCHERE No. 6N/FM13
Height 67 Inches
(Illustrated to Left)

This Torchere is very attractive and we recommend it highly to even the most exacting. The modern art designed Mica Shade with its alternating pearl white and amber toned Mica panels is most exquisite and unusual. It is trimmed with fancy brass binding and measures 8 inches in depth, 7 inches across top and 4 inches across bottom. The modernistic stand is of iron with fancy base, break and column to harmonize. Extreme height including shade 67 inches. Wired complete for one light with pull chain socket. Silk cord and plug furnished. At entrances a pair can be used most effectively.
No. 6N/FM13 Complete........

DAVENPORT LAMP No. 6N/0609/2326½C
Height 49 Inches
(Illustrated to Right)

SHADE: This 17-inch round shade is made of parchment paper and has hand painted banding at top and bottom. Depth 9 inches. This shade is gracefully tapered from a 17-inch diameter at bottom to a 7-inch diameter at top. May be raised, lowered or tilted to any angle since it is mounted on an adjustable swivel fixture. STAND: Fancy iron base with column to harmonize. Fashioned with a three light candle fixture on brass plate and equipped with canopy switch. Height with shade 49 inches. Has an adjustable swivel fixture at top so that lamp can be adjusted to suit individual requirements. Attractive plated finish, heavily gold lacquered. Wired complete and furnished with six feet of silk cord and plug.
No. K6N/0609/2326½C Complete ....

FIRESIDE OR OCCASIONAL TORCHERE
Fashioned with fancy metal overlays and dark crackled, amber colored glass panels. The modernistic stand is fashioned with fancy bridge arm supporting lamp. Fancy iron base on legs with attractive tubing and center break. Has plated finish, heavily gold lacquered. Wired complete for one light with canopy switch. Height 48 inches.
No. 6N/215½F Complete ....

DAVENPORT LAMP No. 6N/0608/2326½C
Height 49 Inches
(Illustrated to Left)

SHADE: 17-inch round Shade fashioned from parchment paper and beautifully hand painted with floral design. This is a very handsome parchment paper shade and is leather bound top and bottom. Is gracefully tapered from a 17-inch diameter at bottom to a 7-inch diameter at top. Depth 9 inches. Mounted on an adjustable swivel fixture. STAND: Fancy iron base with column to harmonize. Fashioned with a three light candle fixture on brass plate and equipped with canopy switch. Height with shade, 49 inches. Has an adjustable swivel fixture at top so that shade can be adjusted in accordance with individual requirements. Pleasingly finished with gold lacquer, plated. Wired complete and furnished with a six foot silk cord and plug.
No. K6N/0608/2326½C Complete ....

FLOOR REFLECTOR No. 6N/FR1
Extreme Height 66 in.
(Illustrated to Right)

An ideal lamp for those desiring indirect illumination. Will illuminate an ordinary size room most satisfactorily. Has fancy stamped brass base, brass tubing and metal reflector. Stand is finished in your choice of Black and Gold, Green and Gold or Red and Gold. Wired complete with pull chain socket for one light. Extreme height is 66 inches. In order to give proper light this reflector requires a 300 Watt bulb. When ordering be sure to specify finish desired.
No. K6N/FR1 Reflector, each...
Note: 300 Watt Bulb can be furnished at $2.65 List Extra.

o. 6N/FM13 Complete.....

No. K6N/0609/2326½C Complete ....

No. K6N/0608/2326½C Complete ....

No. K6N/FR1 Complete.....

BOUDOIR LAMP

Shade: Size 7 inches Octagon shape. Silk Georgette with silk inner and outer lining. Has double row of imported braided ruching trim at both top and bottom rim. Decorated with silk ribbon in center. Choice of Green, Rose or Orchid colors.
Stand: Height 13½ inches. Has brass base with marble onyx center block. Finished in Orchid and Gold. Green and Gold or Rose and Gold to match shade.

TWO CANDLE TABLE LAMP

Shade: Size 12 inches. Oblong shape. Stretched silk on large panels—with attractive silk cord designs. Small side panels pleated. Velvet and Gold Metal trim at top and bottom. All colors listed on top of page.
Stand: Height 15 inches with 5-inch extension. Metal, wired complete for two candle lights, has canopy switch. Finished in Green and Gold or Rose and Gold.

No. K8J/61¾-4004
Complete ......

BOUDOIR LAMP

Shade: Size 8 inches. Silk Georgette with silk inner and outer lining. Ribs trimmed in silk velvet. Top and bottom trimmed in cut out lace. Shade is Octagon shaped. Green, Rose or Orchid colors, optional.
Stand: Height 13½ inches. Has brass base with marble onyx center block. Finished Orchid and Gold, Green and Gold and Rose to match shade.

No. K8J/S50-B1000
Complete ....

THREE CANDLE DAVENPORT LAMP

(Pictured at right)

Shade: Size 15½ inches. Made of Pure Silk with stretched panels. Self made trim with silk braid on ribs. Silk lined. For colors see introductory copy at top of page.
Stand: Davenport style — height 48 inches, with 5-inch extension. Metal finished in Old Gold. Wired complete for three candle lights with canopy turn switch.

No. K8J/183½-3099
Complete ..

No. K8J/S51-B1000
Complete ...

BRIDGE, JUNIOR AND TABLE LAMP ENSEMBLE

In this display we are offering an opportunity of purchasing matched lamps for the home. This is a very new thought in home illumination and this ensemble has been selected because of its great beauty and outstanding intrinsic value.
SHADES: Made of Pure Silk—center panels stretched and decorated with a pleasing design which is fashioned from silk cord twist—side panels neatly pleated. Trimmed effectively with silk braid on top and bottom. Silk lined. Junior Lamp has 18 inch shade, the Bridge Lamp a 12½ inch shade and the Table Lamp a 16½ inch shade. For choice of colors see top of page.
STANDS: Junior is 61 inches high with 5 inch extension. Bridge stand is 54 inches high and is adjustable. They are artistically fashioned from metal—the bridge stand is wired complete with one pull chain socket—the Junior with three candle lights and canopy turn switch. Finished in choice of Old English, Green or Black. The Table Lamp stand is 20 inches high with 5 inch extension. Has all metal base, artistically modeled, and is furnished in Old English, Green and Black colors.

COMPLETE LAMP PRICES
No. K8J/193-1007 Junior Complete..
No. K8J/193¼-2007 Bridge Complete
No. K8J/193¾-4008 Table Lamp
Complete ....

THREE CANDLE JUNIOR LAMP

(Pictured at right)

Shade: Size 18 inches. Made of Pure Silk with stretched panels. Has silk lining and ribs covered attractively with silk braid. Furnished in all colors listed at top of page.
Stand: Is 61 inches high with 5 inch extension. Made from metal and finished only in Old Gold. Wired complete for three candle lights with canopy turn switch.

No. K8J/184-1099
Complete .....

BRIDGE LAMP

(Illustrated above)

Shade: Size 12½ inches. Rounded octagon shape. Made of Pure Silk with stretched panels. Has silk lining and ribs are covered attractively with silk braid. Furnished in all colors listed at top of page.
Stand: Bridge style, adjustable. Height, 54 inches. Made from metal and finished only in Old Gold. Wired complete with one pull chain socket.

No. K8J/184¼-2099
Complete ..

THREE CANDLE JUNIOR LAMP

(Pictured at right)

Shade: Size 18 inches. Rounded octagon shape. Made of Pure Silk with stretched panels. Velvet and silk braid on panels and velvet braid trimming on top and bottom rim. Silk lined. All colors listed at top of page furnished.
Stand: Height, 61 inches. Made entirely from metal and finished in choice of Old Gold, Old English or Black and Old English. Wired complete for three candle lights with canopy turn switch.

No. K8J/187-1096
Complete ..

BRIDGE LAMP

(Pictured above)

Shade: Size 12½ inches. Rounded octagon shape. Made of Pure Silk with stretched panels. Velvet and silk braid on panels and velvet braid trimming on top and bottom rim. Silk lined. All colors listed at top of page furnished.
Stand: Bridge style, adjustable. Height, 54 inches. Fashioned from metal and finished in choice of Old Gold, Old English or Black and Old English. Wired complete with one pull chain socket.

No. K8J/187¼-2096
Complete ....

Floor Lamps

JUNIOR SHADE

2749V 20 inch georgette hexagon shape shade. Color delicately shaded black and white, ombre lined and interlined with peach colored silk. Shirred trim top and bottom. Hand made flower spray decoration. This is one of our very finest shades. **Each**

JUNIOR BASE

5431V A stunning combination of hammered plated metal and genuine white onyx makes a good looking base. The pedestal rests upon a miniature base built over a larger one. **Each**

BRIDGE SHADE

2750V Same as 2749V but in the 12 inch bridge style. **Each**

BRIDGE BASE

5432V Same base as 5431V but in the bridge style. **Each**

TORCHIER

5323V A three light torchier finished in a dull gold with slight tracing of color on the lower spindle turning. Excellent for reception or living room. Usually used as pairs but priced individually. (Bulbs included) **Each**

BRIDGE SHADE

2763V A lovely soft orange georgette with a pink lining to give it tone. The trim is of gold and tan silk braid. Each panel is decorated with a gold medallion. Diameter 12 inches. **Each**

BRIDGE BASE

5446V Spiral stem with break and base of genuine onyx. Finished in Spanish brass. A high grade base at moderate price. **Each**

JUNIOR SHADE

2758V Brocaded stretched silk in bird and cloud design and plaited combination as illustrated. Size 12 inches. Colors taupe over rose or green over gold. **Each**

FLOORETTE

5442V The heavy silk cord is wired and permits the shade to be adjusted. A high grade type of lamp. Finished gold plated brass and lacquered. Genuine onyx base. **Each**

JUNIOR SHADE

2218V A beautiful old rose georgette shade over a firm piece of orange crepe. The scalloped trim is designed in an ivory embroidered net with a gold thread running through it and bound with a fancy braid of gold, green and rose. Size 18 inches. **Each**

JUNIOR BASE

5433V Nothing is more attractive and yet practical than this dark Spanish metal post with the shaded genuine black and grey marble base and trim. **Each**

BRIDGE SHADE

2219V Same as 2218V but in the 12 inch bridge style. **Each**

BRIDGE BASE

5434V Same as 5433V but in the bridge style. **Each**

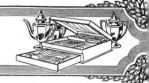

JUNIOR SHADE
2739V Made of leaded Mica in Mosaic design. Rose amber tone tinted green in color. One of our highest grade shades both in workmanship and design.

JUNIOR BASE
5455V A high grade lamp of fluted designed tubing finished in Granada gold plating.

BRIDGE SHADE
2738V Same as 2739V but in the 12 inch bridge style.

BRIDGE BASE
5454V Same as 5455V but in the bridge style.

BRIDGE SHADE
2760V Tailored silk shade of dark tan trimmed in patches of red and bound with red and tan braid gives this shade a distinction. The lining is of peach colored rayon. Diameter 10 inches.

BRIDGE BASE
5444V A good looking base at low price. Post has etched design and octagon base has a hammered brass effect.

BRIDGE SHADE
2761V A very pretty combination of tan georgette and silk embroidered in gold. Tan shirred ribbon and a silk braid of tan and rose form the trimming. Diameter 12 inches.

BRIDGE BASE
5445V Bronze metal lamp with classical lines. Plain footed base, balance has etched design throughout.

SHADE
2212V A silk covered hand made shade. The background is a tan color offset with braid and decorated in black and orange.

"JENNY LIND" LAMP
5299V Lamp is finished in gun metal and gold combination. The base is of 6 pound weight, resting on three Lion Claws fitted with 5/8 inch round brass tubing, trimmed with plain hand turned spindles, finished in gold. Arm is of solid brass tubing fitted with adjustable swivel joint, fancy husk pull chain-socket.

JUNIOR SHADE
2747V Hand decorated parchment shade in tan with orchid and rose flower design. Each section of the octagon shape is laced together with brown lacing producing a most effective appearance. Diameter 20 inches.

JUNIOR BASE
5428V Beautiful decorated antique metal base with delicate green tint. The genuine white onyx trim gives the lamp a most striking appearance.

BRIDGE SHADE
2748V Same as 2747V but in 11 inch bridge style.

BRIDGE BASE
5429V Same as 5428V but in bridge style.

These new creations are attractively fashioned and excellently tailored and finished. All are of standard height—56 inches. All come fitted with two-light cluster, silk cord and plug. All furnished in such beautiful combination of colors, as Orange and Black, Orange and Taupe, Orange and Mulberry, Orange and Blue, Rose and Blue, Rose and Putty, Rose and Champagne, Rose and Tan, Gold and Rose, Gold and Mulberry, Green and Putty, Orchid and Grey, and Orchid and Orchid. The first color represents the lining and the last color the Georgette top.

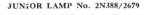

JUNIOR LAMP No. 2N388/2679

SHADE: 22 inch oval shade made in alternate shirred and stretched georgette panels. Two rich and Beautiful Imported tinsel flowers. Trimmed with heavy braid and 6-inch silk fringe.

STAND: 2-light pull chain cluster. Stand attractively finished in stippled Gold and Black.

No. 2N388/2679, Complete....

SHADE OR STAND FURNISHED SEPARATELY IF DESIRED

No. 2N388, Shade, only, each.
No. 2N2679, Stand, only, each.

JUNIOR LAMP No. 2N359/2839

SHADE: 22-inch shade made in shirred Georgette, trimmed with two Imported flowers and braid, and heavy 6-inch silk fringe. A pleasing style and shows up effectively.

STAND: 2-light pull chain cluster. Stand finished in Gold and Black.

No. 2N359/2839, Complete...

SHADE OR STAND FURNISHED SEPARATELY IF DESIRED

No. 2N359, Shade, each.....
No. 2N2839, Stand, each.....

No. 2N388/2679 Complete...

No. 2N359/2839 Complete....

Can furnish a combination of silk and bouillon fringe instead of the heavy silk fringe for $5.35 List Extra. This gives a richer and more exclusive effect to lamp.

JUNIOR LAMP No. 376/2839

SHADE: 24 inch oval shade made in alternate plaited and shirred fan panels. Heavy tinsel braid trimming with silk apron and heavy 6 inch silk fringe.

STAND: 2-light pull chain cluster, long silk pull cords. Finished Gold and Black.

No. 2N376/2839, Complete

SHADE OR STAND FURNISHED SEPARATELY IF DESIRED

No. 2N376 Shade, only...
No. 2N2839 Stand, only.

JUNIOR LAMP No. 393/1428

SHADE: A very attractive and prettily designed shade, 24 inch, stretched georgette top, tinsel lace border. Trimmed with two Imported tinsel flowers, heavy braid and heavy 6 inch silk fringe.

STAND: 2-light pull chain socket, richly carved and finished Black and Gold.

No. 2N393/1428, Complete.

SHADE OR STAND FURNISHED SEPARATELY IF DESIRED

No. 2N393 Shade, each..
No. 2N1428 Stand, each.

No. 2N376/2839 Complete

No. 2N393/1428 Complete.

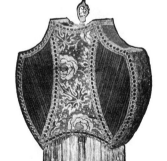

JUNIOR LAMP No. 2N381/1428

SHADE: A design which is most prepossessing in appearance. Symmetrically designed rich stand. 22-inch oblong shade of plated georgette top, lower portion alternate tinsel lace and stretched panels, trimmed with Imported pastel flowers, heavy braid on border and 6-inch silk fringe.

STAND: 2-light pull chain socket, silk pull cords. Hand carved and finished in Gold and Black.

No. 2N381/1428 Complete.

SHADE OR STAND FURNISHED SEPARATELY IF DESIRED

No. 2N381, Shade each.
No. 2N1428 Stand, each.

JUNIOR LAMP No. 2N380/1446

SHADE: Flat shade, 17-inch front and 14 inches in depth. Made of plaited Georgette and stretched tinsel lace. Trimmed with heavy braid and 5-inch bouillon fringe.

STAND: 2-light pull chain socket, silk pull cords. Finished Gold and Black.

No. 2N380/1446 Complete

SHADE OR STAND FURNISHED SEPARATELY IF DESIRED

No. 2N380, Shade, each.........
No. 2N1446, Stand, each.........

Can furnish a combination of silk and bouillon fringe instead of the heavy silk fringe for List Extra. This gives a richer and more exclusive effect to lamp.

JUNIOR LAMP No. 2N382/11014

A design of exclusive charm, expertly tailored of finest materials and nicely finished.

SHADE: 22-inch shade of stretched Georgette top, lower portion alternate, sunburst and tinsel lace panels. Border trimmed with heavy braid and heavy 6-inch silk fringe.

STAND: 2-light pull chain socket, long silk cords. Hand carved with Metal finish.

No. 2N382/11014, Complete.

SHADE OR STAND FURNISHED SEPARATELY IF DESIRED

No. 2N382 Shade, each....
No. 2N11014 Stand, each....

A superb creation in our most exquisite offering in this selling.

SHADE: 24-inch oval shade, plaited georgette. Trimmed with Imported pastel flower, cut-out band on border, heavy 6 inch silk fringe.

STAND: 2-light pull chain socket, silk pull cords. Hand carved stand, metal leaf finish.

No. 2N374/1461, Complete...

SHADE OR STAND FURNISHED SEPARATELY IF DESIRED

No. 2N374 Shade, each.....
No. 2N1461 Stand, each.....

. 2N381/1428 Complete...

No. 2N380/1446 Complete...

No. 2N382/11014 Complete..

No. 2N374/1461 Complete..

Excellent workmanship and high grade materials thruout; solid metal base
and standard; assorted parchment shades in attractive designs; silk cord.

BRIDGE LAMPS

Jr. FLOOR LAMPS

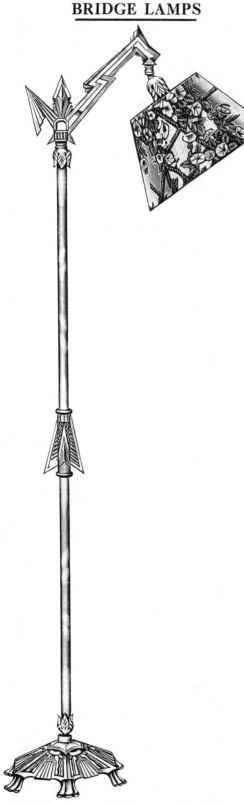

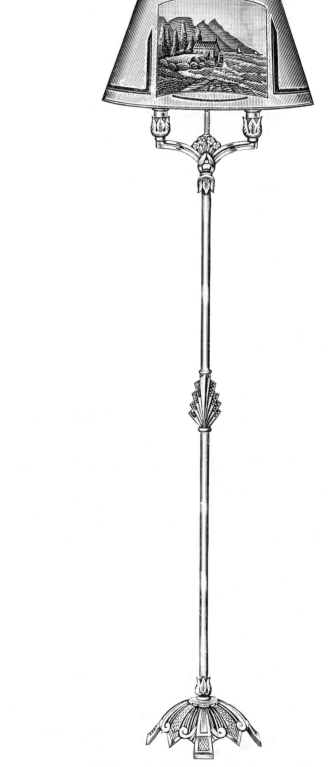

One socket; size of shade at top, 4½″x4½″, at bottom, 10½x10½″ height, overall, 60″.

No. 4600—Weight, each, 20 pounds.

Two sockets; diameter of shade at top, 12″, at bottom, 18″, height, overall, 63″.

No. 5500—Weight, each, 25 pounds.

Jeannette Lamps—Hand Decorated and Colors Fired In. 16-inch shades; height 22 inches. Note that these lamps have patented ring tops. All bases have felt covered bottom. Equipment and packing same as Group No. 500.

GROUP
800

No. 8-805
Finish—Italian Bronze

No. 8-624
Finish—Colonial Brass

No. 8-802
Finish—Antique Gold

No. 8-804
Finish—Black and Gold

No. 8-806
Finish—Venetian

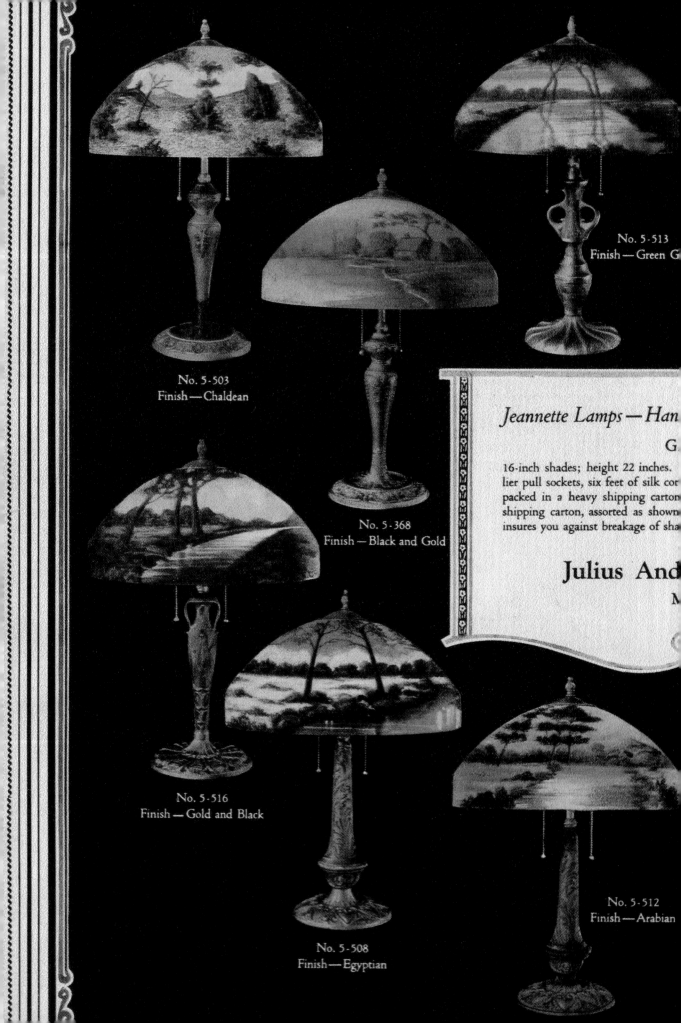

No. 5-503
Finish — Chaldean

No. 5-368
Finish — Black and Gold

No. 5-513
Finish — Green G

No. 5-516
Finish — Gold and Black

No. 5-508
Finish — Egyptian

No. 5-512
Finish — Arabian

Jeannette Lamps — Han

G.

16-inch shades; height 22 inches.
lier pull sockets, six feet of silk cor
packed in a heavy shipping carton
shipping carton, assorted as shown
insures you against breakage of sha

Julius And

M

No. 5-502
Finish—Roman Gold

No. 5-504
Finish—Chaldean

No. 5-515
Finish—Roman Gold

No. 5-514
Finish—Roman Gold

No. 5-522
Finish—Chaldean

No. 5-507
Finish—Arabian

...orated and Colors Fired In

...500

...ps illustrated are equipped with Levo-
...-piece plugs. Each shade is carefully
...breakage. Stands are packed six in a
...ps equipped with patented top which
...ases have felt covered bottom.

...& Sons Co.
...kee

Jeannette Lamps—Hand Decorated and Colors Fired In. 12-inch shades; height 18 inches. Stands are equipped with one push through socket, six feet of silk cord and separable plug. All bases have felt covered bottom. Packed six lamps to a standard package.

GROUP
297

No. 7-512
Finish—Roman Gold

No. 7-515
Finish—Venetian Bronze

No. 7-514
Finish—Gold and Polychrome

No. 7-504
Finish—Bronze

No. 7-518
Finish—Bronze Green

No. 7-507
Finish—Silver and Polychrome

Electric Floor Boudoir, Bed and Desk Lamps

All wired complete and equipped with full length cord and one-piece plug. Bulbs not included.

Electric DESK or BOUDOIR LAMP

S7158—"The Reflector-et." (Mfrs. 540). The newest thing in lamps. Attractive all metal standard with unique footed base, scientifically designed pull socket reflector sheds a soft even light over the entire room, operating independently from the switch controlled 3-light candle cluster. The shade is made of the new exclusive "Dec-Art-Tex" parchment of the leaflette design. Ht. 62 in.
Each....................

S7162—Davonette and Smoker Lamp. (Mfrs. 724). Base is finished in gold and colored enamel, tilting parchment shade is adjustable for raising from 52 to 57 in. high and the harmonizing smoker set consists of cigarette jar and two ash trays. A happy combination of quality, style and price.
Each..............................

S7163—Combination Lamp and Smoker. Enamel base with cleartone parchment shade, hand finished with scroll design in gold relief process, 3-cluster candle type, harmonizing 3-piece smoker set consisting of cigarette jar, ash tray and match holder. An attractive davenport style lamp at a low price. Each

Desk or Boudoir Lamp. (Mfrs. 250.) Height over all, 10 in. Glass base and shade. Spring steel shade holder enameled to match. Completely wired with push socket, cord and plug. Packed each in carton.

S6003—Green.
S6004—Pink.
Doz.,
Each....................

Electric Bed Lamp

S6005 — Bed Lamp. (Mfrs. 151.) Clamp style, easily attached to any bed, standard Edison base, socket with pull chain, 8-ft. cord and plug. Colors, green and mahogany.
1 in cart. Each,

Electric Desk Lamp

S6000—Desk Lamp. (Mfrs. 990.) A beautiful modernistic design, shade adjustable to any angle, base grooved for pen and pencil, tray for paper clips, cigar ashes, etc. Colors, green or mahogany. 1 in carton.

Each....................

Novelty Dice and CARD LAMPS

Your Choice of Either Style at Each,

The most unique and novel appearing electric lamp introduced this season. Both base and shade resemble gigantic size dice, perfectly simulated. Will add distinction and charm to any room environment. Completely wired. Dimensions of lamp are as follows: Height, 11 inches; shade, 3¼ inches square.

S2156—Electric Dice Lamp. Doz., $10.20.
Each................................

S5999 — Same as above, with card spots instead of dice spots. Doz., $10.20. Each....................

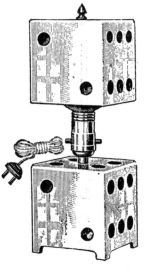

Electric Table, Floor, Bridge and Lounge Lamps

With Shades to Harmonize

Bridge Lamp

S7165—Bridge Lamp. (Mfrs. 100). Metal base of classic style, swivel adjustment on shade, pure silk radium shade with **rayon** taffeta lining, cord and silk covered button.
Each ......

Table Lamp

S7164—Table Lamp. (Mfrs. 800). Attractive metal base, 3-light cluster, candelabra type, adjustable 20 to 25 in., silk radium shade, drum lining. Each..............

STYLES reproduced from Colonial Classics Bridge, table, floor or lounge lamps.

Swivel adjustment on bridge shade.

SHADES of pure silk radium, drum fitted rayon taffeta lining, cord and silk covered button trim.

FIXTURES of the Candelabra type with adjustable extensions.

Tilting shade on Junior.

BASES in a choice of colors: black and gold, green and gold, burgundy and gold or English bronze plated.

Lounge Lamp

S7166—Lounge Lamp. (Mfrs. 400). Ornamental metal standard and base. Classic Colonial style reproduction, 3 lite candelabra style adjustable fixture. Ht. 49-55 in., tilting shade of rayon silk. Each............

Floor Lamp

S7167—Floor Lamp. (Mfrs. 300). Metal base and standard of Colonial Classic style in black and gold, green and gold, burgundy and gold or English bronze plated, 3 lite candelabra style adjustable fixture. Ht. 59-65 in., pure silk 18 in. rayon lined shade. Each ....

Lounge Lamp

S7168—Lounge or Reading Lamp. (Mfrs. 6400). Ornamental metal base and standard in choice of colors listed below, parchment shade, tilting type, 3 lite candelabra style adjustable fixture, ht. 49-55 in. Ea......

STYLES reproduced from Colonial Classics, bridge, table, floor or lounge lamps.

S7168

Swivel Adjustment on Bridge Shade

Bridge Lamp

S7169—Bridge Lamp. (Mfrs. 6100). Base of Colonial Classic style, choice of colors listed below, "Florette" design parchment shade with swivel adjustment. Ea.

Table Lamp

S7170—Table Lamp. (Mfrs. 6800). Art metal base in choice of colors listed below, "Florette" design parchment shade, 3 lite cluster, candelabra type adjustable fixture, 20-25 in. Each ....

S7169

BASES in a choice of colors; black and gold, green and gold and burgundy and gold.

All Lamps Are Exactly As Pictured.

Floor Lamp

S7172—Floor Lamp. (Mfrs. 6300). Colonial Classic type base in black and gold, green and gold or burgundy and gold, "Florette" design parchment shade, 3 lite candelabra style adjustable lamp fixture. Ht. 59-65 in. Each ....

S7172

Quality Lamps at Lowest Prices

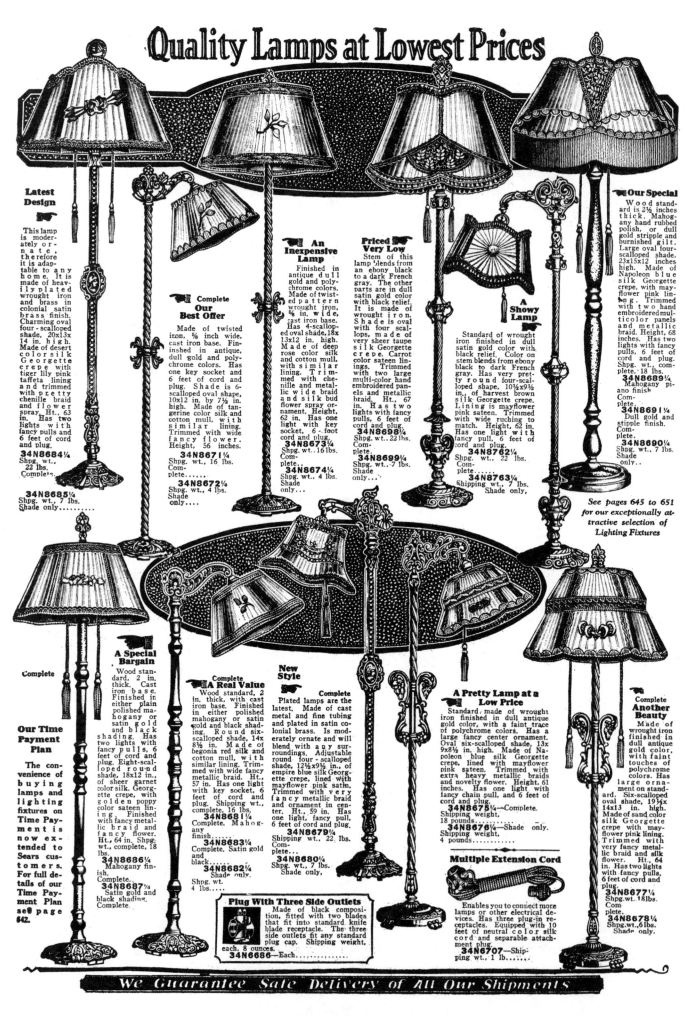

Latest Design

This lamp is moderately ornate, therefore it is adaptable to any home. It is made of heavily plated wrought iron and brass in colonial satin brass finish. Charming oval four - scalloped shade, 20x13x 14 in. high. Made of desert color silk Georgette crepe with tiger lily pink taffeta lining and trimmed with pretty chenille braid and flower spray. Ht., 63 in. Has two lights with fancy pulls and 6 feet of cord and plug.

34N8684¼
Shpg. wt., 22 lbs. Complete.

34N8685¼
Shpg. wt., 7 lbs. Shade only..........

Complete Our Best Offer

Made of twisted iron, ⅝ inch wide, cast iron base. Finished in antique, dull gold and polychrome colors. Has one key socket and 6 feet of cord and plug. Shade is 6-scalloped oval shape, 10x12 in. by 7½ in. high. Made of tangerine color silk and cotton mull, with similar lining. Trimmed with wide fancy flower. Height, 56 inches.

34N8671¼
Shpg. wt., 16 lbs. Complete......

34N8672¼
Shpg. wt., 4 lbs. Shade only....

An Inexpensive Lamp

Finished in antique dull gold and polychrome colors. Made of twisted pattern wrought iron, ⅝ in. wide, cast iron base. Has 4-scalloped oval shade, 18x 13x12 in. high. Made of deep rose color silk and cotton mull, with similar lining. Trimmed with chenille and metallic wide braid and silk bud flower spray ornament. Ht., 62 in. Has one light with key socket, 6 - foot cord and plug.

34N8673¼
Shpg. wt..16 lbs. Complete.

34N8674¼
Shpg. wt.. 4 lbs. Shade only...

Priced Very Low

Stem of this lamp blends from an ebony black to a dark French gray. The other parts are in dull satin gold color with black relief. It is made of wrought iron. Shade is oval with four scallops, made of very sheer taupe silk Georgette crepe. Carrot color sateen linings. Trimmed with two large multi-color hand embroidered panels and metallic braid. Ht., 67 in. Has two lights with fancy pulls, 6 feet of cord and plug.

34N8698¼
Shpg.wt..22 lbs. Complete.

34N8699¼
Shpg. wt..-7 lbs. Shade only...

A Showy Lamp

Standard of wrought iron finished in dull satin gold color with black relief. Color on stem blends from ebony black to dark French gray. Has very pretty round four-scalloped shape, 10½x9½ in., of harvest brown silk Georgette crepe. Lining is mayflower pink sateen. Trimmed with wide ruching to match. Height, 62 in. Has one light with fancy pull, 6 feet of cord and plug.

34N8762¼
Shpg. wt.. 22 lbs. Complete.

34N8763¼
Shipping wt.. 7 lbs. Shade only,

Our Special

Wood standard is 2½ inches thick. Mahogany hand rubbed polish, or dull gold stripple and burnished gilt. Large oval four-scalloped shade, 23x15x12 inches high. Made of Napoleon blue silk Georgette crepe, with mayflower pink lining. Trimmed with two hand embroidered multicolor panels and metallic braid. Height, 68 inches. Has two lights with fancy pulls, 6 feet of cord and plug. Shpg. wt., complete.-18 lbs.

34N8689¼
Mahogany piano finish
Complete.

34N8691¼
Dull gold and stipple finish. Complete.

34N8690¼
Shpg. wt., 7 lbs. Shade only..

See pages 645 to 651 for our exceptionally attractive selection of Lighting Fixtures

Our Time Payment Plan

The convenience of buying lamps and lighting fixtures on Time Payment is now extended to Sears customers. For full details of our Time Payment Plan see page 642.

A Special Bargain

Wood standard, 2 in. thick, Cast iron base. Finished in either plain polished mahogany or satin gold and black shading. Has two lights with fancy pulls, 6 feet of cord and plug. Eight-scalloped round shade, 18x12 in., of sheer garnet color silk Georgette crepe, with golden poppy color sateen lining. Finished with fancy metallic braid and fancy flower. Ht., 64 in. Shpg. wt., complete, 18 lbs.

34N8686¼
Mahogany finish. Complete.

34N8687¼
Satin gold and black shading. Complete.

Complete A Real Value

Wood standard, 2 in. thick, with cast iron base. Finished in either polished mahogany or satin gold and black shading. Round six-scalloped shade, 14x 8½ in. Made of begonia red silk and cotton mull, with similar lining. Trimmed with wide fancy metallic braid. Ht. 57 in. Has one light with key socket, 6 feet of cord and plug. Shipping wt., complete, 16 lbs.

34N8681¼
Complete. Mahogany finish......

34N8683¼
Complete. Satin gold and black.

34N8682¼
Complete. Shade only. Shpg. wt. 4 lbs.

New Style

Plated lamps are the latest. Made of cast metal and fine tubing and plated in satin colonial brass. Is moderately ornate and will blend with any surroundings. Adjustable round four - scalloped shade, 12½x9½ in., of empire blue silk Georgette crepe, lined with mayflower pink satin. Trimmed with very fancy metallic braid and ornament in center. Ht., 59 in. Has one light, fancy pull, 6 feet of cord and plug.

34N8679¼
Shipping wt.. 22 lbs. Complete...

34N8680¼
Shpg. wt., 7 lbs. Shade only,

A Pretty Lamp at a Low Price

Standard, made of wrought iron finished in dull antique gold color, with a faint trace of polychrome colors. Has a large fancy center ornament. Oval six-scalloped shade, 13x 9x8½ in. high. Made of Napoleon blue silk Georgette crepe, lined with mayflower pink sateen. Trimmed with extra heavy metallic braids and novelty flower. Height, 61 inches. Has one light with fancy chain pull, and 6 feet of cord and plug.

34N8675¼—Complete. Shipping weight, 18 pounds.

34N8676¼—Shade only. Shipping weight, 4 pounds...........

Multiple Extension Cord

Enables you to connect more lamps or other electrical devices. Has three plug-in receptacles. Equipped with 10 feet of neutral color silk cord and separable attachment plug.

34N6707—Shipping wt., 1 lb........

Complete Another Beauty

Made of wrought iron finished in dull antique gold color, with faint touches of polychrome colors. Has large ornament on standard. Six-scalloped oval shade, 19½x 14x13 in. high. Made of sand color silk Georgette crepe with mayflower pink lining. Trimmed with very fancy metallic braid and silk flower. Ht., 64 in. Has two lights with fancy pulls, 6 feet of cord and plug.

34N8677¼
Shpg.wt. 18lbs. Complete.

34N8678¼
Shpg.wt.,6 lbs. Shade only.

Plug With Three Side Outlets

Made of black composition, fitted with two blades that fit into standard knife blade receptacle. The three side outlets fit any standard plug cap. Shipping weight, each, 8 ounces.

34N6686—Each......

We Guarantee Safe Delivery of All Our Shipments

NEAT OIL, GAS AND ELECTRIC LAMPS

Buy Them On Credit

All Shipped From Chicago

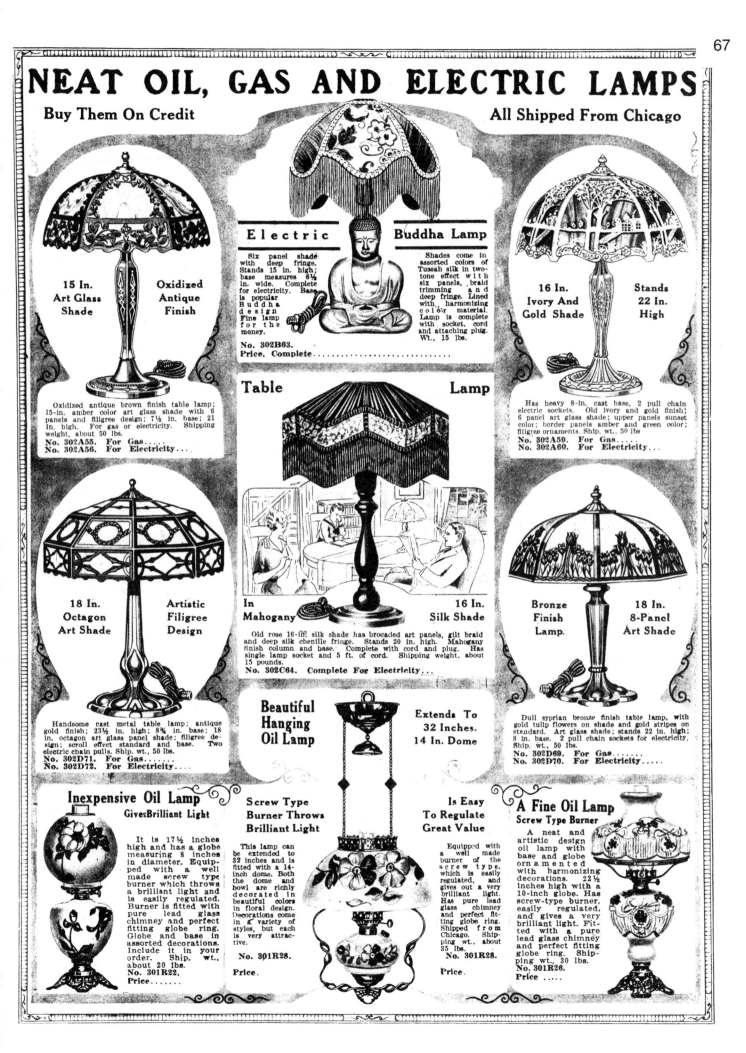

15 In. Art Glass Shade — **Oxidized Antique Finish**

Oxidized antique brown finish table lamp; 15-in. amber color art glass shade with 6 panels and filigree design; 7½ in. base; 21 in. high. For gas or electricity. Shipping weight, about 50 lbs.
No. 302A55. For Gas.....
No. 302A56. For Electricity....

Electric   Buddha Lamp

Six panel shade with deep fringe. Stands 15 in. high; base measures 6½ in. wide. Complete for electricity. Base is popular Buddha design. Fine lamp for the money.
No. 302B63.
Price, Complete.............................

Shades come in assorted colors of Tussah silk in two-tone effect with six panels, braid trimming and deep fringe. Lined with harmonizing color material. Lamp is complete with socket, cord and attaching plug. Wt., 15 lbs.

16 In. Ivory And Gold Shade — **Stands 22 In. High**

Has heavy 8-in. cast base, 2 pull chain electric sockets. Old ivory and gold finish; 6 panel art glass shade; upper panels sunset color; border panels amber and green color; filigree ornaments. Ship. wt., 50 lbs.
No. 302A59. For Gas....
No. 302A60. For Electricity...

18 In. Octagon Art Shade — **Artistic Filigree Design**

Handsome cast metal table lamp; antique gold finish; 23½ in. high; 8¾ in. base; 18 in. octagon art glass panel shade; filigree design; scroll effect standard and base. Two electric chain pulls. Ship. wt., 50 lbs.
No. 302D71. For Gas....
No. 302D72. For Electricity....

Table   Lamp

In Mahogany — **16 In. Silk Shade**

Old rose 16-in. silk shade has brocaded art panels, gilt braid and deep silk chenille fringe. Stands 20 in. high. Mahogany finish column and base. Complete with cord and plug. Has single lamp socket and 5 ft. of cord. Shipping weight, about 15 pounds.
No. 302C64. Complete For Electricity...

Bronze Finish Lamp. — **18 In. 8-Panel Art Shade**

Dull syrian bronze finish table lamp, with gold tulip flowers on shade and gold stripes on standard. Art glass shade; stands 22 in. high; 8 in. base. 2 pull chain sockets for electricity. Ship. wt., 50 lbs.
No. 302D69. For Gas......
No. 302D70. For Electricity.....

Beautiful Hanging Oil Lamp

Extends To 32 Inches. 14 In. Dome

Inexpensive Oil Lamp
Gives Brilliant Light

It is 17½ inches high and has a globe measuring 8 inches in diameter. Equipped with a well made screw type burner which throws a brilliant light and is easily regulated. Burner is fitted with pure lead glass chimney and perfect fitting globe ring. Globe and base in assorted decorations. Include it in your order. Ship. wt., about 20 lbs.
No. 301R22.
Price......

Screw Type Burner Throws Brilliant Light

This lamp can be extended to 32 inches and is fitted with a 14-inch dome. Both the dome and bowl are richly decorated in beautiful colors in floral design. Decorations come in a variety of styles, but each is very attractive.
No. 301R28.
Price.

Is Easy To Regulate
Great Value

Equipped with a well made burner of the screw type, which is easily regulated, and gives out a very brilliant light. Has pure lead glass chimney and perfect fitting globe ring. Shipped from Chicago. Shipping wt., about 35 lbs.
No. 301R28.
Price.

A Fine Oil Lamp
Screw Type Burner

A neat and artistic design oil lamp with base and globe ornamented with harmonizing decorations. 22½ inches high with a 10-inch globe. Has screw-type burner, easily regulated, and gives a very brilliant light. Fitted with a pure lead glass chimney and perfect fitting globe ring. Shipping wt., 30 lbs.
No. 301R26.
Price .....

FLOOR LAMPS, BEDROOM LAMPS, SHADES IN STUNNING DESIGNS

No. 299D54
Stand, $16.50

No. 299B43.
Shade, $14.95

No. 299C51
Stand, $16.75

No. 299C50
Shade,
$17.50

299R20
Stand,
$9.85

299D52
Shade,
$16.49

299A46
Stand,
$8.95

299D55
Shade,
$11.98

302C68
Complete
$3.89

302C67
Complete
$3.97

No. 302C65
Complete
$11.95

All Are Wired For Electricity

No. 299D56. Stand, $17.49
No. 299D57. Shade, 17.95

Has 68-in. standard; 6-in. diameter; 14-in. base; is imitation mahogany finish; 2-light fixture; chain pull; 8 ft. cord and attaching plug; 26-in. shade of shirred tussah silk in blue or rose with floral figured panels; chenille braid trimmed; bead ornaments; deep silk chenille fringe. Ship. wt. of shade, 10 lbs.; of stand, 30 lbs.
No. 299D54. Stand Alone **$16.50**
No. 299B43. Shade Alone **$14.95**

Rose or blue 26-in. silk shade, with two-tone effect silk lining; has deep silk fringe trimmed with chenille braid. Has four figured silk panels and four plain silk panels in shirred effect. Imitation mahogany standard is 68 inches high; 8-ft. cord; 2-piece plug; 14½-inch heavy base; 7-in. column; double lamp sockets. Ship. wt. of shade, 10 lbs.; of standard, 40 lbs.
No. 299C51. Stand Alone **$16.75**
No. 299C50. Shade Alone **$17.50**

Imitation mahogany standard is 68 in. high, 4-in. diameter, fitted with socket and 6 ft. of heavy insulated silk cord. Has double cluster Benjamin socket; 26-inch silk Tussah shade with 8 panels, 4 of plain silk with 4 alternating figured silk panels, all in shirred effect. Fancy braid and fringe. Ship. wt. is about 35 pounds.
No. 299R20. Stand Alone **$9.85**
No. 299D52. Shade Alone **$16.49**

Standard is 68 in. high; 3 in. thick; imitation mahogany finish. Complete with 6 ft. of cord and 1-piece attaching plug. 24-inch shade has 8 panels; these are alternating scalloped and straight panels of fine plain Jap silk and figured silkoline; in rose or blue; 4-in. chenille fringe; mull lining; bound with dainty braid. Shipping weight, about 35 pounds.
No. 299A46. Stand Alone **$8.95**
No. 299D55. Shade Alone **$11.98**

Polychrome gold standard is 67½ in. high. Is very artistic 13-inch base; 2 sockets; 2 pull chains. Cord and plug attachment; 24-inch shade covered with old rose silk Tussah and lined with Jap silk in old gold shade, with pinked edge, shirred top. Trimmed with gold braid; 6-inch fringe; a very rich looking shade. Shipping weight, about 35 pounds.
No. 299D56. Stand Alone **$17.49**
No. 299D57. Shade Alone **$17.95**

Imitation mahogany finish hand polished stand, turned from 1½-inch stock; 4½-inch base; felted bottom. Key socket for electricity; 6-ft. silk cord and plug; about 15 in. high with shade. Silk shade measures about 8 inches in diameter. Choice of old rose or blue. Lined with Tussah silk; bound with gold trimmed braid. Ship. wt., 5 pounds.
No. 302C68. Price, Complete **$3.89**

Adjustable reading lamp. Has 6-ft. cord and screw plug; heavy 12-inch base. Standard turned from 3-inch stock and stands 55 inches high. Finished in imitation mahogany color. The handsome 12-inch silk shade comes in choice of blue, rose or old gold and is trimmed with gold braid and a 3½-inch fringe at bottom. Has an adjustable polished brass bracket. Shade has shirred top. Ship. wt. 30 lbs.
No. 302C65. Price, Complete **$11.95**

Furnished with same standard as No. 302C68 (see description). The silk shade is about 8 inches in diameter. Comes in old rose or blue. Lined with Tussah silk and is neatly bound with gold trimmed braid. Shipping weight, about 5 pounds.
No. 302C67. Complete **$3.97**

All Of These Lamps Shipped From Chicago Warehouse

6031

6082

6022

6003

6012

6013

6114

6103

6113

6104

6105

6115

PARKER LAMPS

6103—Bridge Lamp. All-metal standard; finish Spray Gold with Polychrome; over-all height 57″....................Base only.

6031—Shade. Hand decorated Parchment with futuristic design....Shade only......
    Base and Shade complete.......

6113—Junior Lamp. All-metal standard; finish Spray Gold and Polychrome; over-all height, 60″...............Base only..

6003—Shade. Octagonal mica, hand decorated with laced bindings......Shade only..
    Base and Shade complete.......

6104—Bridge Lamp. All-metal standard; finished in Roman Gold and Polychrome; over-all height, 57″..............Base only..

6012—Shade. Hexagonal Parchment with flowered design...............Shade only.
    Base and Shade complete........

6114—Junior Lamp. All-metal standard; finished in Roman Gold and Polychrome; over-all height 60″...................Base only...

6082—Shade. Decorated Parchment with laced bindings.................Shade only.
    Base and Shade complete........

6105—Bridge Lamp. All-metal standard; finished Spray Gold and Jap Bronze; over-all height 61″...................Base only.

6022—Shade. Hand decorated Parchment in neutral colors............Shade only..
    Base and Shade complete........

6115—Junior Lamp. All-metal standard; finished Spray Gold and Jap Bronze; over-all height 60″..............Base only.

6013—Shade. Hexagonal Crackled Parchment with laced bindings......Shade only..
    Base and Shade complete........

Electric Lamps for Home and Desk

No. 75. DELUXE-A-LITE
A very artfully designed and finished desk lamp. Stand is 18 inches high and finished in Verda Green. Green (white cased inside) shade is 8½ inches long and is adjustable up and down on the stand. Can furnish stands in Verde Green or Antique Gold. This lamp is equipped with 8-foot (underwriters approved) silk cord and 2-piece plug and pull chain socket.
Complete as above......................
Green glass shade only..................

No. 120/704.
ANTIQUE GOLD PLATED
Aladdin Superior Desk Lamp in a modernistic design. Height, 18 inches, Green Shade (white cased inside) adjustable up or down. Equipped with silk cord 2-piece plug and pull chain socket.
No. 122/704.
STATUARY BRONZE PLATED
Otherwise same as above.

No. 111/511. DELUXE-A-WELL
A new attractive and very convenient desk lamp. It equipped with two inkwells and penholder racks. Stand 18 inches high with Green (white cased inside) shade, 8 inches long and adjustable up and down. Stand is fu nished in Pompeian bronze. This lamp is equipped wi 8-foot (underwriters approved, silk cord, 2-piece plug a pull chain socket.
Complete as above......................
Green glass shade only..................

No. 50.
RICH GOLD PLATED
Aladdin Desk lamp complete with silk cord and 2-piece plug.

No. 1335/1745.
GOLD CRINKLED
Aladdin modern table lamp. Shade diameter 16 inches, Stand Height, 20 inches, complete with Cord and plug.
No. 1336/1746.
SILVER CRINKLED
Otherwise same as above.
No. 1337/1747.
RUSSET CRINKLED
Otherwise same as above.

No. 312/722.
BLACK GLAZE
Aladdin End Table Lamp. Shades are Hand Painted, beaded with Black Velvet Binding. Size of Shade 8x9 inches. Height of stand 20 inches, complete with cord and plug.

No. 73. DESK-FLEX
Stand is 15 inches high, shade 6½ inche in diameter. A very handy and reliabl flexible desk lamp. Lamp is wired wit 6-foot (underwriters approved) silk cor 2-piece plugs and turn knob socket. Furn ished in statuary bronze.
Complete..................

No. 521/1970.
LAMP—Complete, with Silk shade, base made of composition white metal, finished in natural colors, bottom covered with felt equipped with cord, socket and plug; size from base to top of socket, 10 inches.

No. 518/4055.
LAMP—Complete with Parchment shade, base made of composition white metal, finished in Nile, bottom covered with felt, equipped with cord, socket and plug; size from base to top of socket 13 inches high.

No. 519/205.
LAMP—Complete with silk shade, base made of com position white metal, finished in Nile, bottom covered wit felt, equipped with cord socket and plug; size from base t top of socket 10½ inches high.

Bed Lights, Boudoir Lamps, and Candeliers

2285V Bedlight. Georgette with sateen lining. Fully wired and a very quick selling item. Width 10 inches. Colors, rose, gold and orchid.

2804V An ornament which will most effectively grace the mantel or end-table. This candelier, which is brass with a slight green cast, stands 15 inches in height. The shade is orange glass, having a crackled appearance.

2797V One of our best bedlights. A new design in oval shape. Size 9½ inches. A rosette center and overlay of lace on side panels makes a very attractive and beautiful appearance. Colors, rose, orchid, or green.

2796V Our leader in popular priced bedlights and a wonderful value. A very attractive shape and furnished with pull chain socket. Colors, gold, orchid, or rose.

2799V Oval shaped shade, 8 inch size, made of georgette and silk lined. Color, rose over rose.

2562V Two figure colonial character lamp. An imported china base. Detail and workmanship is very fine for such a low priced lamp. Rose color on a white background.

2803V Candelier. Made of metal in black and gold finish. Dark red metal flowers and green leaves give a pleasing effect. Makes a good special sale item. Height 13 inches. Bulb not included. Lots of 12.

2811V Tan parchment shade bound at top and bottom with a mingled gold and brown leatherette. A rose cluster forms the trim. Diameter 8 inches.

2812V Urn shaped pottery base, decorated in gold and rose buds. Mounted on brass stand. Height 10 inches. Complete

2798V An unusual little pottery base with an attractive design. A most essential addition for the lovliest of bed-room suites. The silk tailored shade in tan bears the same pattern. Lamp may be had in blue, green or orchid. Height 12 inches. Diameter of shade 8 inches Complete

2823V A plaited linen shade with bands of light green, orchid and pink velvet ribbon. A beautiful shade especially designed for companion lamp 2554V. Size 8 inches.

2554V Something new in a lamp base. Lustre china finish, designed as a flower pot with Dresden flowers to represent growing plant. The big range of colors in the foliage and flowers gives a very pleasing effect. Height 9 inches.

2732V An inexpensive little metal and wood lamp with plaited parchment shade. Three colors, rose, yellow and green. Complete

1664V Georgette shade with lace trimmings. Very dainty and pretty. Size 7 inches. Colors, green over coral or orchid over orchid.

2561V Imported china lamp base with colorings of orchid and green. Shepherdess figure with sheep designs.

2824V One of our best boudoir shades in an oval shape. Made of georgette and lined with silk. Two bands of lace on a georgette ruffle give a very dainty effect. Diameter 10 inches. Colors: rose over gold or honeydew over peach.

2563V A two figure imported china base so popular for a boudoir lamp. The colorings are a light blue and canary on a white background. Height 11 inches.

2806V This smart looking candelier with handles at either side is a very pretty piece for a living room or reception hall. May be had in gold or silver. Height 15 inches.

2469V A clever quaint little bronze lantern, set on an artistic dragon base. Amber glass panels protect the bulb. Height 15 inches.

2468V A similar lantern, a draped maiden figure serving as base. Height 14 inches.

Novelty Electric Table and Desk Lamps

No. 257—Novelty Electric Lamp. Handsomely designed with metal base and shade in chased etched effect assorted green, rose, blue, silver and gold color finishes with contrasting striped trim. Height, 12 inches. Complete with push-type switch, socket, cord and plug.

Each.............................
Per dozen.........................

No. 884—Indirect Light Electric Desk Lamp. All metal in durable bronze finish with contrasting marble effect base trim and brass fittings. Efficient indirect light design, complete with switch, cord and plug. Height, 17½ inches. Shade diameter, 11½ inches.

Each.............................
Per dozen.........................

No. 273—Modernistic Electric Lamp. Chromium plated metal base and shade, with center section of white frosted glass with raised clear glass banded decorations. Complete with regulation cord and plug. Height overall, 11½ inches.

Each.............................
Per dozen.........................

No. 287—Novelty Glass Electric Lamp. Attractive frosted glass base and shade in assorted two-one red and white, green and white, and blue and white pastel color combinations. Colorful decorative design on side of shade. Height, 10⅞ inches. Complete with pull-type switch, cord and plug.

Each.............................
Per dozen.............

No. 254 — Glass Boudoir Lamp. Cut glass effect glass base and fancy shade in assorted crystal, amber and rose colors. Decorative metal wreath in gold finish is attached. Height, 12½ inches. Complete with switch, cord and plug.

Each.................
Per dozen......

No. 274—Novelty Chrome Golfer Electric Lamp. Striking chrome plated all-metal construction with realistic golfer figure attached to side of base. Supplied complete with push-type switch, regulation cord and plug. Height over all, 11½ inches.

Each.................
Per dozen......

No. 295—Sportsman's Electric Desk Lamp. All chrome finished metal with flexible arm and round style shade. Assorted Football, Golfer and Bowler figures attached to base. Complete with switch, cord and plug. Height, 15 inches.

Each.........................
Per dozen...........

No. 893 — Electric Desk Lamp with Ash Tray. Made of oxidized bronze finish metal with flexible arm and removable copper plated ash tray in base. Lamp socket has snap switch, and shade is silver finished inside. Diameter of base, 8½ inches. Complete with cord and plug.

Each.....................
Per dozen......

No. 294—Electric Desk Lamp. Made entirely of metal with flexible arm, socket and shade in gleaming chromium finish. Modernistic base in black colored crackle finish. An ideal lamp for desk use at an unusually low price. Height, 14 inches; shade diameter, 6 inches.

Each.................
Per dozen......

Amazing Values in Low Priced Electric
Table Lamps

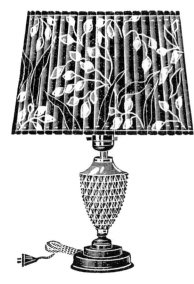

No. 864—Crystal Glass Electric Table Lamp. Truly an astounding lamp value! Handsomely styled round metal base in assorted green, ivory and maroon colors with wood column inset in light maple finish and cut glass effect crystal glass column section. Cellophane wrapped pleated parchmentized paper shades in color combinations to match. Height, 15¼ inches. Complete with push-type switch socket, cord and plug. One dozen assorted in carton.

Each...

Per dozen.......................................

A SUPER VALUE!

No. 277—Glass Base Electric Table Lamp. Beautiful cut glass effect assorted orchid, rose, green and amber color glass vase style base with polished nickel plated socket and fittings. Handsome cellophane wrapped fancy pattern pleated parchmentized paper shade. An exceptional value at our low price. Height, 15½ inches. Complete with regulation cord, push-type switch socket and plug.

Each..............................

Per dozen..................

No. 861—Crystal Glass Electric Table Lamp. A super-value offering! Beautifully styled clear crystal glass base with polished nickel plated fittings and handsome cellophane wrapped fluted parchmentized paper shade in fancy design color combinations to match. Height, 16 inches.

Each...

Per dozen...................................

No. 262—Modern Electric Table Lamp. Beautiful carved effect ivory onyx glass base with gold finished column inset and cellophane wrapped fluted parchmentized white paper shade having colored decorations. Height, 15¾ inches. Complete with push-type switch socket, regulation cord and plug.

Each...

Per dozen...................................

No. 290—Colonial Glass Electric Table Lamp. Appealing new style consisting of a frosted glass base and removable upper shade in assorted rose, green, blue and white colors with colorful contrasting decorations in assorted wreath and floral designs. The clear glass chimney projection at top and the silver finished metal shade fitting add to the realistic "oil lamp" appearance of this attractive number. Height, 13⅛ inches. Complete with switch, regulation cord and plug.

Each...

Per dozen...................................

No. 259—Modern Glass Base Electric Table Lamp. Very attractively styled with handsomely designed fancy glass base in appealing assorted green, rose and white colors and strikingly beautiful cellophane wrapped parchmentized paper shade in matching color combinations. A super-value at our low price. Height, 13¼ inches. Complete with switch, cord and plug. Packed one dozen assorted colors in a carton.

Each...

Per dozen...................................

MODERNISTIC ELECTRIC TABLE LAMPS
Alabaster, Glass and Metal Bases

No. 250—Modern Electric Table Lamp. Combination gilt metal and milky white glass base with crystal glass and gold finished column insets. Elegant cellophane wrapped figured white and gold color silk shades with white and gold fancy braid edging. Height, 21 inches. Complete with push-type switch socket, regulation cord and plug.

Each ....

Each (in lots of 6).............

No. 869—Genuine Alabaster Electric Table Lamp. Distinctively designed base of carved effect Alabaster in ivory color with cellophane wrapped finely pleated white Claire de Lune shade having white ribbon edging and bow decoration. An exceptionally beautiful lamp. Height, 20 inches. Complete with push-type switch socket, regulation cord and plug.

Each ....

Each (in lots of 6)........

No. 894—Modern Electric Table Lamp. Elaborate cut glass effect lower section and standard with fancy gold finished metal base. Elegant cellophane wrapped semi-transparent parchmentized paper shade with beautiful harmonizing color decorations and fancy braided edges. Height, 20 inches. Complete with switch-type socket, regulation cord and plug.

Each...................................

Each (in lots of 6).............

No. 267—Crystal Glass Electric Table Lamp. Elegantly designed style made of cut glass effect glass sections and crystal glass drops with gilt filigree metal column inset and fancy gold finished base. Attractive cellophane wrapped figured parchmentized paper shades in assorted white and gold colors with ribbon bow trimming. Height, 17½ inches. Complete with push-type switch socket, regulation cord and plug.

Each...................................

Each (in lots of 6).............

No. 868—Genuine Alabaster Electric Table Lamp. Distinctively designed base of carved effect genuine Alabaster in assorted white and ivory colors with matching cellophane wrapped Homespun woven fabric covered parchmentized paper shades having fancy braided edging. An exceptionally beautiful lamp with genuine appeal. Height, 19¾ inches. Complete with push-type switch socket, regulation cord and plug.

Each...................................

Each (in lots of 6)........

No. 276—Crystal Glass Electric Table Lamp. Distinctively designed gilt metal base with cut glass effect crystal and gold finished metal column insets and crystal drops. Cellophane wrapped figured parchmentized paper fluted shades in assorted white and gold colors with ribbon bow decorations. Height, 17½ inches. Complete with push-type switch socket, regulation cord and plug.

Each...................................

Each (in lots of 6)...........

ORNAMENTAL ELECTRIC TABLE LAMPS
WITH METAL BASES

No. 284—Modern Electric Table Lamp. Base is handsomely designed in green metallic color with beautiful gilt decorations and trim. Appealing cellophane wrapped white parchmentized paper shade having decorations in color combinations to match. Complete with switch, regulation cord and plug. Height, 18½ inches.

Each ....
Each (in lots of 6).............

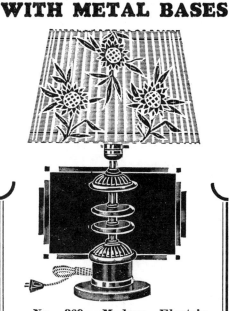

No. 269 — Modern Electric Table Lamp. Distinctively styled fancy design metal base in assorted bronze, ivory and green colors with rich gold contrasting trim. Beautiful cellophane wrapped pleated parchmentized paper shades in handsome matching color combinations. Height, 16¾ inches. Complete with push-type switch socket, regulation cord and plug.

Each ....
Per dozen........................

No. 268—Modern Electric Table Lamp. Features a beautifully designed metal base in assorted green, ivory and brown colors with contrasting rich gold trim. Attractive cellophane wrapped parchmentized paper shades with decorations in color combinations to match. Complete with push-type switch, regulation cord and plug. Height, 19¾ inches.

Each ....
Per dozen.........................

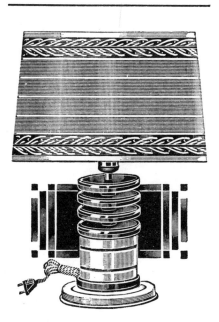

No. 892—Modern Electric Table Lamp. Handsomely designed metal base in assorted rose and ivory, green and ivory, and black and ivory color combinations with contrasting nickel finished trim. Appealing cellophane wrapped parchmentized paper shade in beautiful color combinations to match. Height, 15¾ inches. Complete with cord and plug.

Each ....
Per dozen............................

No. 270 — Modern Electric Table Lamp. Distinctively styled fancy design metal base in assorted green, black and Terra Cotta red colors with rich gold contrasting trim. Beautiful cellophane wrapped parchmentized paper shades in handsome matching color combinations. Complete with push type switch, regulation cord and plug. Height, 16 inches.

Each ....
Per dozen........................

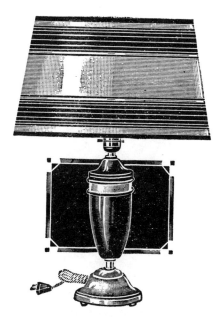

No. 886—Modern Electric Table Lamp. Very beautifully styled with metal base in assorted bronze and white colors with rich gold contrasting trim. Handsome cellophane wrapped parchmentized paper shades in strikingly attractive color combinations to match. Height, 20 inches. Complete with push-type switch socket, regulation cord and plug.

Each ....
Per dozen.........................

IRON CANDLESTICK
(Pictured to Right) ☞

6½-inch fancy oblong embossed open work design base. Height, 14 inches. Finished in Polychrome and wired complete. Equipped with canopy switch. Furnished as illustrated, less electric bulb. Very attractive on the buffet when used in pairs.
No. 6N/DC4 Each.

No. 6N/DC4

METAL CANDLESTICK
☜ *(Pictured to Left)*

5-inch fancy oval base. Height, 11 inches. Finished in rich Polychrome and wired complete. Equipped with handy canopy switch. Furnished as illustrated above, less bulb. Trimmed with six glass pendants. Fine workmanship and attractive low price feature this selling.
No. K6N/DC1 Each.

ILLUMINATED FRUIT AND FLOWER CENTERPIECE

A very artistic and decorative centerpiece for the dining table or buffet. Wired for 4 lights. Spread 13 inches. Height, 16½ inches. Diameter of fruit bowl, 9½ inches. Finished in Polychrome and furnished complete as shown, less bulbs. This article is decidedly new this season and would make a most charming and distinctive wedding or anniversary gift. Excellent workmanship throughout notwithstanding being priced very reasonable.
No. 6N/FB4 Each.............................

No. 6N/DC1

IRON CANDLESTICK

Fashioned with fancy iron base. Height, 14½ inches. Finished in Polychrome and wired complete. Equipped with handy canopy switch. Furnished as illustrated, less bulb. Trimmed with glass pendants.
No. K6N/DC2 Each.......................

IRON CANDLESTICK

8-inch fancy hexagon base. Richly finished in Polychrome. Wired complete and equipped with canopy switch. Height 10½ inches. Four glass teardrops furnished. Ideal for gift purposes.
No. K6N/BC1 Each.......................

Three Charming Radio or Desk Lamps

END, RADIO OR DESK LAMP

A new creation this season. Exquisitely beautiful when illuminated. 5½-inch Mica octagonal shade of alternate Amber and White Mica panels. Enriched with artistic hand painted design on white panels. Trimmed with brass binding. One-light, 7-inch fancy oblong weighted base. Extreme height, 11½ inches. Stand is plated finish, heavily gold lacquered and wired complete with push socket, silk cord and plug. Nicely made and finished and priced very low.
No. 6N/GN3 Each.........................

ADJUSTABLE PIANO OR DESK LAMP

Fashioned with attractive metal over-lay pattern and art glass panels, amber color. Wired complete for one light with pull chain socket. Shade measures 8 inches in width. Height of lamp, 12 inches. The metal stand is richly finished in Polychrome. This is a very practical lamp and at the extremely low price we are quoting it is certainly an outstanding value. Complete with silk cord and plug.
No. 6N/1026 Each.........................

END, RADIO OR DESK LAMP

At an attractive low factory price we are offering the attractive lamp shown above. One light, 7-inch fancy round embossed base. Height, 15 inches. Diameter shade, 4½ inches. Georgette covered, enhanced with attractive heavy ruching trimming. Stand richly finished in Polychrome and wired complete with push socket, silk cord and plug.
No. 6N/GN2 Each.....................

LAMP WITH ILLUMINATED WORLD GLOBE

Current events of international scope are unfolding daily and it is certainly convenient to follow them when you have a globe of the world. This charming and practical lamp is fitted with a 6-inch colored glass illuminated world globe which makes it doubly interesting. Has heavy brown colored marble base, 5x5 inches, with gold plated metal parts. Height 10 inches.

No. K8W/491 Each...........

LAMP WITH ILLUMINATED WORLD GLOBE

The student of geography and all those who follow current events closely will appreciate the practical as well as the decorative qualities of this artistic lamp. Fashioned with fancy cast triangular metal base, fitted with three ramshead ornaments surmounted by illuminated colored glass 6-inch world globe. Finished in black and gold. Height, 13 inches.

No. K8W/675 Each...........

ORNAMENTAL RADIO OR TABLE LAMP

A statuette of a Mexican Girl in dancing attire is used very effectively in the fashioning of this beautiful radio or table lamp. The material and artistic workmanship entering into the construction of this model are of an excellent quality throughout. Base measures 7¼x4½ inches, overall height of lamp, 17 inches. Fitted with 5-inch crackled glass globe, canopy switch, detachable plug, and 7 feet of silk cord. Supplied in your choice of the following finishes: Royal Bronze, Pompeian Green, Polished Silver Oxidized Plate or Old Gold Plate. These finishes fully described on opposite side of page. A highly acceptable gift item.

No. 8V/14084 Each......................

ORNAMENTAL RADIO OR TABLE LAMP

An unusually artistic figure of grace and charm has been selected which gives this unique lamp a touch of Grecian Art that is at once pleasing and acceptable. When illuminated the figure stands out in silhouette relief. The base measures 9x4 inches—overall lamp height, 11½ inches. Lamp is fitted with a 5-inch glass globe, canopy switch, detachable plug and seven feet of silk cord. It is supplied in four beautiful finishes: ROYAL BRONZE—A very dark finish, almost a black, with crevices relieved in green. POMPEIAN GREEN—Handsome Jade Green of high lustre. POLISHED SILVER OXIDIZED—Genuine silver plating. OLD GOLD PLATE—Genuine 24 carat gold plate, and relieved. (Specify preference.)

No. 8V/14044 Each........................

ORNAMENTAL RADIO OR TABLE LAMP

A superb police dog, excellently modelled at lifelike attention is surmounted on the base which measures 9x4 inches. Length of dog from nose to tip of tail, 12 inches. Overall lamp height, 13 inches. Fitted with 5-inch crackled glass globe, canopy switch, detachable plug, and 7 feet of silk cord. Supplied in choice of Royal Bronze or Old Gold Plate finishes. (State preference.)

No. 8V/14000 Each.................................

"GIRL AND BOOK" ORNAMENTAL LAMP

An exquisitely attractive radio or table lamp—beautifully sculptured. The subject is well chosen and exactingly presented by the craftsmen who have fashioned this popular and attractive lamp. Base measures 4¾x5¾ inches. Lamp overall height, 13 inches. Fitted with 5-inch glass globe, canopy switch, detachable plug and 7 feet of silk cord. Choice of Polished Silver Oxidized Plate or Old Gold Plate.

No. 8V/12979 Each...................

LAMP WITH ILLUMINATED WORLD GLOBE

You can hardly afford to be without this charming and practical lamp. In following current events of the day you will find this globe of the world lamp most convenient. The gold plated, metal, footed base measures 6x6 inches and is fitted with a 6-inch illuminated glass world globe. Height of lamp, 9 inches.

No. 8W/492 Each.............................

"DANCING GIRL" ORNAMENTAL LAMP

A clever radio lamp, with cylindrical mottled art glass globe, graceful figure of dancing girl attached to top of globe. When globe is illuminated a most artistic effect is produced. Base 4¾x4¾ inches. Overall lamp height, 14¼ inches. Fitted with canopy switch and 7 feet of silk cord. Supplied in Old Gold Plate or Brush Silver Plate only. (Specify preference.)

No. 8V/14077 Each.....................

ATTRACTIVE AND
CAPTIVATING
FIRST SIGHT

ADDS A TOUCH
OF BEAUTY TO
THE HOME

FLAMES
Scene-In-Action Radio-Table Lamp

This model brings three complete and individual scenes to the user, each rivaling the other in beauty and realism. On one panel is pictured a vicious forest fire, raging madly, rapidly destroying massive trees and nearing a hunter's cabin on the edge of a clearing; on another panel, a ship taking fire after an encounter with pirates, its hulk feeding the swirling flames; and on the third panel, a deer and its young seeking safety in a pool of water after having been driven to the edge by an avid fire which has invaded their forest home. This lamp provides a never-ending source of interest to the watcher. Encased in a beautiful pressed steel mounting pleasingly Copper plated and lacquered. Fully equipped with bulb, silk cord and plug. Size 9¼x5¾ inches. Weight approximately 2½ lbs. packed.

No. K3540 "Flames" Scene-In-Action Radio-Table Lamp, Each.....................

COLONIAL FOUNTAIN
Scene-In-Action Radio-Table Lamp

Beautiful in design and color, the Colonial Fountain's gentle spray never fails to command intense interest. The graceful fountain continuously spouts a gentle stream of phosphorescent water, which, as it again descends, is transformed into rainbow hues of mist. Surrounding the fountain is a beautiful colonial court backed by stately columns. In the background, huge southern pines rise in splendor against a typical summer sky. The natural and lifelike color of this scene adds beauty and distinction to any room. Encased in a beautiful and artistic lightweight metal frame, finished in pewter. When lighted the figures in foreground stand out in silhouette relief. Complete with bulb, switch, silk cord and plug. Size 10½x9 inches.

No. 3521 Colonial Fountain "Scene-in-Action" Radio-Table Lamp. each.......................................

NIAGARA FALLS
Scene-In-Action Radio-Table Lamp

The Niagara Falls Model, size 5½x9½ inches, brings to your home a true, colorful reproduction of Niagara itself in action. You see the River above peacefully traveling it course, Canadian hills in the background, Goa Island in its prominence, dividing the two greatest Falls in the world—the American an Canadian Niagaras. You see this majestic body of water continuously falling to th rocks below, the rising spray with its rainbow colors glistening in a summer sun, the historic "Maid of the Mist" winding through turbulent waters of whirlpool rapidity, as the roaring River again settles down to its cours of travel below the falls. All this you actually SEE IN ACTION, just as you see it a Niagara Falls. Equipped with incense burner Complete with bulb, silk cord and plug.

No. K3522 Niagara Falls "Scene-in-Action" Radio-Table Lamp, each.............

REALISTIC
SCENIC
MOTION

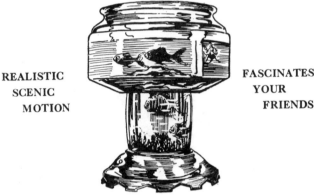

FASCINATES
YOUR
FRIENDS

SCENE-IN-ACTION AQUARIUM

This is the latest offering in the famous Scene-in-Action line. It is distinguished from all other forms of animated lighting effects; the above aquarium must really be seen to be fully appreciated. The base is finished in burnished silver. The Pedestal is equipped with SCENE-IN-ACTION, enabling you to visit the ocean depths. You see submarine life in its natural state—mammoth fish swimming about, ocean currents briskly churning a sandy bottom, and every natural color brought out to its best advantage. The one-gallon bowl on the pedestal has a transparent crystal rock in its bottom. Colored light rays, projected from the bulb below, throw myriads of reflected color on the fish in the bowl above. Equipped with bulb, switch, silk cord and plug. Size, 12x14 inches.

No. 3523 "Scene-in-Action" Aquarium, each...................

THE SERENADER
Scene-In-Action Radio-Table Lamp

The Serenader is created from beautifully molded white metal, finished in antique bronze and gracefully set off by a panel of ground-edge glass. It pictures a dreamer's castle in the air, with a pool of glistening water. When lighted, it gives forth a blend of colors never before produced. We call special attention to the richness in design of metal and glass. If you appreciate statuary bronze, you will want this charming lamp because of its lifelike detail. Rippling moonlight rays, concerted with shifting shadows, create an atmosphere of witchery which only moonlight scenery can produce. Complete with switch, bulb, silk cord and plug. Size 13x11 inches.

No. 3524 The Serenader "Scene-in-Action" Radio-Table Lamp, each.................

JAPANESE TWILIGHT
Scene-In-Action Radio-Table Lamp

This design is one of the most fascinating home lighting effects ever created. Turning on th switch, you behold a softly lighted scene depicting the tranquil waters of a hidden lake at th base of Fujiyama in its ageless glory, as see through the eyes of an artist traveling in th Orient. You see the silver beams of a full Japanese moon reflected by the rippling water. Thi delightful scene is encased in a beautiful whit metal frame of strictly modernistic design, finished in Antique Silver. Size 13½x9 inches. Complete with bulb, switch, silk cord and plug. You too can enjoy the romantic spell cast by a fu Japanese moon.

No. 3525 Japanese Twilight "Scene-in-Action Radio-Table Lamp, each..................

SCENE-IN-ACTION TABLE LAMP

A practical Table Lamp—the urn shaped vase base is molded after classical Grecian lines, and is beautifully set off by a harmonizing parchment paper shade. Wired complete with two pull chain sockets which operate independently of SCENE-IN-ACTION unit in vase. Comes complete with action bulb, silk cord and plug. A very unique and distinctive table lamp. Height, 25 inches.

CHOICE OF TWO MODELS

No. 3526 is carried out in striking colors of red and black, the vase being of opaque black glass. Inserted in one side of the base is an impressive scene portraying a merchant schooner, burning after an attack by pirates. Ravishing flames tint the sky a dull red to its horizon, and the blue water reflects the story. A distance away the pirates gloatingly watch their prey meet its doom. On the opposite side a forest ablaze is shown, raging flames approaching the water. A deer and its young find themselves pressed to the edge of the pool, trapped. Furious flames, piercing the gloomy forest, are grimly realistic.

No. 3526 Table Lamp, each...

In model No. 3527 a green color scheme is carried out, as peaceful an atmosphere as No. 3526 is sensational. On one side of the green vase base, two maidens in the costume of Colonial times, are seen gazing at two graceful swans swimming about in clear, placid water. In the center, a fountain spurts in stately streams. Luxuriant shrubbery encloses the pool, and in the background is a colonnade characteristic of the period which this scene depicts. On the opposite side of the base is a romantic moonlight scene showing a young cavalier wooing his lady love on the balcony above, with music. Lending atmosphere is a pool of luminous water, reflecting moonlight rays as they beat gently on a fountain, gorgeous in design, which emits glistening, symmetrical streams of water. Shadows throw the entire scene into relief.

No. 3527 Table Lamp, each.......

RIPPLES
Scene-In-Action Radio-Table Lamp

A Lamp designed to fit the utmost requirements of refinement and high quality. Each of the three panels on this lamp bears a different scene—on one you see a young lover serenading his sweetheart, with an appropriate and romantic background of a luminous fountain, spraying gentle stream of water; on another panel, a silhouette of a hidden lake front, my terious shadows, and the moon casting a soft radiance over all; a the third panel scene depicts a Sampan at rest for the night in the shadow of the harbor, quiet, serene, and peaceful. This lamp brings actual pictures of life. Encased in a beautiful pressed steel mounting which is finished in lacquered Chrome plate. Fully equipped with bulb, silk cord and plug. Size 9¼x5¾ inches. Weight approximately 2½ lbs. Packed.

No. K3541 "Ripples" Scene-In-Action Radio-Table Lamp, Each ....

FOREST FIRE
Scene-In-Action Radio-Table Lamp

The Forest Fire Model, size 5½x9½ inches, is so realistic in it color action scenes, you hardly will believe your eyes. Here you se a dense northern forest, stately pines, a hunter's cabin, with ragin fire traveling in its path; black smoke clouds, rolling skyward, th cabin rapidly taking flame, and the massive trees slowly succumbin to the intense heat. All of this you actually SEE IN ACTIO It's a sight you'll never forget, and a lamp you'll never be withou once you see it. Scene-in-Action Lamps serve as the finishing tou in lighting effects for every home. Equipped with incense burne Complete with bulb, silk cord and plug.

No. K3529 Forest Fire "Scene-In-Action" Radio-Table Lamp, each....................................

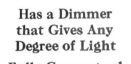
**Any Degree
of
Light**

**The Lamp
With
Many Lights**

Love Bird Design
No. 7K79/79

*(Description
to Right)*

BIRD DESIGN MULTI-LITE LAMP
(Patented)
Six Changes of Light
(Pictured at Right)

Height over all 18 inches. Solid Metal Base in Ebony and Gold, Mahogany and Gold, or Gold and Black. Square shade in Oil Treated Linen, richly painted in five colors. Crystal line Treated—the very latest design. Beautiful and artistic.

No. 7K79/78 Bird Design Multi-Lite Lamp (State Finish). Complete..

LOVE BIRD DESIGN MULTI-LITE LAMP
(Patented)
Six Changes of Light
(Pictured at Left)

Height over all 15 inches. 11-inch oval shade. Solid Metal Base, richly finished with choice of Ebony and Gold Trim, Mahogany and Gold Trim, Gold and Black, Egyptian Bronze and Butler Silver. Oil Treated hand painted linen center in six colors. Rose, Gold, Green Silk Ends.

No. 7K79/79 Love Bird Design Multi-Lite Lamp (State Finish).
Complete ....

**Has a Dimmer
that Gives Any
Degree of Light**

Fully Guaranteed

Bird Design
No. 7K79/78

*(Description
to Left)*

THE NURSERY LAMP

GIVE THE BABY WARM MILK AT ANY HOUR OF NIGHT WITHOUT ANY TROUBLE

The latest creation of a baby-loving inventor. Keeps baby's milk at an even temperature and gives a soothing glow of light.

GIVES ANY DEGREE OF LIGHT SAVES CURRENT

Guaranteed against defective workmanship. Should the element burn out, it will be replaced at practically cost.

A NECESSITY WHERE THERE'S A BABY

A necessity in every home where small children drink milk, because it keeps milk at even temperature. Suitable for Nursery, hospitals, etc.

Milk will warm in 1½ hours. By turning light down to its lowest point it will keep it at its same temperature all night. Also gives a low night light. Use 40 or 50-watt bulb.

White metal richly embossed stand, finished in Baby Blue, Pink or Ivory, decorated. 9-inch linen shade, oil treated, decorated in natural colors and trimmed with ruching. Height, 11½ inches. Complete with cord and plug.

No. 7K425 Nursery Lamp (State Finish). Complete ....

Showing Nursery Lamp Without Shade (Patented)

F. O. B. INDIANA FACTORY

Showing Nursery Lamp with Shade

80

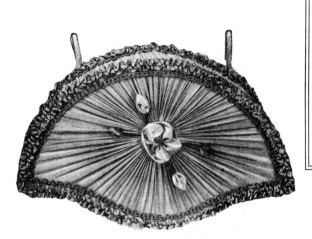

No. 7K/020 BED LAMP—PATENTED
SILK BED LAMP

A beautiful and artistic Shade that has a special feature. You can **DIM** your light to any degree—from full candle-power to the very lowest. A low light at night is everyone's delight. This is entirely new and no bedroom is complete without this convenience. The shade, measuring 12 inches in length and 7½ inches in height, is a gem in itself. Fashioned from a very good quality of silk, trimmed with decorative flowers and braid. It captivates your admiration on sight. Available in the following lovely colors: Blue, Orchid, Rose, Green and Tangerine. Will not get hot or burn out on any light up to and including 40 watts. Convenient, serviceable and ornamental. (Specify color preference when ordering.)

No. 7K/020 Silk Bed Lamp. Each................................

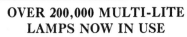

ORNAMENTAL MULTI-LITE LAMP

As an end table or boudoir lamp this excellent pattern is unsurpassed for beauty and utility. This lamp incorporates the famous Multi-lite feature—the invention that makes six degrees of light possible. In cases of illness you cannot estimate the worth of such a lamp in the bedroom. At such times softer lighting effects are very essential—Multi-lite will serve efficiently and also prove economical by saving electric current. Our latest design Multi-lite lamp. The artistic oval metal base is finished in bright Polychrome colors. The 8-inch Oval Silk Shade with its decorative flowers is available in the following colors: Green, Rose, Taupe and Gold. Constructed by skilled craftsmen. An ideal Wedding, Christmas or Anniversary Gift. Height, 14 inches.

No. 7K/012/012
Ornamental Lamp.
Each ....

No. 7K/012/012 LAMP—PATENTED

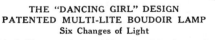

MULTI-LITE BOUDOIR LAMP
(Patented)
Six Changes of Light

This is one of the most exquisite styles in the ever-increasing popular MULTI-LITE lamps (Patented) which offers six changes of light. Has a solid metal base, most artistically embossed and richly finished in Pale Gold decorated in Green and Rose. The beautiful Zazza Silk Shade measures 6 inches in diameter and comes in a lovely Rose or Tangerine color, neatly trimmed with rich braid and enhanced with a beautiful flower decoration. Height 10 inches. It is nicely finished throughout, irrespective of the low price prevailing in this important selling. Complete with 2-piece plug and six foot cord. Makes a splendid Christmas gift or a birthday remembrance.

No.	Color Shade
7K21/21R	Rose
7K21/21T	Tangerine

F. O. B. INDIANA FACTORY

THE "DANCING GIRL" DESIGN
PATENTED MULTI-LITE BOUDOIR LAMP
Six Changes of Light

8-inch Hexagon shade, richly painted in three colors on Oil Treated Linen—Green or Rose Tint. Solid metal base 8½ inches high, furnished in Ebony trimmed with Gold, Mahogany trimmed with Gold, or Gold trimmed with Black. Complete height overall, 14 inches. Will not get hot or burn out on any light up to and including 40 watts. Works on direct or alternating current. Is expertly constructed and faultlessly finished and a real value at price quoted.

No. 7K68/81 (State Color), each.............

THE "PEACOCK DESIGN"
PATENTED MULTI-LITE BOUDOIR LAM
Six Changes of Light

One of the most popular and most magnificent de the manufacturers make. It is very attractive in ap ance, and will enhance surroundings in the home. H overall, 14 inches. Oil treated Linen shade on two embodying six colors in decoration, which is richly painted. The two ends are of pleated silk in colo Tangerine, Rose or Green, with Black Tassels, enr with gold braid. Solid metal base, richly embosse finished with choice of Ebony with Gold Trim, M any with Gold Trim, Gold with Black Trim, or F tian Bronze, expertly executed.

No. 7K17/70 (State Color), each.............

BOUDOIR LAMP

1-light push socket, 6-inch shade in metal overlay design. Two art glass panels in Amber, Blue or Sunset Glass. Imported glass prisms suspended from each side of stand. Height, 14 inches. Stand finished in Ivory or Gold. (Specify color and finish when ordering.)

No. 2N220   Each..........

BOUDOIR LAMP

1-light push socket, 7-inch hand painted shade, scenic effect. Height, 16 inches.   Stand finished in Ivory or Polychrome. (Specify finish stand.)

No. 2N226   Each..........

BOUDOIR LAMP

1-light key socket, 7-inch shade in overlay design, four panels in amber or sunset art glass. Height, 17 inches; finish, ivory and rose or gold polychrome. (Specify color and finish.)

No. 2N213   Each..........

BOUDOIR LAMP

1-light push socket, 6-inch shade in metal overlay, six panels in sunset or amber art glass. Height, 15 inches; finish, gold and polychrome or ivory and rose. (Specify color and finish.)

No. 2N215   Each..........

BOUDOIR LAMP

1-light pull chain socket. Closed top, hexagonal shape.   Six art glass panels.   Height, 15 inches. Stand attractively finished in Ivory and Rose, or Polychrome. A distinctive new creation, faultlessly constructed and priced reasonably low. (Specify finish stand wanted when ordering.)

No. 2N215½   Each.........

BOUDOIR LAMP

One light push button socket. Moulded "Vitreo" stand mounted on a metal base, finished in Japanese Blue, Black or Jade Green. Artistically decorated Parchment 10-inch shade.   Height, 15 inches. These beautiful stands are very lustrous and attractive. (Specify color stand when ordering.)

No. 1C301B   Each.........

BOUDOIR LAMP

One light push button socket. Base is constructed of moulded pottery and finished in lustrous Rose, Black or Yellow colors with 7-inch shade to match in a corresponding color.   Height, 14½ inches.   Would make an ideal Holiday or Birthday gift. (Specify color stand wanted when ordering.)

No. 1C300   Each..........

BOUDOIR LAMP

One light push button socket. Base is constructed of moulded pottery and finished in Chinese Blue, Black or French Blue, with 7-inch shade to match of a corresponding color.   Old Grecian design. Height, 14½ inches. Ideal for the boudoir or davenport end table. (Specify color stand wanted when ordering.)

No. 1C299   Each..........

BOUDOIR LAMP

1-light push socket, 4-inch shade, metal over silk, in rose, gold or blue; finish ivory or rose, or gold polychrome, height, 12 inches. (Specify color and finish.)

No. 2N217   Each.

BOUDOIR LAMP

1-light push socket, 6-inch shade, metal over silk in blue, rose or gold; finish, ivory and rose or gold and polychrome.   Height, 12 inches.   (Specify color and finish.)

No. 2N219   Each...

BOUDOIR LAMP

One light key socket. Eight inch shirred silk shade in Rose, Blue or Gold colors.   Stand in Mahogany finish. Height, 15½ inches. Nicely tailored and finished and priced very low in this selling.   (Be sure to specify color shade wanted when ordering.)

No. 2N22/1119 Each.

BOUDOIR LAMP

One light key socket. Eight inch silk shade in Rose, Blue or Gold colors.   Stand in Mahogany finish.   Height, 15½ inches.   Nicely tailored and finished.   Suitable for the boudoir or davenport end table.   (Be sure to specify color shade wanted when ordering.)

No. 2N23/1119 Each.

BOUDOIR LAMP

One light key socket. Eight inch hand painted chemically treated and stiffened voile shade, coated with fine small glass beads.   This gives it a frosted effect and is very charming in appearance. Stand finished in Birch Mahogany.   H e i g h t , 15½ inches. You will greatly admire one of these style lamps for your boudoir.

No. 2N02   Each.....

No. L 450
Ivory and Pink.

No. L 436
BOUDOIR LAMP.

Shade: 5 inches.   Height: 12 inches.
Silk Shade,   Colors: Blue, Old Rose
or Gold. Metal Base.
Finish: Ivory.

No. L 402
Gold and Blue.

No. L 455
Ivory and Gold.

No. L 413
Ivory.

No. L 446
Ivory and Tan.

No. L 454
Gold and Green.

ART METAL ELECTRIC LAMP CLOCKS

Each with 6 ft. cord and plug, operate on 110-120 volt alternating current only. Lamp operates independent of Clock.

W3055—Lamp Clock (Mfrs. 275). Composition white metal case, ornate and artistic design, depth of base 11 in., height of base and shade 15¼ in., oxidized bronze or green gold finish, cellophane wrapped rayon shade, completely wired, 110 to 120-volt A.C. 60 cycle.
Each ....

No. 275

Combination Electric Coach Clock Lamp (Mfrs. 612). Height, 18¼ inches; length, 13 inches; depth, 3¼ inches. All metal, Period model Coach, gold, silver or bronze finish, cellophane wrapped decorated rayon shade, reliable electric movement, silver finish dial, sweep second hand. 1 in carton.

W3072—Gold Finish.
W3072B—Bronze Finish
W3072S—Silver Finish
Each..............................

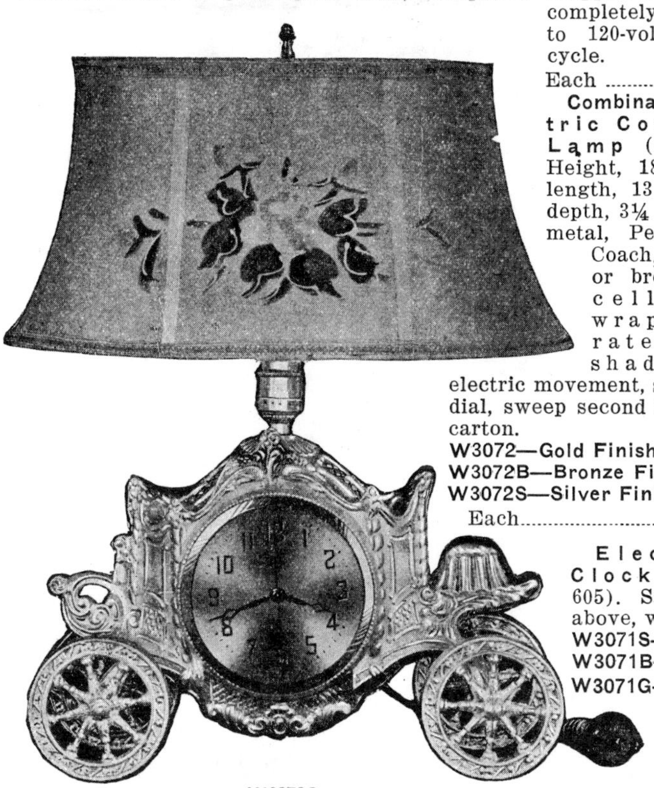

W3072G

Electric Clock (Mfrs. 605). Same as above, without lamp and shade. 1 in carton.

W3071S—Silver Finish.
W3071B—Bronze Finish.
W3071G—Gold Finish. Each..................................

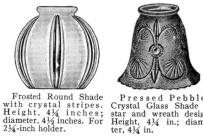

Electric Lighting Glassware

White Satin Finish Fancy Glass Shade. Embossed in classic fluted design. Height, 5½ in.; diameter, 4¾ inches. For 2¼-inch holder.
34A9287..........

Border is tinted in light brown. Height, 5 inches; diameter, 4¼ inches. For 2¼-inch holder.
34A9012........

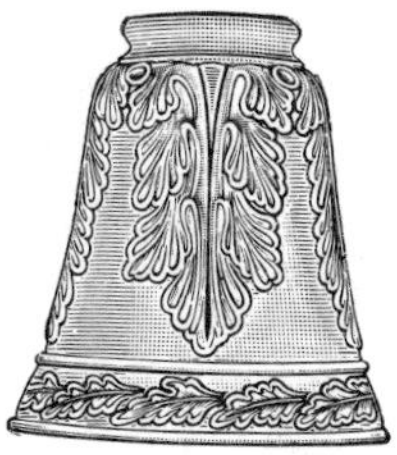

White Satin Finish Bell Shape Glass Shade. Embossed in oak leaf design. Height, 5¼ in.; diameter, 4¾ inches.
34A9253.......

Fancy Frosted Glass Shade in panel design. Height, 5½ inches; diameter, 4 inches. For 2¼-inch holder.
34A9088.......

Complete.......

Frosted Satin Finish Glass Shade, raised design in red rose. Height, 5½ inches; diameter, 4¼ inches. For 2¼-inch holder.
34A9204.....

Cone Shape Reflector with 2¼-inch opening at top. Made of metal, enameled green on the outside and white on the inside. Takes a 2¼-inch holder.
34A9455—*8-Inch*.......
34A9456—*10-Inch*.......

Hand Painted Glass Shade. Border is light blue and garlands in purple flowers. Height, 5 inches; diameter, 4¼ inches. For 2¼-inch holder.
34A9110.........

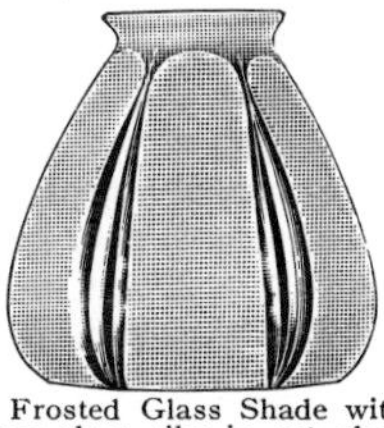

Frosted Glass Shade with deep clear ribs in cut glass style. Height, 4½ inches; diameter, 4¾ inches. For 2¼-inch holder.
34A9179.........

Frosted Glass Bell Shape Blown Shade. Height, 4⅛ inches; diameter, 4½ inches.
34A9015.....

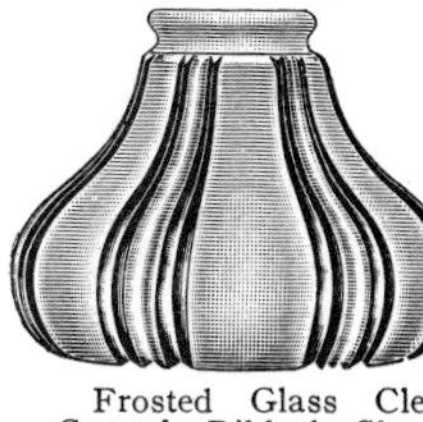

Frosted Glass Clear Crystal Ribbed Shade. Height, 4 inches; diameter, 6 inches. For 2¼-inch holder.
34A9087.........

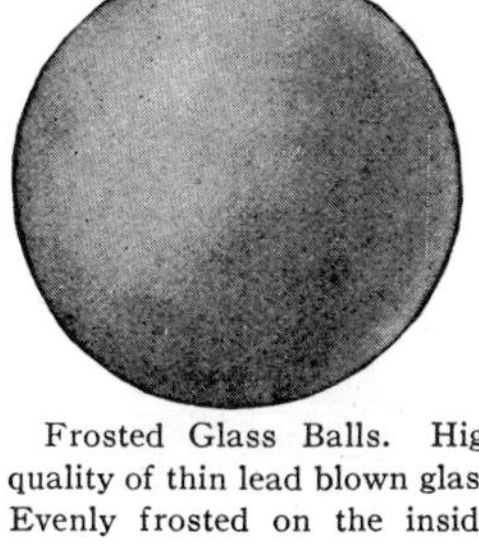

Frosted Glass Balls. High quality of thin lead blown glass. Evenly frosted on the inside. For use on fixtures, ceiling lights, ceiling bands, etc.

	Holder, In.	Size, In.	Each
34A9225	3¼	6	
34A9226	3¼	7	
34A9227	3¼	8	
34A9228	4	8	

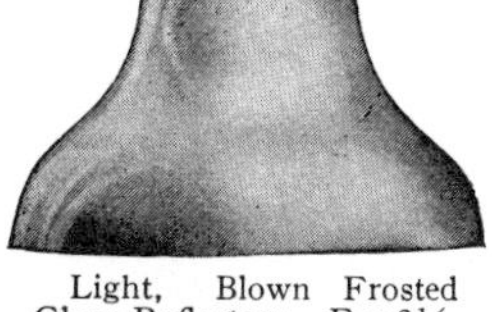

Light, Blown Frosted Glass Reflectors. For 2¼-inch holder.

34A9400 — 25-watt. Height, 4¼ inches; diameter, 6 inches.........

34A9401 — 40 or 60-watt. Height, 4½ inches; diameter, 7 inches.........

34A9402 — 100-watt. Height, 5 inches; diameter, 8 inches.............

Fancy Ribbed Frosted Glass Shade. Height, 4¾ inches; diameter, 4½ in. For 2¼-inch holder.
34A9248..........

White Satin Finish Fancy Glass Shade in flower design. Height, 5 inches; diameter, 4½ inches. For 2¼-inch holder.
34A9010...........

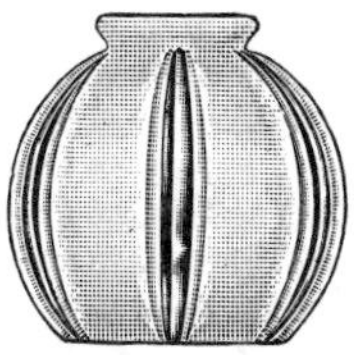

Frosted Round Shade with crystal stripes. Height, 4¼ inches; diameter, 4½ inches. For 2¼-inch holder.
34A9083.........

Pressed Pebbled Crystal Glass Shade in star and wreath design. Height, 4¼ in.; diameter, 4¼ in.
34A9001.........

No. L 7000
BOUDOIR LAMP.

Shade: 8 inches. Height: 13½ inches.
Shirred Georgette Shade with Gold Embroidered Bands and Floral touches in harmony. Silk Lined. Colors: Old Rose; Blue; Old Rose, Blue Lined; Blue, Gold Lined. Metal Base.
Finish: Ivory and Polychrome.

No. L 31
BOUDOIR LAMP.

Shade: 5 inches. Height: 13½ inches.
Silk Shade, Silk Lined. Colors: Blue, Old Rose Lined; Old Rose with Old Rose Lining; or Gold, Old Rose Lined. Metal Base.

Finish: Ivory.

No. L 822
ILLUMINATED BASE TABLE LAMP. THREE LIGHTS.

Shade: 18 inches. Height: 26 inches.
Artistically painted glass panels harmonizing with metal work in Polychrome, Empire Gold, Antique Gold or Florentine Finishes.

ELECTRIC LIGHT SHADES

Deep cone, porcelain green outside, white inside, for 2¼ in. holder.

Without Holder.

No. 627E— 7 in. ..
No. 630E—10 in. ..

Deep cone tin, green outside white inside, standard for 2¼ in. holder.

No. 408E— 8 in. ...
No. 410E—10 in. ...
No. 412E—12 in. ...

Hubbell, deep cone tin, green outside, white inside, holder attached.

No. 5440E— 8 in. ..
No. 5441E—10 in. ..

Diam. 6¾ in., height 3¾ in., for 60 watt lamp and less, equipped with snap on holder, aluminum frosted inside.

SOLID BRASS

No. 1186E—Brush Brass,
per dozen ....

No. 1185½E—"Hand" shade, green out side, aluminum frosted inside, 6 in. long, 3¾ in. wide, 1½ in. deep, with shade holder ......

ALL SHADES PACKED LOOSE

ELECTRIC LIGHT SHADES

Flat tin, silver plated glass mirror reflector, green outside, for 2¼ in. holder, without holder socket and bulb.

Throws powerful divergent light.

No. 1910E—10 in..
No. 1914E—14 in...

Opal, scalloped. For 2¼ in. holder.

No. 556E—6 in. ....

Flat flint. For 2¼ in. holder.

No. 610E—10 in. .

For 3¼ in. Holder.

No. 614E—14 in. .
No. 616E—16 in. ..

Deep cone, opal, crimped. For 2¼ in. holder.

No. 967E—7 in. ...

Flat, opal, crimped. For 2¼ in. holder.

No. 958E— 8 in. ....
No. 960E—10 in. ....

ALL SHADES PACKED LOOSE

REFLECTORS
"MOONSTONE DORIC"

Nos. V200E to 1202E.
HOLDERS NOT FURNISHED.

Moonstone Doric Reflectors are designed to give the highest possible efficiency where used in connection with light source of great brilliancy producing the best results for maximum of diffusion—minimum of glare—distribution of the fixtures, eye comfort, color of light.

The light transmitted by Moonstone Doric Reflectors is totally different compared to opal, opalescent, ground glass or prismatic shades. The Moonstone Doric Reflectors are free from shadows or dark spots when lighted. The entire surface is diffusive and of marble whiteness, soft and pleasing. Since the introduction of high efficiency light source oculists say eyestrain has largely increased. The Moonstone Doric Reflector will relieve the eyes. No other globe can compare with Moonstone for effective street illumination. Maximum of distribution and no shadows. Pure white free from sharp uncertain light rays and shadows.

No. 1213E

No. 1200E—Diam. 5 in., depth 3½ in., fitter 2¼ in., for 25 watt lamps,
....
SIX DOZEN IN A BARREL

No.1201E—Diam. 5¾ in., depth 4⅛ in., fitter 2¼ in., for 40 watt lamps,
....
FIVE DOZEN IN A BARREL

No. 1202E—Diam. 7¼ in., depth 4¾in., fitter 2¼ in., for 60 watt lamps,
....
THREE AND ONE-HALF DOZEN IN A BARREL

No. 1213E—Diam. 11 in., depth 4½ in., fitter 2¼ in., for 100 watt lamps,
....
ONE AND ONE-HALF DOZEN IN A BARREL

Tungsten Lamps
Wire Drawn Tungsten Filament Lamps
Standard Edison Base—110 Volts

NOTICE

The electric lamps shown on this page **cannot** be used with current generated from private electric plants having an output of less than 110 volts.

For 28-32-volt electric lamps for private or farm lighting plants write for Circular R7246LF.

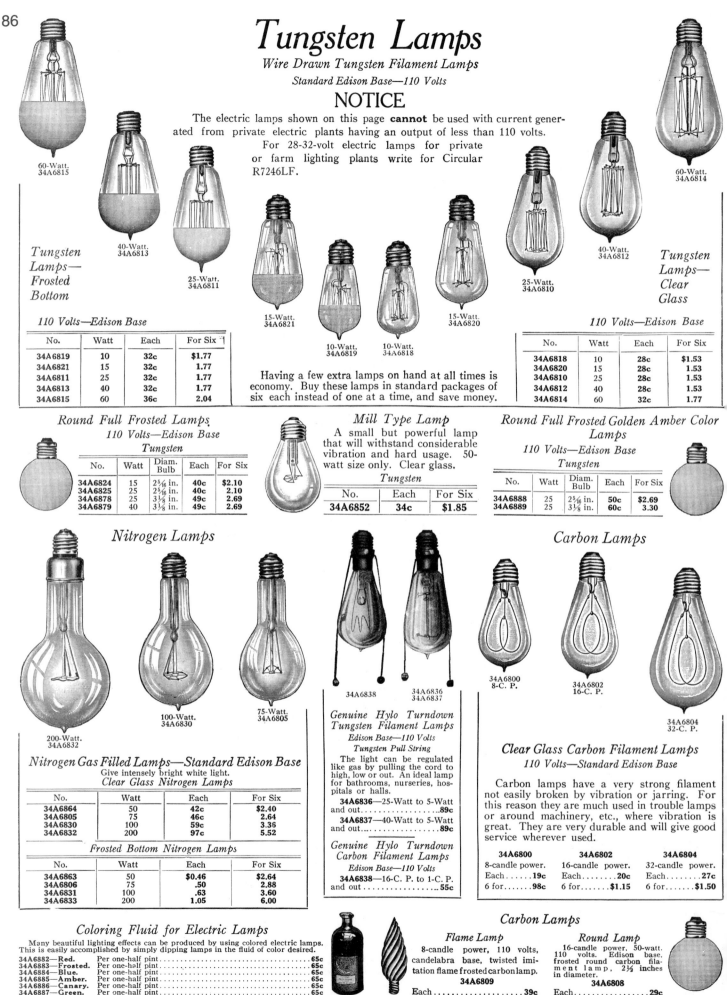

60-Watt. 34A6815

40-Watt. 34A6813

25-Watt. 34A6811

15-Watt. 34A6821

10-Watt. 34A6819

10-Watt. 34A6818

15-Watt. 34A6820

25-Watt. 34A6810

40-Watt. 34A6812

25-Watt. 34A6811

60-Watt. 34A6814

Tungsten Lamps— Frosted Bottom

110 Volts—Edison Base

No.	Watt	Each	For Six
34A6819	10	32c	$1.77
34A6821	15	32c	1.77
34A6811	25	32c	1.77
34A6813	40	32c	1.77
34A6815	60	36c	2.04

Having a few extra lamps on hand at all times is economy. Buy these lamps in standard packages of six each instead of one at a time, and save money.

Tungsten Lamps— Clear Glass

110 Volts—Edison Base

No.	Watt	Each	For Six
34A6818	10	28c	$1.53
34A6820	15	28c	1.53
34A6810	25	28c	1.53
34A6812	40	28c	1.53
34A6814	60	32c	1.77

Round Full Frosted Lamps
110 Volts—Edison Base
Tungsten

No.	Watt	Diam. Bulb	Each	For Six
34A6824	15	2⁵⁄₁₆ in.	40c	$2.10
34A6825	25	2⁵⁄₁₆ in.	40c	2.10
34A6878	25	3⅛ in.	49c	2.69
34A6879	40	3⅛ in.	49c	2.69

Mill Type Lamp
A small but powerful lamp that will withstand considerable vibration and hard usage. 50-watt size only. Clear glass.
Tungsten

No.	Each	For Six
34A6852	34c	$1.85

Round Full Frosted Golden Amber Color Lamps
110 Volts—Edison Base
Tungsten

No.	Watt	Diam. Bulb	Each	For Six
34A6888	25	2⁵⁄₁₆ in.	50c	$2.69
34A6889	25	3⅛ in.	60c	3.30

Nitrogen Lamps

200-Watt. 34A6832

100-Watt. 34A6830

75-Watt. 34A6805

Nitrogen Gas Filled Lamps—Standard Edison Base
Give intensely bright white light.
Clear Glass Nitrogen Lamps

No.	Watt	Each	For Six
34A6864	50	42c	$2.40
34A6805	75	46c	2.64
34A6830	100	59c	3.36
34A6832	200	97c	5.52

Frosted Bottom Nitrogen Lamps

No.	Watt	Each	For Six
34A6863	50	$0.46	$2.64
34A6806	75	.50	2.88
34A6831	100	.63	3.60
34A6833	200	1.05	6.00

34A6838

34A6836 34A6837

Genuine Hylo Turndown Tungsten Filament Lamps
Edison Base—110 Volts
Tungsten Pull String

The light can be regulated like gas by pulling the cord to high, low or out. An ideal lamp for bathrooms, nurseries, hospitals or halls.

34A6836—25-Watt to 5-Watt and out.................89c

34A6837—40-Watt to 5-Watt and out.................89c

Genuine Hylo Turndown Carbon Filament Lamps
Edison Base—110 Volts

34A6838—16-C. P. to 1-C. P. and out.................55c

Carbon Lamps

34A6800 8-C. P.

34A6802 16-C. P.

34A6804 32-C. P.

Clear Glass Carbon Filament Lamps
110 Volts—Standard Edison Base

Carbon lamps have a very strong filament not easily broken by vibration or jarring. For this reason they are much used in trouble lamps or around machinery, etc., where vibration is great. They are very durable and will give good service wherever used.

34A6800	34A6802	34A6804
8-candle power.	16-candle power.	32-candle power.
Each......19c	Each........20c	Each........27c
6 for......98c	6 for......$1.15	6 for......$1.50

Coloring Fluid for Electric Lamps
Many beautiful lighting effects can be produced by using colored electric lamps. This is easily accomplished by simply dipping lamps in the fluid of color desired.

34A6882—Red. Per one-half pint 65c
34A6883—Frosted. Per one-half pint 65c
34A6884—Blue. Per one-half pint 65c
34A6885—Amber. Per one-half pint 65c
34A6886—Canary. Per one-half pint 65c
34A6887—Green. Per one-half pint 65c

Carbon Lamps

Flame Lamp
8-candle power, 110 volts, candelabra base, twisted imitation flame frosted carbon lamp.
34A6809
Each....................39c

Round Lamp
16-candle power, 50-watt. 110 volts. Edison base, frosted round carbon filament lamp, 2½ inches in diameter.
34A6808
Each.................29c

Prices on Application

INCANDESCENT ELECTRIC LAMPS

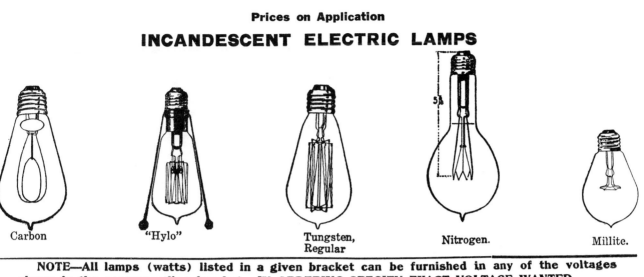

Carbon   "Hylo"   Tungsten, Regular   Nitrogen.   Millite.

NOTE—All lamps (watts) listed in a given bracket can be furnished in any of the voltages shown in the corresponding bracket. IN ORDERING SPECIFY EXACT VOLTAGE WANTED.

No. 105E— CARBON

Voltage	Watts	Efficiency, W. P. C.	Std. Pkg.	Clear Each.
110	10	4.15	250	$0.22
	30	3.23	250	.22
	60	2.97	250	.22
220	60	3.69	250	.25

No. 107E—
HYLO—MAZDA—PULL STRING

Voltage.	Watts.	Approx. C.P.	Std. Pkg.	Clear Each.
110	25	20	100	$1.00
	40	32	100	1.00

No. 108E—
TUNGSTEN FOR INDIVIDUAL LIGHTING PLANTS

Voltage	Watts	Style Bulb	Diam., Bulb, in.	Length, Overall. in.	Stand. Pkg.	Clear Each
32	Nos.					
	15	S17	2⅛	4⅝	100	$0.40
	25	S19	2⅜	4⅝	100	.40
	40	S19	2⅜	4⅝	100	.40
	50	S19	2⅜	5¼	100	.40

No. 116E—
NITROGEN FOR INDIVIDUAL LIGHTING PLANT

Voltage	Watts.	Style Bulb.	in. Overall.	Stand. Pkg.	Clear Each.
32	15	PS18	5½	100	.65
	25	PS20	5½	100	$0.65
	50	PS20	5½	50	.65
	75	PS22	6⅛	50	.75
	100	PS25	7⅛	24	1.10

MILLITE LAMPS

Concentrated Filament (Tugsten)
Shock Proof Factory Mill Type.

Voltage 110   **No. 119E**

Watts	Diam. Bulb	Style Bulb	Length In. Overall	Std. Pkg.	Clear Each
25	2⅜	P19	5¼	100	$0.45
50	2⅜	P19	5¼	100	.45
C0	2⅜	P19	5¼	100	.55

No. 109E—TUNGSTEN

Tungsten—Regular and Nitrogen Types.
Medium Screw Base—except where otherwise indicated.

Voltage.	Watts.	Style Bulb.	Diam., in.	Length, in. Overall	Stand. Pkg.	Clear Each.
110 and 115	10	S17	2⅛	4⅝	100	$0.40
	15	S17	2⅛	4⅝	100	.40
	25	S19	2⅜	5¼	100	.40
	40	S19	2⅜	5¼	100	.40
	50	S19	2⅜	5¼	100	.40
	60	S21	2⅝	5½	100	.45
	100	S30	3¾	7⅞	24	1.00

					Nos. 109E	**F112E**
220	25	S19	2⅜	5¼	100	$0.45	$0.50★
	50	S19	2⅜	5¼	100	.45	.50★
	100	S30	3¾	7⅞	24	1.15	1.25★

No. 110E—NITROGEN

Voltage	Watts	Style Bulb	Diam. Bulb, in.	Lgth, in. Overall	Stand. Pkg.	Clear Each
110 and 115	50	PS20	2⅝	5¾	50	$0.65
	75	PS22	2¾	6⅛	50	.70
	100	PS25	3⅛	7⅛	24	1.00
	150	PS25	3⅛	7⅛	24	1.40
	200	PS30	3¾	8⅜	24	1.90
	300†	PS35	4⅜	9¾	24	2.80

					No. F110E
110 and 115	500†	PS40	5	10	12	$4.15★
	750†	PS52	6½	13⅜	8	5.75★
	1000†	PS52	6½	13⅜	8	6.70★

No. 118E—DAYLIGHT NITROGEN

Voltage	Watts.	Style Bulb.	in. Overall	Stand. Pkg.	Each. Clear
110 and 115	75	PS22	6⅛	50	$0.80
	100	PS25	7⅛	24	1.15
	150	PS25	7¼	24	1.65
	200	PS30	8⅜	24	2.20

†Fitted with "Mogul" Screw Base.

★ Items Marked Thus ★ Are Shipped From Factory Only.

88

Electric Seashells and Novelty Lamps

No. 282—Decorative Seashell Electric Lamp. Consists of a large genuine seashell, containing a concealed electric bulb, set into a colorfully painted plaster-composition base featuring natural shell decorations. Natural shell colorings are brought out when lamp is lighted. Approximate width, 8½ inches; approximate height, 6½ inches. Complete with cord, plug and bulb.

Each.................................
Per dozen.........................

No. 283—Decorative Seashell Electric Lamp. Consists of a painted composition base decorated with assorted genuine seashells in natural colors and having star shaped background shell featuring figure of a boy fishing. Concealed electric bulb produces marvelous effect when lighted. Approximate width, 9 inches; approximate height, 7 inches. Complete with cord, plug and bulb.

Each.................................
Per dozen.........................

No. 280—Decorative Seashell Electric Lamp. Consists of a painted plaster-composition base decorated with genuine seashells in natural colorings and showing figure of a boy fishing. Large shell in back with concealed electric bulb producing marvelous color effects when lighted. Approximate width, 8½ inches; approximate height, 6¾ inches. Complete with regulation cord, plug and bulb.

Each.................................
Per dozen.........................

No. 882—Marine Buoy Design Electric Lamp. Made of highly polished burnished brass to represent a buoy with ivory enameled guards around frosted white glass globe. Has bell at top which rings when lamp is tipped. Complete with thumb switch, regulation cord and plug. Height, 8¾ inches.

Each.........................
Per dozen...........

No. 252—Electric Bridge Lamp. White opal glass decorated with the four card suit designs in black and red colors. Nickel trim. Complete with switch, cord and plug. Height, 10 inches.

Each.....................
Per dozen......

No. 264—Electric Bridge Lamp. White opal glass with scotty dog decorations in red and black colors. Nickel trim. Complete with switch, cord and plug. Height, 10 inches.

Each.....................
Per dozen........

No. 883—Marine Lantern Electric Lamp. Distinctively designed of polished burnished brass with fancy frosted white glass globe and brass finished handle. Height, 9 inches including handle. Complete with pull type chain switch socket, regulation cord and plug.

Each.........................
Per dozen...........

No. 261—Novelty Dog Lamp. Made of glass with the new step-up base and has dice shaped shade with printed dog figures. Complete with switch and regulation cord and plug. Height, 9½ inches.

Each.........................
Per dozen.............

No. 881—Marine Lantern Electric Lamp. Made of highly polished burnished brass to represent a marine lantern. Supplied with assorted color frosted globes including red, green and white. Complete with regulation cord and plug. Height, 8¾ inches.

Each.........................
Per dozen...........

These Are the Kind of Novelties That Captures the Public's Fancy

Attractive Ocean Shell Electric Lamps

NEPTUNA Roaring with trident glory of a mighty Southern Sea, Nature brings these gloriously hued transluscent Conche Shells. Carefully processed and polished to bring out the full natural colors. Artistically mounted on a heart shell of harmonizing color and contour. Wired complete with 6-ft. silk cord, plug and candelabra socket.

S5976—Shell Lamp. (Mfrs. 11). Average dimensions: Height 8½ in., width 6 in., length 9 in. Individually boxed, 12 to carton. Doz., $9.50.
Each ....

SILHOUETTE This irresistible All-Shell creation with its Abalone Pearl shade reflects the full glory and beauty of Nature's restful deep-sea hues combined with the romantic glamour of tropical moonbeams. Its shimmering iridescent beauty blends perfectly with any mural decorations, making it an ideal occasional lamp of many uses. Mounted on attractive heart shell base. Wired complete with 6-ft. silk cord, plug and candelabra socket.

S5977—Shell Lamp. (Mfrs. 12). Average dimensions: Height 9½ in., width 5 in., length 5½ in. Individually boxed, 12 to carton. Doz., $9.50.
Each ....

 S5977

 S5976

Modernly Designed Electric Lamps

No. 22

Beautiful Models Completely Equipped With Globes

All of the dependability of satisfying service that good workmanship and materials can give. Never before has so much been offered for so little. Have all of the pulling power of price appeal, along with a gorgeous beauty—but, best of all, lasting quality—actually equaling lamps offered at a great deal more.

Made of white composition metal molded into artistic and ornamental bases finished in oxidized bronze with glass globe to match as follows:

S22—Athletic girl, 13¾ in. high, 2¾ in. wide.
S24—Dancing girl, 13¼ in. high, 7 in. wide.
12 in carton complete with globes.
Electric Lamps.
Each ....
Less than carton lots. Each..........

In Lots of 12 (1 carton) Our Price Only Each

No. 24

QUAINT AND NOVEL STYLED LAMPS
Both Numbers We List Are Excellent Items for Premium and Promotion Use

Colonial Style Lamp

S5978—Electric Colonial Chimney Lamp. (Mfrs. 410). An unusually attractive lamp that has proven to be a fast seller. Has solid copper shade and base with hammered effect. Glass chimney. Standard size socket and turn knob switch. Silk cord and plug. Height 12½ inches. Each..........

Milk Stool Style Lamp

S5979—Milk Stool Lamp. (Mfrs. 769). Height 10 in., width 6 in., copper bowl and shade, turned wood legs, push through switch in socket, wired complete with cord and plug. 1 in carton. Doz. ....$9.00. Each........

GLASS BASE ELECTRIC TABLE LAMPS
EXCELLENT VALUES

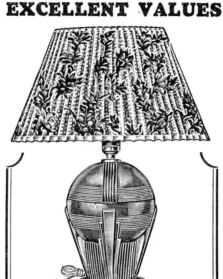

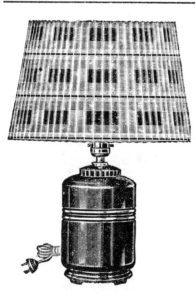

No. 859—Glass Base Electric Table Lamp. Exceptionally beautiful style with artistically designed glass base in assorted green, rose, rust and burgundy colors. Supplied with elegant fluted parchmentized paper cellophane wrapped shades in matching designs and color combinations. Complete with switch, cord and plug. Height, 15¾ inches. Packed 6 assorted colors in a carton. (No less sold.)

Per dozen..............................

No. 876—Modern Glass Base Table Lamp. Handsome large size fancy design base in assorted green and peach colors with cellophane wrapped beautiful pleated parchmentized paper shade in matching color combinations. Height, 19½ inches. Complete with switch, cord and plug. Packed 6 assorted colors in a carton. (No less sold.)

Per dozen......................

No. 877—Glass Base Table Lamp. Distinctive fluted design inside frosted base in assorted popular colors with contrasting colored decorations. Cellophane wrapped parchmentized paper shade in beautiful color combinations to match. Height, 17½ inches. Complete with switch cord and plug.

Each..............................

Per dozen..............................

No. 854—Glass Electric Table Lamp. Distinctively styled base of glass in assorted green, white, and maroon colors with contrasting metallic foil trim. Supplied with beautiful pleated style cellophane wrapped parchmentized paper shades in appealing color combinations to match base. Height, 18 inches. Complete with push-type switch socket, regulation cord and plug. Packed 6 assorted colors in a carton. (No less sold.)

Per dozen..............................

No. 856—Modern Glass Base Electric Table Lamp. Handsome large size fancy design glass base in assorted white, green and maroon colors with cellophane wrapped beautiful pleated parchmentized paper shade in matching color combinations. Height, 17¾ inches. Complete with switch, cord and plug. Packed 6 assorted colors in a carton. (No less sold.)

Per dozen......................

No. 853—Glass Electric Table Lamp. Artistically designed three-section effect base of glass in assorted green, white and maroon colors with contrasting metallic foil decorative trim. Handsomely styled pleated parchmentized paper cellophane wrapped shades in appealing color combinations to match base. Height, 19½ inches. Complete with switch, cord and plug. Packed 6 assorted colors in a carton. (No less sold.)

Per dozen..............................

ELECTRIC TABLE LAMPS

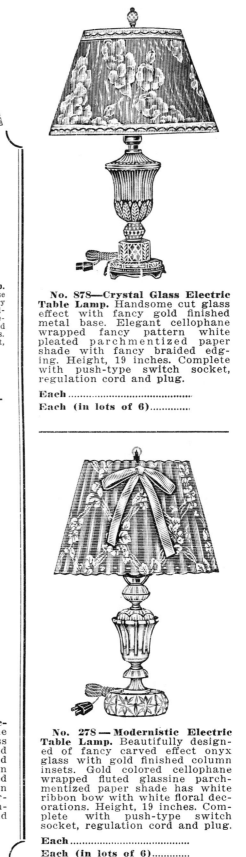

No. 251—Crystal Glass Electric Table Lamp. Elegantly designed base of crystal glass sections with gilt and nickel plated metal fancy column insets. Attractive tan homespun woven fabric covered parchmentized paper shade in matching harmonious colors with fancy braided edging. Height, 20¼ inches. Complete with push-type switch pocket, regulation cord and plug.

Each ....

Each (in lots of 6) ....

No. 266—Modern Electric Table Lamp. Appealingly designed gilt finish metal base with combination gold finish metal, ivory colored glass and fancy crystal glass column insets. Cellophane wrapped fancy design white glassine fluted parchmentized paper shade to match. Height, 17 inches. Complete with push-type switch socket, regulation cord and plug.

Each ....

Each (in lots of 6) ....

No. 878—Crystal Glass Electric Table Lamp. Handsome cut glass effect with fancy gold finished metal base. Elegant cellophane wrapped fancy pattern white pleated parchmentized paper shade with fancy braided edging. Height, 19 inches. Complete with push-type switch socket, regulation cord and plug.

Each ....

Each (in lots of 6) ....

No. 265—Modern Electric Table Lamp. Elaborately styled base in gilt finished metal with appealing onyx glass column and crystal glass inset. Cellophane wrapped gold colored fluted glassine parchmentized paper shade having white floral and ribbon bow decorations. Height, 19 inches. Complete with push-type switch socket, regulation cord and plug.

Each ....

Each (in lots of 6) ....

No. 289—Crystal Glass Electric Table Lamp. Handsome cut glass effect crystal glass base and column with gold finished metal fittings and trim. Beautiful fancy pattern cellophane wrapped pleated parchmentized paper shades in assorted white and gold colorings. Height, 17¾ inches. Complete with switch, cord and plug.

Each ....

Each (in lots of 6) ....

No. 278 — Modernistic Electric Table Lamp. Beautifully designed of fancy carved effect onyx glass with gold finished column insets. Gold colored cellophane wrapped fluted glassine parchmentized paper shade has white ribbon bow with white floral decorations. Height, 19 inches. Complete with push-type switch socket, regulation cord and plug.

Each ....

Each (in lots of 6) ....

TABLE LAMPS

LIBRARY

No. P6035E—2-light pull chain, 8 in. cast base, 19 in. shade in overlay, 8 upper and 8 lower panels, upper portion in amber, lower portion in green glass, height 25 in., finish gold and green with 6 ft. of cord and plug, w't boxed approximately 60 lbs. ....

ONE IN A BOX

No. P6015—2-light pull chain, 8 in. cast base, 18 in. shade in overlay conventional design, 8 panels in amber glass, height 24 in., finish brown and gold with 6 ft. of cord and plug, w't boxed approximately 60 lbs. ....

ONE IN A BOX

LIBRARY

No. P6020E—2-light pull chain socket, 7½ in. cast base, 18 in. shade in overlay urn design, 8 panels in sunset glass, height 24 in., finish gold and green with 6 ft. of cord and plug, w't approximately 55 lbs., each ....

ONE IN A BOX

No. P6038E—2-light pull chain, 8 in. cast base, 18 in. shade in overlay rose basket design, 6 panels in amber or ambergreen glass, height 24 in., finish gold and green or brown and green with 6 ft. of cord and plug, w't boxed approximately 50 lbs. ....each

ONE IN A BOX

LIBRARY

No. P6037E—2-light pull chain, 8 in. cast base, 18 in. shade in overlay drape design, 8 panels in amber-green, height 24 in., finish antique gold with 6 ft. of cord and plug, w't approximately 55 lbs., each ....

ONE IN A BOX

No. P709E—1-light key socket, 6½ in. cast base, 14 in. shade in overlay, 4 panels in green glass, height 17 in., finish antique brass with 6 ft. of cord and plug, w't approximately 35 lbs. ....

ONE IN A BOX

TABLE LAMPS

No. P6042E — Two light pull chain, with 19½ in. shade, eight upper and eight lower panels, two tone glass, upper amber, lower sunset, height 24 in., finished in gold and green, with 6 ft. of cord and plug, w't each 80 lbs. ....each

ONE IN A BOX

P6042½E—**Lighted base,** two pull chains in shade, diameter of shade 19½ in., eight upper and eight lower panels, two tone glass, upper amber, lower blue, height 24 in., finished in polychrome, with 6 ft. of cord and plug, w't each 80 lbs. ..each

ONE IN A BOX

BOUDOIR LAMPS

No. P215E—One light, key socket, 6 in. shade, in overlay, six panels in amber glass, height 16 in., finished in ivory and rose, with 6 ft. of cord and plug, w't each 25 lbs., each ....

ONE IN A BOX

P210E—One light, key socket, 7½ in. shade in overlay, four panels in sunset glass, height 17 in., finished in ivory and rose, with 6 ft. of cord and plug, w't each 25 lbs. each ....

ONE IN A BOX

DINING-ROOM DOMES

No. P1037E—22 in., 8 panels with overlay at the bottom of panels and a ruby piece of glass between each section, depth of dome 13 in., length of fixture 36 in., making length over all 49 in., finish brush brass, 2-light electric key socket, w't packed approximately 60 lbs. ....each

ONE IN A BOX

No. P6018E—22 in., overlay scenic design, ten upper and ten lower panels, top panels amber, bottom blue to resemble water, depth of dome 14 in., length of fixture 36 in., making length over all 50 in., 2-light electric key socket, w't packed approximately 65 lbs. ....each

ONE IN A BOX

Two light, 16-inch Shade in metal overlay, eight upper and eight lower panels. Two-tone art glass. Height, 21 inches. Finish, Polychrome or Gold and Green stand, which specify when ordering.
No. 2N6093½ Specify finish. Each.....................

Two light. 18-inch shade in metal overlay. Eight panels in Amber or Sunset glass. Height 22 inches. Stand finished in Polychrome or Gold and Green, which specify when ordering.
No. 2N6037½ Specify finish. Each.....................

LIGHTED BASE TABLE LAMP
One light in shade, one light in base. Height, 21 in Diameter of shade, 16 inches. Three-tone art glass. beautifully finished in Polychrome.
No. 2N6050 Each ....

Two light. 18-inch shade in metal overlay. Six upper and six lower panels. Two-tone art glass. Height, 24 inches. Finish of Stand, Antique Gold, Polychrome, or Gold and Green, which specify when ordering.
No. 2N6002 Specify finish. Each.....................

Two light. 18-inch Shade in metal overlay. Six upper and six lower panels. Two-tone art glass. Height, 24 inches. Stand finished in Polychrome or Antique and Polychrome. Very attractive.
No. 2N6051½ Specify finish, Each.....................

Two light. 20-inch shade in metal overlay. Eight upper eight lower panels, two-tone art glass. Height, 24 inches. Stand most exquisitely finished in rich Polychrome.
No. 2N6047½ Each ....

LIGHTED BASE TABLE LAMP
Two lights in shade, one light in base. 19½-inch shade in metal overlay. Eight upper and eight lower panels. Two-tone art glass. Height, 24 inches. Stand attractively finished in Polychrome.
No. 2N6047-35 Each ....

LIGHTED BASE TABLE LAMP
Two lights in shade, one light in base. 20-inch shade in metal overlay. Three tone art glass. Height, 26 inches. Stand magnificently finished in rich Polychrome.
No. 2N6045 Each ....

LIGHTED BASE TABLE LAMP
Two lights in shade, one light in base. 20-inch Sha metal overlay. Three-tone art glass panels. Height, 26 in Stand richly finished in Polychrome. A very high number.
No. 2N6046-40 Each ....

No. L 2800
VASE LAMP. TWO LIGHTS.

Height: 23 inches. 2 Lights.   Teakwood Base.
Finish: Mirror Black with Decoration in Gold.

BASE NO. T 2805
VASE LAMP. TWO LIGHTS.

No. L 2810
VASE LAMP. TWO LIGHTS.

Height: 23 inches. 2 Lights.   Teakwood Base.
Finish: Mirror Black.

Height: 23 inches. 2 Lights.   Teakwood Base.
Finish: Tokanabe.

SILK SHADE

2793V A shade which is certain to enhance the beauty of any living room. Designed in plaited georgette interlined with a stretched silk. A combination of gold, silver and brown braid form a very pretty trim. Colors, rosewood ombre over rose or black and white ombre over peach.

TABLE BASE

2792V A combination of white onyx and gold plated fittings produces an ultra-smart looking base. A lamp which makes a strong appeal to the fastidious. One of our best table lamps. Height 25 inches.

2801V A real utility lamp suitable for bedroom, end-table or den. Has a claw foot base, silver plated with fittings to match. The marbleize stem in a mottled pattern adds charm to the silver effect. Height 12 inches.

2802V Square style oblong parchment shade. 8 inch size, tan color with brown lacings. Dark red decoration in corners and bird design makes this a very attractive shade.

ART MODERNE LAMP

2716V Art moderne is very beautifully characterized in this striking lamp of black metal mounted with a stem of tan. Figures of red, green, and black form a most distinctive trim. The shade, which is made of heavy parchment, is perfectly matched with the base, both in color and design. Lamp complete.

2815V A small lamp shade in keeping with the art moderne idea. Oblong shape, 9 inches long, silver grey color with black and gold decorations. A very striking shade especially when used with 2814V base as illustrated.

2814V Gold and black metal base with a crystal glass break in center. True modernistic lines are featured in this lamp base. Height 10½ inches.

PARCHMENT SHADE

2779V Artistically decorated parchment shade with flower designs in pastel colors. Laced at top and bottom with leather lacing. Diameter inches.

TABLE BASE

2778V A most distinctive imported china urn vase of ivory highly decorated in hand painting of variegated colors set on green metal stand. Height 24 inches.

PARCHMENT SHADE

2781V Same as 2779V, but 1? inch diameter.

TABLE BASE

2780V Same as 2778V, but ?0 inch height.

SHADE

1827V Luminous velvasheen parchment shade of design always pleasing. Decorated blending colors having Chinese pheasant predominating. Oval shape 16 inches in diameter.

TABLE BASE

1828V Beautiful imported mirror black vase decorated in gold Chinese pheasant. Equipped with adjustable socket extending from 24 inches to 27 inches.

END TABLE LAMP

Same as above except height of base 22 inches and diameter of shade 12 inches.
1082V Shade.
1083V Base.

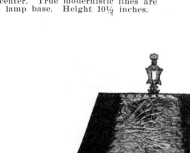

PARCHMENT SHADE

2791V A very neat looking shade of tan parchment hand decorated in raised work. Attractive conventional design of blue, black, and red. Bound in gold leatherette. Diameter 18 inches.

TABLE BASE

2790V A highly ornamented base surmounted on white onyx creates a stunning effect. The three outstanding nymph figures give a most desirable distinction. Gold plated or silver.

PARCHMENT SHADE

2777V A most popular number is this crackled parchment shade, the six sides of which are laced together with leather. The floral blend of tan, red and green is lacquered in between the parchment. Diameter 16 inches.

TABLE BASE

2776V A substantially built good looking base of antique bronze. Height 21 inches.

6202—Table Lamp. All metal base; height 11½″; pleated Georgette Shade, interlined. Colors of base and shade: Rose, Blue, Green, Orchid. State color wanted........

6212—Table Lamp. All metal base, finished Roman Gold and Blue; height 14″; shade, Parchment, hand decorated......

6222—Vanity Lamp. All metal base; height 18½″. Finished: Antique Ivory and Rose; Antique Ivory and Blue; Antique Ivory and Green; Antique Ivory and Orchid. Shade, silk. Colors: Blue, Rose, Green and Orchid. State color wanted..............

6204—Table Lamp. All metal base; Polychrome finish; height 23″; Parchment shade, hand decorated, in assorted designs.

6205—Table Lamp. All metal base; finished Roman Gold and Polychrome; height 24″; colored Parchment shade, hand decorated in assorted designs.................

6206—Table Lamp. All metal base; finish Assyrian Gold and Blue; height 25″; hexagonal crackled Parchment shade, decorated, with laced bindings..............

6214—Table Lamp. All metal base; finished in Flemish copper; height 23½″. Shade, hexagonal decorated Parchment, laced binding with colored leatherette. Assorted designs.

All of the above lamps fitted with 6 ft. cord, push socket and 2-piece separable plug.

PARKER LAMPS

6203—Table Lamp. Mottled glazed base; height 22½″. Colors: Brown mottled, Blue mottled, Green mottled. Parchment shade decorated with Gesso Scroll. Furnished in colors to match the base. State color wanted . . . .

6213—Table Lamp. All metal base; finished in Gold and Black relief; height 23″; hexagonal Parchment shade, decorated.

6215—Table Lamp. All metal base; finish, Roman Gold and Blue; height 23¼″; hexagonal Parchment, decorated.

6225—Table Lamp. All metal base; Roman Gold and Polychrome finish; height 23″; octagonal mica shade, hand-decorated with laced binding . . .

6216—Table Lamp. All metal base; spray Gold and Baby Blue finish; height 23½″; pleated taffeta shade, interlined. Colors: Green, Blue, Orchid and Rose . . .

All of the above lamps fitted with 6 ft. cord, push socket and 2-piece separable plugs.

6216

6215

6203

6213

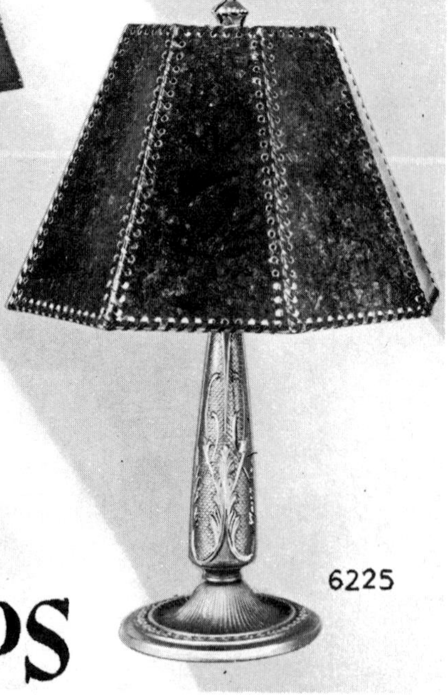

6225

PARKER LAMPS

Beautiful Basket of Flowers

34A8040—*As shown*............................,

This basket of flowers is very pretty, whether illuminated or not. The large roses are pink in color and have a small electric light bulb in the center, the same color as the flower. The basket is made of wicker, finished in tiffany green gold color and is well filled with flowers and green leaves. Can be used on 110-volt electric current only. Shipping weight, 10 pounds.

Conventional Electric Portable

34A8046—*As shown*............................,

This is really a beautiful lamp. Finished in antique gold (the appearance of tarnished gold). Height, 22 inches. Diameter of shade, 16 inches. The shade is ornamented with six amber onyx color glass panels at top and six border panels in blended red at bottom. This is a lamp you will appreciate and admire. It is made of metal and is complete with two chain pull sockets, 6 feet of cord and plug. Shipping weight, 35 pounds.

Flower Portable

34A8057—*As shown*....................... ...

Flowers and foliage are always pleasant to look at. The shade of this lamp, with its pretty arrangement of hand painted leaves and flowers, creates in your mind that pleasant feeling of spring. The eight amber green glass panels form a pleasing background for the metal parts of the shade. The base is made of metal and is in keeping with the design of the shade. The metal parts of this lamp which are not colored are in ancient gold finish. Height of portable, 22 inches. Shade, 17 inches in diameter. Complete with two chain pull sockets, 6 feet of cord and plug. Shipping weight, 35 pounds.

Gold and Gray Stipple Portable

34A8028—*As shown*.................

Height, 26 inches. Round shade, 19 inches wide. Elaborate wood standard in dull and burnished gold finish, decorated with gray stipple work. Top of shade, delft blue silk and cotton crepe. Lining, gold color silk. Double blue artificial silk fringe, 5½ inches long. Heavy two-tone Jap silk ruching with picoted edges. Has two chain pull sockets, 6 feet of cord and plug. Shipping weight, 15 pounds.

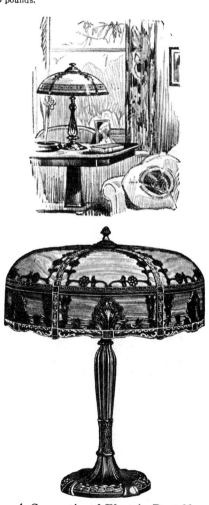

A Conventional Electric Portable

34A8016—*As shown*............................

The finish of this beautiful electric portable is polychrome, an artistic blending of red and green on a pretty background of antique gold color. Into the frame of the shade are fitted six large amber onyx color glass panels with six blended red panels in the border. Height, 22 inches. Shade is 18 inches wide. Made of metal and has two chain pull sockets, 6 feet of cord and plug. Shipping weight, 35 pounds.

Two-Light Electric Portable

34A8152—*As shown*.................

Height, 25 inches. Shade, 19½ inches in diameter across corners. Antique gold finish. Ornamental square metal base and standard beautifully embossed in flower and medallion design, supporting an eight-panel metal overlaid shade. The upper panels of the shade have amber color art glass and the border panels amber green art glass, overlaid with metal in artistic latticework, flower and bird design. Complete with two chain pull sockets, 6 feet of cord and plug. Shipping weight, 45 lbs.

Your Living Room Can Be Made More Attractive With a Table Lamp

A New Style Lamp

34A8048—*As shown*...........................

This lamp is made of metal. Height, 21 inches. Shade, 14 inches in diameter. One of the latest designs both in style and finish. The finish is polychrome, a wonderfully artistic blend of red, green and gold on a beautiful background of soft brown color. The shade is fitted with six beautiful amber onyx color glass panels. You will admire this lamp when you see it. Completely wired, with one push button socket, 6 feet of cord and plug. Shipping weight, 30 pounds.

A Real Value

34A8010—*As shown*...............

The base and shade of this pretty electric table lamp are decorated with raised hand tinted flowers and leaves. There are six amber onyx colored glass panels mounted in the shade. The height is 21 inches and the shade is 16 inches wide. It is fitted with two chain pull sockets, 6 feet of cord and plug. Shipping weight, 40 pounds.

Brown and Gold Color

34A8038—*As shown*.............

The brown and gold color finish is very popular because it is so striking in its appearance. The background is all in brown color with raised flowers and leaves in gold color relief. The shade is 18 inches wide and is fitted with 6 amber onyx art glass panels with vermilion color in border. Height, 22 inches and made of metal, has 6 feet of cord and plug with two chain pull sockets. Shipping weight, 50 pounds.

Silver and Polychrome Portable

34A8050—*As shown*..................

The latest finish for portable lamps is silver and polychrome. The entire lamp is silver plated, after which it is decorated a beautiful color blending of red, blue and green. Height of lamp, 23 inches. The shade is 18 inches in diameter and is fitted with six onyx color glass panels. Complete with two chain pull sockets, 6 feet of cord and plug. Shipping weight, 40 pounds.

Hand Painted Glass Shade

34A8044—*As shown*....................

The entire shade of this lamp is made of glass and beautifully hand painted in scenery effect. The standard and base are finished in French bronze and embossed in leaf design. Height, 21 inches. Width of shade is 14 inches. Equipped with one key socket, 6 feet of cord and plug. Shipping weight, 40 pounds.

Two-Light Electric Portable

34A8004—*As shown*....................

Height, 25 inches. Shade, 18 inches wide. Antique gold color finish. Ornamental metal base and standard embossed in fluted and leaf design, supporting an eight-panel metal overlaid shade. The upper panels of the shade have amber color art glass and the border panels blue art glass overlaid with metal in artistic scenery design. Complete with two chain pull sockets, 6 feet of cord and plug. Shipping weight, 50 pounds.

34A8199............
An unusually attractive lamp for decorative purposes about the house or for restaurant tables. The finish is antique gold effect with green relief. An artistically embossed cast metal standard supports a cast metal round openwork shade with six panels in Japanese tea garden design, lined with rose color silk. Wired to push socket, with 6 feet of cord and attaching plug. Height, 14½ inches. Diameter of shade, 8¼ inches. Shipping weight, 6 pounds.

34A8181............
Height, 11 inches. Base, 4 inches in diameter, made of brass in white ivory finish, hand decorated in delicate pink flowers and bird design. Round 8-inch shade of champagne color silk in delicate pink flower and bird design. Rose color silk lining and fancy braid trimming. Complete with 5 feet of white cord, plug and 16-candle power round frosted carbon Edison base bulb. Shipping weight, 6 pounds.

Bedroom and Dressing Table Lamps

34A8023—*As shown*..
Height, 11 inches. Width of shade, 8 inches. Pottery base finished in glazed black color. The shade is made of transparent cloth called "glace." Hand painted in black silhouette figures on a background of pleasing orange color. Equipped with push button socket, 6 feet of cord and plug. Shipping weight, 6 pounds,

34A8194............
Height, 12½ inches. Base, 3¾ inches in diameter. Metal base and standard in white ivory finish, decorated in pink flower and leaf design. Delft blue 7-inch silk shade, lined with rose silk and trimmed with gilt braid, decorated with blue forget-me-nots. Complete with push socket, 6 feet of white cord and plug, *but without bulb*. Shipping weight, 6 pounds.

34A8205............
A very popular and attractive lamp in old ivory finish. The metal standard and base are cast in artistic Adam design. Beautiful hexagonal cast metal panel shade, double lined with pink color silk. Wired to push socket, with 6 feet of cord and attaching plug. Height, 13½ inches. Diameter of shade, 6½ inches. An ordinary 25-watt lamp should be used. Lamp not included in price. Shipping weight, 7 pounds.

34A8026—*As shown*.....
Height, 14 inches. Glass shade, 8 inches at widest part. The base is made of metal in white enamel finish. The shade is rose color glass in quilted effect. Equipped with push button socket, 6 feet of cord and plug. Shpg. wt., 8 lbs.

Brownie's Shoe Candlestick
34A8192...............
This Brownie Shoe Lamp is a novel little candlestick and is sure to attract attention. Can be used on a dresser, a small table, on the mantel shelf, above the fireplace, on the buffet, and many other places. It is made of metal. The shoe is finished in silver, with a red buckle. The candle is a natural wax color and is fitted with a 16-candle power flame lamp. Complete with electric light bulb, 6 feet of cord and plug. Height, 8½ inches. Shipping weight, 3 pounds.

34A8116—*As shown*....
Polychrome Boudoir Lamp. Embossed and finished in old ivory and polychrome colors. Metal shade is 4½ inches wide, and has open panels, is double lined with rose color silk. Wired to key socket, 6 feet of cord and attaching plug. Height, 11 in. Shipping weight, 4 pounds.

34A8173............
An exceedingly attractive and beautiful metal lamp in old ivory and polychrome finish. It has a taper column standard and fancy design base with leaves and scroll in colors. The square shade has panels ornamented with floral spray, tinted in red and green colors, and amber glass panels. Wired to push socket, with 6 feet of cord and attaching plug. Height, 14½ inches. Diameter of shade, 6 inches. Shipping weight, 8 pounds.

34A8198...........
Height, 15 inches. Diameter of shade, 6 inches. Metal base and standard in old ivory finish, handsomely embossed in imitation of trunk of a tree. This standard supports a fancy pattern satin finish glass shade. The shade is richly embossed in lotus leaf and flower design. Complete with one key socket, 6 feet of cord and plug. Shipping weight, 8 pounds.

34A8171...........
A neat dresser lamp. Made of wood and finished in mahogany. The shade is hexagonal and is made of old rose color silk, with an applied spray of green leaves and berries. It is 13½ inches high; diameter of shade, 7 inches. Has a key socket for one electric light, 6 feet of cord and plug. Shipping weight, 5 pounds.

Mahogany Finish Electric Portable
34A8183........................
Height, 25½ inches. Base, 8 inches in diameter. Colonial design birch standard in dull mahogany finish. Old rose color silk shade, 19¾ inches in diameter, with 3½-inch scalloped curtain with alternating panels of pink rose silk in beautifully figured and plain pattern. Lined with old rose mull and trimmed with combination gilt and pink rose fancy braid and 3½-inch chenille fringe. Fitted with two-light chain pull cluster, 6 feet of cord and plug. Shipping weight, 12 pounds.

34A8174...........
Boudoir lamp. The natural color fruit is also suggestive of the dining room. The base is made of composition and the shade is blue silk with applied spray of green leaves and berries, trimmed with gilt braid, top and bottom. Height, 13 inches. Shade, 6 inches wide. Has key socket, 6 feet of cord and plug. Shipping weight, 6 pounds.

34A8176.........
An inexpensive yet very attractive electric lamp with pink rose vase shape pottery standard and black wood base. The shade is 7 inches in diameter, made of paper, decorated with red poppy flower and green leaves on a shaded background. Wired to push socket and has 6 feet of cord and attaching plug. Height, 12 inches. Shipping weight, 4 pounds.

High Grade Piano, Desk and Multi-Lite Lamps at Factory Prices

EXPERTLY MADE AND FINISHED   PRICED VERY LOW

Featured in this selling are the MULTI-LITE LAMPS AS SHOWN. Six changes of light. These MULTI-LITE lamps are for use in hospitals, nurseries, sickrooms, bedrooms, and where a low light is required. Will not get hot or burn out on any light up to and including 40 watts. Dim your light—save current. These articles make practical and useful gifts which immensely please the recipient.

GIFTS OF UTILITY

ADJUSTABLE PIANO LAMP

A charming and most prepossessing style in a very high grade adjustable piano lamp. One-light pull chain, rich conventional design, 9-inch shade. Five panels in Amber art glass, extreme height, 12 inches. Beautifully finished in either Gold and Green or Polychrome. Complete with silk cord and plug.

No.	Finish
2N209GG	Green and Gold
2N209P	Polychrome

MULTI-LITE BOUDOIR LAMP
Six Changes of Light

Think of the practicability of this beautiful boudoir lamp—six changes of light—any degree of dimness and the utmost in brightness. Very attractive stand which measures 7 inches high in a choice of several beautiful colors as quoted. Nicely tailored silk shade. Complete height, 14 inches. Shade also furnished in most charming colors. Complete with silk cord and plug.

No. 25P17/17A Ivory and Gold Base with Gold
Shade, each............................
No. 25P17/17B Ivory and Pink Base with Pink
Shade, each............................
No. 25P17/17C Ivory and Orchid Base with
Orchid Shade, each....................
No. 25P17/17D Ivory and Blue Base with Blue
Shade, each............................

PIANO OR DESK LAMP

A high grade piano or desk lamp which would make a most practical gift. Workmanship and finish measure up to the highest standard. One light pull chain, metal overlay, 8-inch shade. Two panels in Amber or Sunset art glass. Extreme height, 12 inches. Stand attractively finished in Polychrome or Antique Gold. Complete with cord and plug.

No.	Finish
2N1027A	Polychrome Stand, Amber Glass............
2N1027B	Polychrome Stand, Sunset Glass............
2N1027C	Antique Gold Stand, Amber Glass...........
2N1027D	Antique Gold Stand, Sunset Glass...........

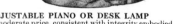

ADJUSTABLE PIANO OR DESK LAMP

At a moderate price, consistent with integrity embodied in workmanship and finish, we offer this magnificent piano or desk lamp portrayed above. One-light pull chain. Metal overlay, 8-inch shade, 2 panels in Amber or Sunset art glass. Extreme height, 12 inches. Stand richly finished in Antique Gold or rich Polychrome. Complete with silk cord and plug.

No.	Finish
2N1026A	Antique Gold Stand, Amber Glass.....
2N1026B	Antique Gold Stand, Sunset Glass.....
2N1026C	Polychrome Stand, Amber Glass.......
2N1026D	Polychrome Stand, Sunset Glass.......

ADJUSTABLE PIANO OR DESK LAMP

A design of unusual beauty, coupled with best of workmanship and finish, makes this lamp a very desirable number. One-light pull chain. Artistic metal overlay 6½-inch shade, 4 panels in Amber or Sunset art glass. Stand finished in Copper, Bronze or Polychrome. Height, 16 inches. Complete with silk cord and plug.

No.	Finish
2N211A	Copper Stand, Amber Glass...........
2N211B	Copper Stand, Sunset Glass...........
2N211C	Bronze Stand, Amber Glass...........
2N211D	Bronze Stand, Sunset Glass...........
2N211E	Polychrome Stand, Amber Glass........
2N211F	Polychrome Stand, Sunset Glass........

FLEXIBLE ARM DESK LAMP

For detailed work in the home, these practical flexible lamps are very serviceable and convenient. This number is especially priced and represents especial value. One-light key socket. Brass Parabola shade. Finished Verdi Green, Bronze or Brass. Complete with cord and plug.

No.	Finish
2N1019A	Verdi Green
2N1019B	Bronze
2N1019C	Brass

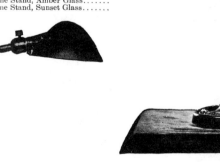

MULTI-LITE TABLE LAMP
Six Changes of Light

A large Boudoir or small size table lamp. Featured in construction is the six changes of light—any degree of dimness to the utmost in brightness. Often you will wish to dim the light to give the room that soft pleasing effect and the MULTI-LITE fulfills this requirement. Complete height, 17 inches. Diameter of shade, 11¼ inches. Shade is oil treated silkaline, floral design in colors to harmonize with base. Colors of base are Gold trimmed in Black and Ebony trimmed in Gold. Complete with cord and plug.

No.	Finish
25P79/106A	Gold trimmed in Black....................
25P79/106B	Ebony trimmed in Gold...................

FLEX-LITE ADJUSTABLE DESK LAMP

Highly ornamented metal base and can be furnished in Pompeian, Old Ivory or Flemish finish. The flexible armored arm can be bent or adjusted and will hold its position, directing the light where wanted. Size, 6½x7x9 inches. Complete with cord and two-piece plug.

No.	Finish
1C204P	Pompeian
1C204OI	Old Ivory
1C204F	Flemish

Those Seeking Newly Designed, Distinctive and Exclusive Merchandise Should Consult This Showing for Artistic, Beautiful and Rare Creations

The lamps are decidedly New. The construction, designs and finish are very charming and prepossessing. All lamps come complete with silk cord and plug.
EXCEPTIONAL AS WEDDING OR HOLIDAY GIFTS

BOUDOIR LAMP
Genuine lustre finish. Carved Teakwood base. 1-light push pin socket. Base obtainable in Gold, Blue, Rose and Orange. 7-inch silk top and silk lined shade with gold braid trimmed top and bottom. Made in colors to harmonize with stand. Height 12 inches. Priced very low.
No. 2M4/S310 Complete . .

TABLE LAMP
Japanese pottery vase base. Hand carved Teakwood Base. One light push pin socket. The color of the pottery base is a rich bronze. Fitted with an attractive 10-inch silk shade in a harmonizing color to match. It is especially priced and represents wonderful value. Height 16 inches.
No. 2ML77/S323 Complete.............

TABLE LAMP
Genuine Imported lustre vase lamp furnished in Orchid, Black or Gold. 16 inches high, single push button socket light, Teakwood base. 12-inch hand painted parchment shade to match vase. Expertly decorated and finished. Very attractive and prepossessing in appearance.
No. 2ML104/S408 Complete.............

TABLE LAMP
Decorated Imported Chinese vase lamp, 16 inches high. One light push button socket, mounted on a hand carved Teakwood base. Furnished with a 10-inch Parchment shade to match. The design is made in colors Green and Blue with a black background. Very pretty.
No. 2M640 Complete.....

BOUDOIR LAMP
Twelve-inch boudoir lamp in genuine lustre finish. Carved Teakwood base and single light push key socket. May be had in Gold, Blue, Rose and Orange. 7-inch hand painted parchment shade in colors to match stand. Work is skillfully executed.
No. 2ML637/S301 Complete.............

TABLE LAMP
Twenty-four-inch table lamp made of the new and popular black and gold Chinese vase. Handsomely decorated and equipped with 2-light pull chain socket and Teakwood base. 20-inch oval shade, made of stretched Georgette top, lined and interlined with silk and 6-inch double silk fringe and skirt. Trimmed with gold braid and black and gold ruching. Shade obtainable in all colors. (Specify preference.) A charming lamp and priced very low.
No. 2ML103/S150 Complete...................

TABLE LAMP
Twenty-two-inch beautifully decorated Imported Japanese table lamp, equipped with 2-light pull chain socket and genuine Teakwood base. 18-inch Colonial parchment shade, decorated to match base of lamp. It is profusely decorated in a most artistic and captivating color combination. Distinctively new and exclusive and very high grade.
No. 2ML110/110 Complete.......................

TABLE LAMP
Twenty-four-inch Imported Chinese lustre table lamp, equipped with 2-light pull chain socket. Hand carved Teakwood base. This genuine lustre vase lamp may be had in black, gold, blue or rose. 22-inch oval shade made of georgette with four brocaded lace panels. Lined and interlined with silk. Has 6-inch double silk fringe and skirt and is obtainable in harmonious colors to match vase.
No. 2ML32/S148 Complete.......................

TABLE LAMP
Imported Chinese pottery vase lamp equipped with 2-light pull chain cluster, carved Teakwood base. Can be had in brown pottery only with hand painted design in black and gold. 20-inch oval georgette shade with panels of black lace, trimmed with gold braid top and bottom and 6-inch silk fringe. Obtainable in all colors. Specify preference.
No. 2ML28/158 Complete.............

SMOKING STAND
Beautiful hand wrought iron, finished in Antique gold leaf polychrome. Balanced with heavy cast metal base, artistically finished. A splendid holiday gift and a real convenience for the home. Height, 30 inches.
No. 2M979 Each.....

SMOKING STAND
Exceptionally handsome smoking stand, made of hand wrought iron, beautifully finished in dark natural metal polychromed. A symmetrical design, nicely balanced and properly weighted. Height 27½ inches.
2M976 Each.........

SMOKING STAND
A delightfully graceful pattern finished in Antique polychrome. Deep removable ash receptacle and individual grooves for three cigars or cigarettes. Also equipped with match holder. Heavy cast base. A real piece of art. Height 30 inches.
No. 2M975 Each....

TABLE LAMP
Twenty four-inch Imported Table Lamp made of Genuine Satsuma pottery vase in antique bronze. 2-light pull chain cluster. Carved Teakwood base. 18-inch scalloped gold shade made of shirred georgette top. Lined and interlined with silk and trimmed with gold and black braid and 6-inch double silk fringe. A rare and unusual exquisite charming lamp.
No. 2ML26/165 Complete.............

Novelty Desk and Aeroplane Lamps and
Scale of Justice Centerpieces

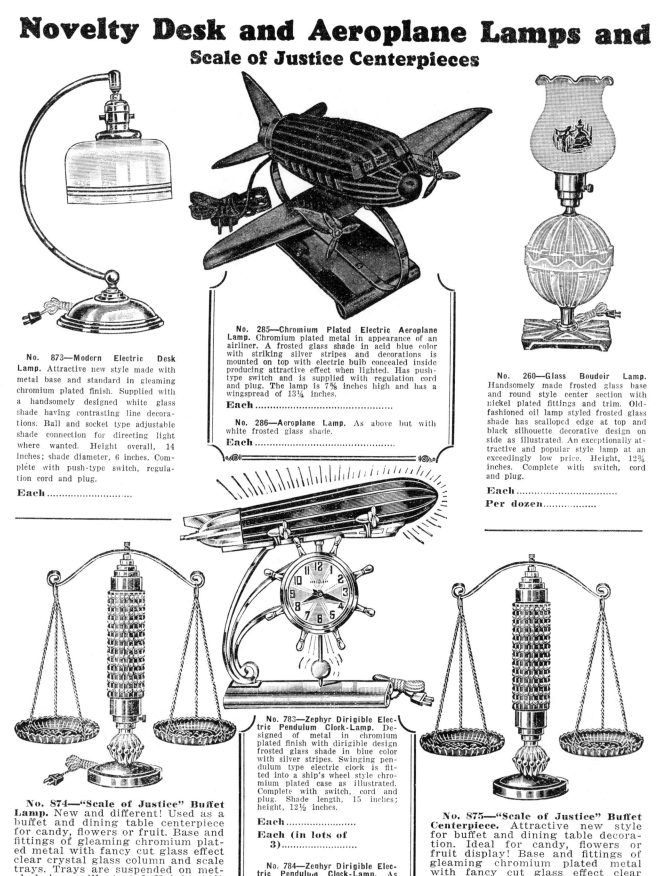

No. 873—Modern Electric Desk Lamp. Attractive new style made with metal base and standard in gleaming chromium plated finish. Supplied with a handsomely designed white glass shade having contrasting line decorations. Ball and socket type adjustable shade connection for directing light where wanted. Height overall, 14 inches; shade diameter, 6 inches. Complete with push-type switch, regulation cord and plug.

Each ....

No. 285—Chromium Plated Electric Aeroplane Lamp. Chromium plated metal in appearance of an airliner. A frosted glass shade in acid blue color with striking silver stripes and decorations is mounted on top with electric bulb concealed inside producing attractive effect when lighted. Has push-type switch and is supplied with regulation cord and plug. The lamp is 7⅝ inches high and has a wingspread of 13¼ inches.

Each ....

No. 286—Aeroplane Lamp. As above but with white frosted glass shade.

Each ....

No. 260—Glass Boudoir Lamp. Handsomely made frosted glass base and round style center section with nickel plated fittings and trim. Old-fashioned oil lamp styled frosted glass shade has scalloped edge at top and black silhouette decorative design on side as illustrated. An exceptionally attractive and popular style lamp at an exceedingly low price. Height, 12¾ inches. Complete with switch, cord and plug.

Each ....

Per dozen ....

No. 874—"Scale of Justice" Buffet Lamp. New and different! Used as a buffet and dining table centerpiece for candy, flowers or fruit. Base and fittings of gleaming chromium plated metal with fancy cut glass effect clear crystal glass column and scale trays. Trays are suspended on metal chains as illustrated. Height, 14¾ inches. Complete with switch, cord and plug.

Each ....

Per dozen ....

No. 783—Zephyr Dirigible Electric Pendulum Clock-Lamp. Designed of metal in chromium plated finish with dirigible design frosted glass shade in blue color with silver stripes. Swinging pendulum type electric clock is fitted into a ship's wheel style chromium plated case as illustrated. Complete with switch, cord and plug. Shade length, 15 inches; height, 12½ inches.

Each ....

Each (in lots of 3) ....

No. 784—Zephyr Dirigible Electric Pendulum Clock-Lamp. As above but with white frosted shade.

Each ....

Each (in lots of 3) ....

No. 875—"Scale of Justice" Buffet Centerpiece. Attractive new style for buffet and dining table decoration. Ideal for candy, flowers or fruit display! Base and fittings of gleaming chromium plated metal with fancy cut glass effect clear crystal glass column and scale trays. Trays are suspended on metal chains as illustrated. Height, 14¾ inches.

Each ....

Per dozen ....

No. L 746

TABLE LAMP. TWO LIGHTS.

Shade: 21 inches.   Height: 25½ inches.
Hand Decorated Panels and Fired. Metal Base.
Finish: Antique Gold.

No. L 796

TABLE LAMP. TWO LIGHTS.

Shade: 18 inches.   Height: 23 inches.
Amber Panels. Metal Base.
Finish: Dobre Grey.

No. L 743

TABLE LAMP. TWO LIGHTS.

Shade: 18¾ inches.   Height: 25 inches.
Hand Decorated Panels and Fired. Metal Base.
Finish: Rustic Bronze.

No. L 1595½
TABLE LAMP. THREE LIGHTS.

Shade: 18 inches.   Height: 26½ inches.
Hand Painted: Triple Decoration, "The Waterfall at Mountain's Top."
Metal Base.
Finishes: Mediæval Gold or Silver.

No. L 794
TABLE LAMP. TWO LIGHTS.

Shade: 18 inches.   Height: 26½ inches.
Hand Decorated Panels and Fired. Metal Base.
Finish: Verde Green.

No. L 742
TABLE LAMP. TWO LIGHTS.

Shade: 16 inches, Round. Height: 22½ inches.
Hand Painted Shade. Metal Base.
Finish: Antique Bronze.

No. L 739
TABLE LAMP. TWO LIGHTS.

Shade: 16 inches.   Height: 20½ inches.
Hand Decorated Panels and Fired. Metal Base.
Finish: Antique Bronze.

No. L 740
TABLE LAMP. TWO LIGHTS.

Shade: 16 inches.   Height: 20½ inches.
Hand Decorated Panels and Fired. Metal Base.
Finish: Verde Green.

No. L 782
TABLE LAMP. TWO LIGHTS.

Shade: 16 inches.   Height: 21½ inches.
Amber Panels. Metal Base.
Finish: Antique Green.

No. L 1615½ C
TABLE LAMP. TWO LIGHTS.

Shade: 16 inches. Hand Painted: "Snowbound."
Height: 24 inches.   Metal Base.
Finish: Imperial Gold.

No. L 1615½ A
TABLE LAMP. TWO LIGHTS.

Shade: 16 inches. Hand Painted: "The Old Homestead."
Height: 24 inches.   Metal Base.
Finish: Barbedienne.

No. L 1615½ B
TABLE LAMP. TWO LIGHTS.

Shade: 16 inches. Hand Painted: "The Clearing."
Height: 24 inches.   Metal Base.
Finish: Browntone.

No. L 1568½

TORCHERE.

Cylinder: 7 x 2¾ inches.   Height: 14¼ inches.

Hand Painted Glass Cylinder.   Gold Plated Base.

No. L 1506½

TABLE LAMP.   TWO LIGHTS.

Shade: 16 inches.   Height: 22½ inches.

Hand Painted: "The Afterglow."   Metal Base.

Finish: Barbedienne.

No. L 1474½

TABLE LAMP.   TWO LIGHTS.

Shade: 15 inches.   Height: 19 inches.

Hand Painted: "The Cool Valley Stream."

Finish: Barbedienne.

No. L 3106
BOUDOIR LAMP.

Shade: 8 inches.   Height: 14 inches.
Hand Painted: "Rustic Homestead" in
Autumn Tones.   Metal Base.
Finish: Florentine.

No. L 3107
BOUDOIR LAMP.

Shade: 8 inches.   Height: 14 inches.
Hand Painted: "Old Holland Scene" in
Tones of Green and Pink.   Metal Base.
Finish: Antique Gold.

No. L 726
BOUDOIR LAMP.

Shade: 9x5¾ inches. Height: 13¼ inches.
Hand Decorated Panels and Fired for
Permanency of its Design. Metal Base.
Finish: Zarta Bronze.

No. L 3132
BOUDOIR LAMP.

Shade: 8 inches.   Height: 14 inches.
Hand Painted: "An Autumn Brook" in
Tints of Pink.   Metal Base.
Finish: Ivory.

No. L 3133
BOUDOIR LAMP.

Shade: 8 inches.   Height: 14 inches.
Hand Painted: Tones of Warm Orange
and Green.   Metal Base.
Finish: Matt Copper.

Handel Lamps

No. 5353

No. 5409

No. 5234.

No. 5307

No. 5442

No. 5121

Handel Lamps

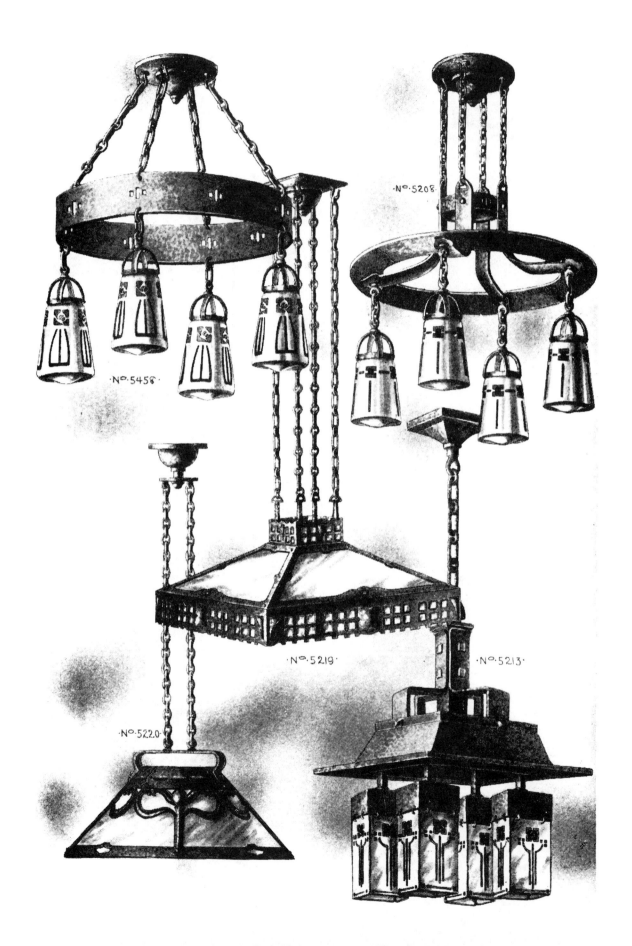

No. 5458

No. 5208

No. 5219

No. 5220

No. 5213

Handel Lamps

·Nº·5110·

·Nº·5281·

·Nº·5378·

·Nº·5265·

·Nº·5408·

Handel Lamps

·N°·5289·

·N°·5447·

·N°·5446·

·N°·5420·

·N°·5376·

·N°·5387·

·N°·5381·

Handel Lamps

·Nº·5363·

·Nº·5421·

·Nº·5404·

·Nº·5422·

·Nº·5380·

Handel Lamps

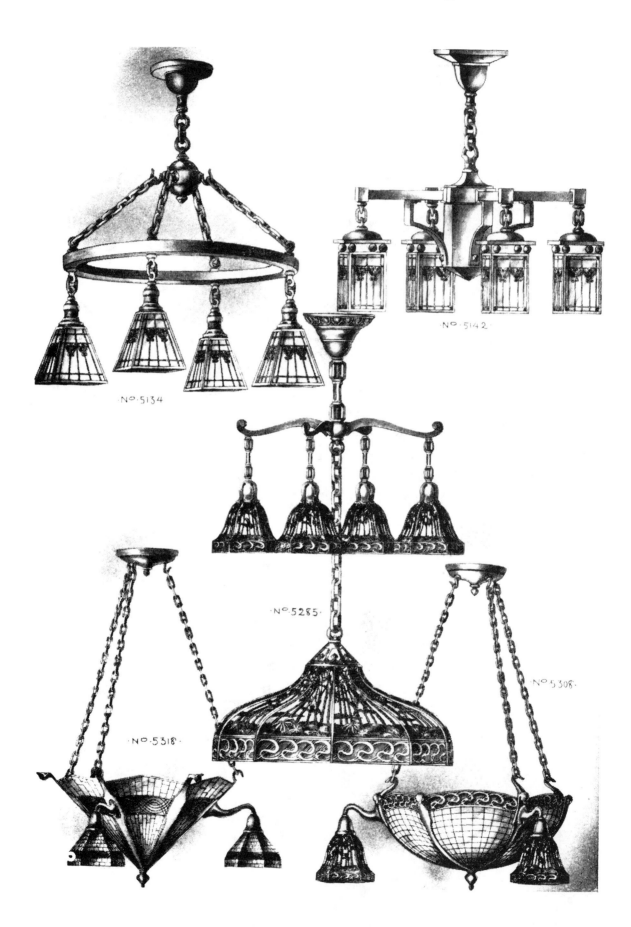

Nº 5134

Nº 5142

Nº 5285

Nº 5318

Nº 5308

Handel Lamps

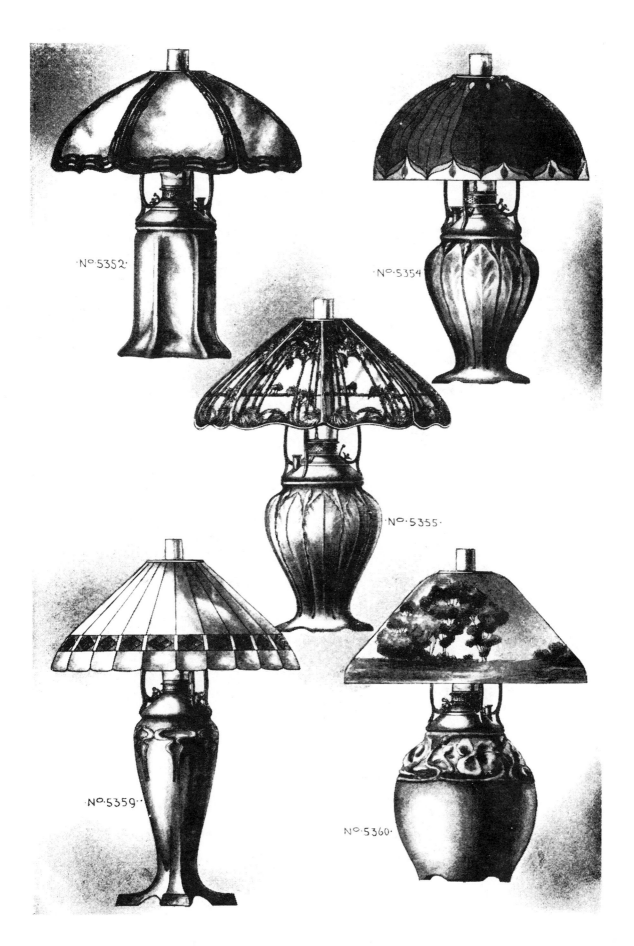

·Nº·5352·

·Nº·5354·

·Nº·5355·

·Nº·5359·

·Nº·5360·

Handel Lamps

·Nº·5440·

·Nº·5345·

·Nº·5451·

·Nº·5059·

·Nº·5254·

·Nº·5339·

·Nº·5066·

EMERALITE

"Hurts no eyes—no purse"

5230

(Cut opposite)

A VERY practical and efficient reading lamp can be used with 60-watt tungsten or smaller lamps. Shade 12 inches in diameter, base 8 inches in diameter.

Price. Satin Brass Finish. Complete with EMERALITE glass shade, pull socket, six feet silk cord and plug   each,

6513 *(Cut opposite)*

FOR small desks and writing tables; has switch in base, and all wiring concealed, shade and arm adjustable to any angle; base heavily weighted and felt covered. Height, 17 inches.

Price. Complete with shade, socket, switch, six feet silk cable:

	Each
Satin Brass Finish,	$10.00
Bronze Finish . .	10.50

180

(Cut opposite)

SIMILAR to 5230, only smaller shade, 10 inches in diameter; total height of lamp 17 inches. Can be used with 25, 40 or 60 watt tungsten lamps.

Price. Satin Brass Finish. Complete with EMERALITE glass shade, push socket, six feet silk cord and plug . each,

EMERALITE

"Makes reading in bed a pleasure"

Attached to Horizontal Bar

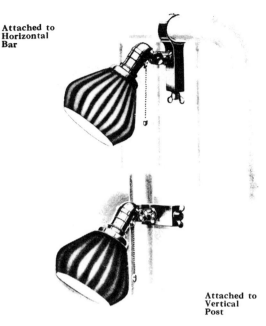

Attached to Vertical Post

0615 M, Bed Lamp

A NEW and practical bed lamp which can be attached to any round or square, vertical or horizontal bed post, of any diameter, regularly furnished with clamp to fit posts from 1 inch to 2¼ inches diameter, larger clamps to order. Clamp is felt-lined and operated by thumb-screw in end of fixture. By loosening small thumb-screw on side, the shade and socket can be turned 90 degrees as shown in small cut. Shade has special shape to concentrate light on small area for individual reading. The smallest and neatest bed fixture on the market; very substantial and practical. Thumb screw can be detached, thus locking fixture in position.

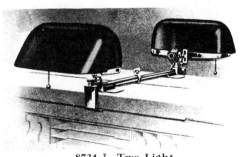

8734 L, Two-Light

FOR similar use as 8734 A C two-light, telescoping arm regularly furnished for 20-inch minimum and 28-inch maximum combined width of desk tops, special sizes to order.

120

EMERALITE
"Has the eye shield on the light"

8734 X D

FOR use with roll-top desk or piano, shade adjustable to any angle, arm rigid.

EMERALITE

'Is kind to your eyes"

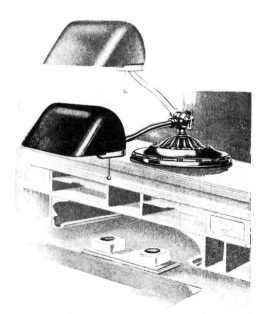

8734 A C

FOR use on roll-top desk or piano. Base, 8 inches diameter. Arm and shade each adjustable to any angle.

EMERALITE

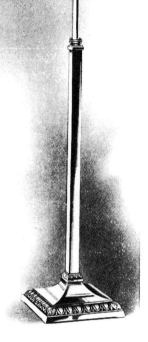

**8734
Floor
Lamp**

AN excellent lamp for reading or sewing and general use in the home. Column is adjustable in height, from 32 to 58 inches. Base, 9 inches square, and heavily weighted. Silk cable enters at base and coils inside when stem is raised or lowered.

PRICE GUIDE

(To simplify, fractions have been dropped from item numbers)

Page 1
34A 5677 - **$125+**
34A 5683 - **$125+**
34A 5685 - **$150+**
34A 5518 - **$175+**
34A 5634 - **$100+**

Page 2
34A 5587 - **$125+**
34A 5595 - **$175+**
34A 5017 - **$25+**
34A 5586 - **$150+**
34A 5090 - **$25+**

Page 3
34A 5631 - **$125+**
34A 5676 - **$125+**
34A 5136 - **$25+**
34A 5624 - **$100+**
34A 5137 - **25+**

Page 4
34A 5803 - **$135+**
34A 5804 - **$190+**
34A 5103 - **$80+**

Page 5
34A 5750 - **$125+**
34A 5239 - **$50+**
34A 5757 - **$125+**
34A 5711 - **$50+**
34A 5242 - **$200+**
34A 5709 - **$75+**

Page 6
34A 4609 - **$45+**
34A 4613 - **$50+**
34A 5796 - **$75+**
34A 5810 - **$95+**
34A 5797 - **$50+**
34A 5765 - **$135+**

Page 7
34A 5114 - **$25+**
34A 7041 - **$40+**
34A 5119 - **$25+**
34A 5264 - **$70+**
34A 5249 - **$75+**
34A 5245 - **$30+**
34A 5250 - **$50+**
34A 5251 - **$40+**

Page 8
34A 4607 - **$75+**
34A 4615 - **$100+**
34A 5426 - **$75+**
34A 5780 - **$150+**
34A 5778 - **$100+**
34A 5809 - **$140+**

Page 9
34A 4611 - **$60+**
34A 5225 - **$75+**
34A 5227 - **$50+**
34A 5278 - **$100+**

Page 10
34A 5783 - **$110+**

Page 11
34A 5132 - **$25+**
34A 5133 - **$25+**
34A 5424 - **$50+**
34A 5423 - **$50+**
34A 5279 - **$75+**
34A 5276 - **$90+**

Page 12
34A 5472 - **$110+**
34A 5473 - **$125+**
34A 5444 - **$80+**
34A 5445 - **$95+**

Page 13
34A 5596 - **$100+**
34A 5592 - **$100+**
34A 5019 - **$50+**
34A 5781 - **$250+**
34A 4810 - **$100+**

Page 14
34A 5038 - **$15+**
34A 5039 - **$20+**
34A 5450 - **$70+**
34A 5212 - **$40+**
34A 5207 - **$35+**
34A 5268 - **$60+**

Page 15
34A 5005 - **$25+**
34A 5006 - **$35+**
34A 5406 - **$100+**
34A 4808 - **$100+**
34A 5442 - **$100+**
34A 5408 - **$100+**

Page 16
34A 5179 - **$25+**
34A 5056 - **$25+**
34A 5728 - **$175+**
34A 5771 - **$100+**
34A 5139 - **$25+**
34A 5775 - **$125+**

Page 17
34A 5755 - **$150+**
34A 5731 - **$75+**
34A 5759 - **$85+**
34A 5807 - **$85+**
34A 5219 - **$50+**
34A 5741 - **$125+**
34A 5795 - **$125+**
34A 5724 - **$50+**

Page 18
34A 5589 - **$125+**
34A 5600 - **$100+**

Page 19
34A 5284 - **$80+**
34A 5272 - **$80+**
34A 5805 - **$100+**
34A 5753 - **$110+**

Page 20
34A 5265 - **$75+**
34A 5013 - **$40+**
34A 5220 - **$85+**
34A 5233 - **$15+**
34A 5234 - **$15+**
34A 5756 - **$100+**
34A 5246 - **$40+**
34A 5723 - **$150+**

Page 21
34A 5029 - **$25+**
34A 5040 - **$25+**
34A 5041 - **$25+**
34A 5739 - **$150+**
34A 5790 - **$80+**
34A 5248 - **$50+**

Page 22
34A 5427 - **$50+**
34A 5419 - **$75+**
34A 5412 - **$75+**
34A 5084 - **$25+**
34A 5085 - **$25+**
34A 5088 - **$25+**
34A 5089 - **$25+**

Page 23
7T/182PC - **$35+**
7T/661 6BS - **$140+**
7T/661 6BB - **$125+**
7T/661 5CS - **$165+**
7T/661 5CB - **$150+**
7T/CR1 - **$20+**
7T/2602 - **$35+**
7T/84PC - **$20+**

Page 24
34A 5421 - **$140+**
34A 5407 - **$110+**
34A 5080 - **$15+**
34A 5081 - **$20+**
34A 5409 - **$110+**

Page 25
34A 5425 - **$110+**
34A 5417 - **$110+**
34A 5077 - **$15+**
34A 5078 - **$20+**
34A 5415 - **$110+**

Page 26
34A 5416 - **$110+**
34A 5452 - **$110+**
34A 5198 - **$30+**
34A 5199 - **$40+**
34A 5241 - **$55+**
34A 5168 - **$35+**
34A 5169 - **$60+**

Page 27
34A 4806 - **$200+**
34A 4804 - **$200+**
34A 5462 - **$600+**
34A 4800 - **$200+**
34A 5464 - **$800+**
34A 4802 - **$125+**

Page 28
34A 5252 - **$75+**
34A 4902 - **$55+**
34A 5253 - **$60+**
34A 4903 - **$60+**
34A 5256 - **$40+**
34A 4916 - **$30+**
34A 4904 - **$55+**

Page 29
34A 4614 - **$95+**
34A 4612 - **$95+**
34A 4608 - **$40+**
34A 5142 - **$20+**
34A 4630 - **$35+**
34A 7038 - **$40+**
34A 4600 - **$75+**

Page 30
34A 5689 - **$75+**
34A 5688 - **$50+**
34A 5761 - **$100+**
34A 5715 - **$85+**
34A 5714 - **$60+**
34A 5216 - **$75+**
34A 5215 - **$75+**
34A 5232 - **$100+**
34A 5280 - **$65+**
34A 4636 - **$95+**

Page 31
34A 4818 - **$65+**
34A 5226 - **$50+**
34A 5214 - **$65+**
34A 5144 - **$20+**
34A 5141 - **$20+**
34A 5230 - **$50+**
34A 5224 - **$75+**
34A 4814 - **$20+**
34A 4962 - **$100+**
34A 4816 - **$30+**
34A 4700 - **$100+**
34A 4812 - **$40+**

Page 32
34A 7048 - **$40+**
34A 4975 - **$70+**
34A 7052 - **$40+**
34A 5283 - **$75+**
34A 5255 - **$75+**
34A 5259 - **$60+**
34A 5269 - **$200+**
34A 5257 - **$100+**

Page 33
34A 4960 - **$85+**
34A 3205 - **$175+**
34A 5291 - **$125+**
34A 5030 - **$40+**
34A 5018 - **$55+**
34A 5032 - **$60+**

Page 34
34A 5138 - **$25+**
34A 5015 - **$40+**
34A 5016 - **$40+**
34A 8577 - **$800+**
34A 8567 - **$350+**
34A 5050 - **$40+**
34A 5001 - **$45+**
34A 5004 - **$45+**
34A 5002 - **$45+**

Page 35
34A 4982 - **$90+**
34A 7020 - **$40+**
34A 7011 - **$40+**
34A 7023 - **$45+**
34A 7043 - **$40+**
34A 7021 - **$40+**
34A 7045 - **$35+**
34A 7022 - **$35+**
34A 8580 - **$800+**
34A 4980 - **$60+**
34A 7034 - **$40+**
34A 5499 - **$25+**
34A 7024 - **$40+**

Page 36
34A 4913 - **$50+**
34A 4910 - **$40+**
34A 4909 - **$35+**
34A 4911 - **$55+**
34A 8552 - **$2500+**
34A 4908 - **$55+**
34A 7556 - **$40+**
34A 4625 - **$45+**
34A 4905 - **$45+**
34A 7554 - **$40+**

Page 37
34A 4628 - **$45+**
34A 4626 - **$50+**
34A 7040 - **$40+**
34A 5244 - **$45+**
34A 5140 - **$20+**
34A 4977 - **$45+**
34A 4610 - **$55+**

Page 38
34A 5440 - **$80+**
34A 5764 - **$60+**
34A 5438 - **$70+**
34A 5439 - **$60+**

Page 39
34A 5177 - **$25+**
34A 5178 - **$35+**
34A 5802 - **175+**
34A 5270 - **$150+**
34A 5460 - **$60+**
34A 5243 - **$85+**

Page 40
34A 7069 - **$50+**
34A 7081 - **$70+**
34A 7076 - **$35+**
34A 7013 - **$35+**
34A 7079 - **$55+**
34A 7061 - **$45+**
34A 7083 - **$65+**
34A 7067 - **$30+**
34A 7018 - **$65+**
34A 7093 - **$55+**

Page 41
For Reference Only

Page 42
34A 5261 - **$125+**
34A 5260 - **$80+**
34A 4535 - **$150+**
34A 4927 - **$100+**
34A 4626 - **$75+**
34A 4623 - **$75+**
34A 4563 - **$110+**

Page 43
34A 8029 - **$40+**
34A 8409 - **$50+**
34A 8412 - **$60+**
34A 8025 - **$40+**
34A 8415 - **$60+**
34A 8441 - **$70+**
34A 8435 - **$175+**

Page 44
7T/800C - **$250+**
7T/4600CT - **$1000+**
7T/7800B - **$200+**
7T/2402/S - **$50+**
7T/2402/B - **$50+**
7T/4600D - **$1000+**
7T/7205 - **$40+**

Page 45
34A 8251 - **$250+**
34A 8235 - **$250+**
34A 8239 - **$250+**
34A 8710 - **$250+**
34A 8706 - **$250+**

Page 46
34A 8068 - **$125+**
34A 5650 - **$165+**
34A 8405 - **$175+**
34A 8069 - **$125+**

Page 47
2N 369/12569 - **$125+**
2N 383/41 - **$125+**
2N 367/11001 - **$125+**
2N 392/1179 - **$125+**
2N 370/12529 - **$125+**
2N 353/1179 - **$125+**
2N 397/1303 - **$125+**
2N 368/1159 - **$125+**

Page 48
34A 8628 - **$150+**
34A 8702 - **$175+**
34A 8217 - **$150+**
34A 8714 - **$200+**
34A 8718 - **$175+**

Page 49
34A 8118 - **$60+**
34A 8120 - **$150+**
34A 8123 - **$150+**
34A 8209 - **$125+**
34A 8259 - **$150+**
34A 8626 - **$150+**
34A 8111 - **$75+**
34A 8624 - **$125+**

Page 50
K6N/0126/1385 - **$200+**
K6N/0106/1350 - **$200+**
K6N/0112/1354 - **$200+**
K6N/0120/1390 - **$200+**
K6N/051 - **$225+**
K6N/0100/1353 - **$225+**
K6N/059/1350 - **$225+**

Page 51
K6N/0709/V102 - **$125+**
K6N/0708/V103 - **$125+**
K6N/0705/V103 - **$125+**
K6N/0700/V101 - **$125+**
K6N/0610/V101CP - **$75+**
K6N/0611/V108 - **$75+**
K6N/0613/V104 - **$75+**
K6N/0612/2307 - **$75+**

Page 52
K5H/3051 - **$75+**
K5H/5055 - **$75+**
K5H/5054 - **$75+**
K5H/1050 - **$75+**
K5H/2014-2 - **$75+**
K5H/1044 - **$75+**
K5H/5077 - **$75+**
K5H/4053 - **$75+**
K5H/4052 - **$75+**
K5H/1051 - **$75+**

Page 53
2M 2569 BR - **$150+**
2M 2678 BR - **$100+**
2M 2879 BR - **$150+**
2M 2539 G - **$150+**
2M 111 BR - **$150+**
2M 96F - **$150+**
2M 80H - **$150+**
2M 114 BR - **$175+**

Page 54
1008-2382 - **$125+**
1011-2384 - **$125+**
1001/2392 R - **$125+**
1000-2381 - **$125+**
1005-2383 - **$125+**
1006-2390 - **$125+**
1002-2393 - **$125+**
1005-V219 - **$125+**
1011-2381 - **$125+**
1008-2382 - **$125+**

Page 55
6N/736/V10 - **$125+**
6N/741/1390 - **$125+**
K6N/776/2324 - **$125+**
6N/726/V101 - **$125+**
K6N/725/1383 - **$125+**
K6N/729/1390 - **$125+**
K6N/736/2307 - **$125+**
K6N/726/1393 - **$125+**

Page 56
F581/F1001 - **$75+**
8W/367 - **$250+**
8W/347 - **$250+**
R636/R6063 - **$90+**
K8W/660 - **$250+**
R622/R4391 - **$75+**
T554/5252 - **$450+**
T596/T6001 - **$75+**
R109/4310 - **$100+**

Page 57
K6N/2362 - **$150+**
6N/2364 - **$150+**
K6N/2361 - **$150+**
6N/2360 - **$150+**
K6N/203 - **$150+**
6N/FM13 - **$200+**
0609/2326C - **$100+**
6N/215F - **$200+**
K6N/FR1 - **$100+**
0608/2326C - **$100+**

Page 58
551-B1000 - **$90+**
61-4004 - **$110+**
850-B1000 - **$105+**
183-3099 - **$100+**
184-1099 - **$105+**
187-1096 - **$100+**
193-1007 - **$100+**
193-2007 - **$110+**
193-4008 - **$85+**
184-2099 - **$100+**
187-2096 - **$100+**

Page 59
2729V - **$25+**
5431V - **$110+**
2750V - **$25+**
5432V - **$150+**
5323V - **$100+**
2763V - **$25+**
5446V - **$125+**
2758V - **$25+**
5442V - **$150+**
2218V - **$25+**
5433V - **$125+**
2219V - **$25+**
5434V - **$150+**

Page 60
2739V - **$125+**
5455V - **$75+**
2738V - **$150+**
5454V - **$85+**
2760V - **25+**
5444V - **$80+**
2761V - **$25+**
5445V - **$85+**
2212V - **$25+**
5299V - **$80+**
2747V - **$25+**
5428V - **$85+**
2748V - **$25+**
5429V - **$100+**

Page 61
2N 388/2679 - **$175+**
2N 359/2839 - **$175+**
2N 376/2839 - **$175+**
2N 393/1428 - **$175+**
2N 381/1428 - **$175+**
2N 380/1446 - **$175+**
2N 382/11014 - **$175+**
2N 374/1461 - **$190+**

Page 62
4600 - **$75+**
5500 - **$75+**

Page 63
S7158 - **$80+**
S7162 - **$140+**
S7163 - **$140+**
S6003 - **$75+**
S6004 - **$75+**
S6005 - **$40+**
S2156 - **$140+**
S6000 - **$100+**
S5999 - **$140+**

Page 64
S7165 - **$130+**
S7164 - **$80+**
S7166 - **$140+**
S7167 - **$110+**
S7168 - **$140+**
S7169 - **$130+**
S7170 - **$75+**
S7172 - **$110+**

Page 65
34N 8694 - **$175+**
34N 8700 - **$150+**
34N 8667 - **$150+**
34N 8692 - **$175+**
34N 8669 - **$175+**
34N 8696 - **$150+**

Page 66
34N 8684 - **$110+**
34N 8671 - **$85+**
34N 8673 - **$75+**
34N 8698 - **$100+**
34N 8762 - **$110+**
34N 8689 - **$175+**
34N 8686 - **$100+**
34N 8681 - **$110+**
34N 8675 - **$110+**
34N 8677 - **$110+**

Page 67
302A56 - **$1000+**
302B63 - **$175+**
302A60 - **$1000+**
302C64 - **$125+**
302D72 - **$1000+**
301R22 - **$250+**
301R28 - **$350+**
301R26 - **$200+**
302D70 - **$750+**

Page 68
Floor Lamps - **$175+**
Table Lamps - **$75+**

Page 69
All Lamps - **$75+**

Page 70
75 - **$110+**
120/704 - **$150+**
120/704 - **$150+**
111/511 - **$175+**
50 - **$50+**
1335/1745 - **$225+**
1336/1746 - **$225+**
1337/1747 - **$225+**
312/722 - **$175+**
73 - **$35+**
521/1970 - **$75+**
518/4055 - **$120+**
519/205 - **$120+**

Page 71
285V - **$30+**
2797V - **$30+**
2803V - **$40+**
2796V - **$50+**
2562V - **$50+**
2804V - **$80+**
2812V - **$75+**
2732V - **$35+**
2798V - **$110+**
2554V - **$50+**
2561V - **$50+**

2563V - **$125+**
2806V - **$40+**
2469V - **$75+**
2468V - **$80+**

Page 72
257 - **$110+**
884 - **$60+**
273 - **$110+**
287 - **$75+**
254 - **$110+**
274 - **$110+**
295 - **$75+**
893 - **$40+**
294 - **$40+**

Page 73
864 - **$40+**
277 - **$40+**
861 - **$40+**
262 - **$75+**
290 - **$75+**
259 - **$60+**

Page 74
250 - **$60+**
869 - **$75+**
894 - **$60+**
267 - **$75+**
868 - **$75+**
276 - **$75+**

Page 75
284 - **$60+**
269 - **$60+**
268 - **$60+**
892 - **$75+**
270 - **$60+**
886 - **$45+**

Page 76
6N/DC4 - **$40+**
K6N/DC2 - **$40+**
6N/FB4 - **$125+**
K6N/DC1 - **$40+**
K6N/BC1 - **$40+**
6N/GN3 - **$65+**
6N/1026 - **$125+**
6N/GN2 - **$100+**

Page 77
8V/14044 - **$175+**
K8W/491 - **$150+**
K8W/675 - **$175+**
8V/14084 - **$175+**
8V/14000 - **$75+**
8V/12979 - **$175+**
8W/492 - **$175+**
8V/14077 - **$135+**

Page 78
K3540 - **$100+**
3521 - **$100+**
K3522 - **$100+**
3523 - **$175+**

3524 - **$125+**
3525 - **$100+**
3526 - **$125+**
K3541 - **$80+**
3527 - **$125+**
K3529 - **$80+**

Page 79
7K79/78 - **$65+**
7K79/79 - **$60+**
7K425 - **$125+**

Page 80
7K/020 - **$30+**
7K/012/012 - **$60+**
7K68/81 - **$75+**
7K21/21R - **$50+**
7K21/21T - **$50+**
7K17/70 - **$75+**

Page 81
2N 220 - **$125+**
2N 226 - **$175+**
2N 213 - **$150+**
2N 215 - **$130+**
2N 215 1/2 - **$130+**
1C 301B - **$75+**
1C 300 - **$50+**
1C 299 - **$50+**
2N 217 - **$75+**
2N 219 - **$75+**
2N 22/1119 - **$50+**
2N 23/1119 - **$60+**
2N 02 - **$60+**

Page 82
L450 - **$250+**
L436 - **$125+**
L455 - **$250+**
L402 - **$250+**
L413 - **$250+**
L446 - **$250+**
L454 - **$250+**

Page 83
W 3055 - **$125+**
W 3072 - **$125+**
All Shades - **$30+**

Page 84
L 7000 - **$75+**
L 31 - **$80+**
L 822 - **$1000+**

Page 85
All Glass Shades - **$30-50·**
All other shades - **$5-25+**

Page 86
For reference only

Page 87
For reference only

124

Page 88
282 - **$30+**
283 - **$40+**
280 - **$40+**
882 - **$50+**
252 - **$60+**
264 - **$60+**
883 - **$40+**
261 - **$45+**
881 - **$40+**

Page 89
S5976 - **$25+**
S5977 - **$25+**
S22 - **$150+**
S24 - **$175+**
S5978 - **$25+**
S5979 - **$25+**

Page 90
859 - **$35+**
876 - **$75+**
877 - **$40+**
854 - **$60+**
856 - **$70+**
853 - **$60+**

Page 91
251 - **$65+**
266 - **$70+**
878 - **$60+**
265 - **$75+**
289 - **$75+**
278 - **$75+**

Page 92
All lamps - **$850+**

Page 93
P6042E - **$800+**
P215E - **$200+**
P1037E - **$1000+**
P6042E - **$800+**
P210E - **$200+**
P6018E - **$1000+**

Page 94
All lamps - **$750+**

Page 95
L2800 - **$80+**
L2805 - **$85+**
L2810 - **$85+**

Page 96
2792V - **$40+**
2801V - **$50+**
2716V - **$100+**
2814V - **$100+**
2778V - **$60+**
1828V - **$85+**
2790V - **$75+**
2776V - **$50+**

Page 97
6202 - **$30+**
6205 - **$80+**
6222 - **$35+**
6204 - **$85+**
6212 - **$35+**
6214 - **$85+**
6206 - **$85+**

Page 98
All lamps - **$85+**

Page 99
34A 8046 - **$800+**
34A 8040 - **$125+**
34A 8057 - **$800+**
34A 8028 - **$175+**
34A 8016 - **$800+**
34A 8152 - **$800+**

Page 100
34A 8010 - **$600+**
34A 8048 - **$600+**
34A 8038 - **$600+**
34A 8050 - **$600+**
34A 8044 - **$500+**
34A 8004 - **$800+**

Page 101
34A 8199 - **$45+**
34A 8181 - **$45+**
34A 8023 - **$60+**
34A 8194 - **$45+**
34A 8205 - **$45+**
34A 8026 - **$80+**
34A 8192 - **$50+**
34A 8116 - **$45+**
34A 8173 - **$125+**
34A 8198 - **$80+**
34A 8171 - **$45+**
34A 8183 - **$125+**
34A 8174 - **$45+**
34A 8176 - **$60+**

Page 102
2N 209 - **$125+**
25P17 - **$60+**
2N 1027 - **$125+**
2N 1026 - **$125+**
2N 1019 - **$25+**
25P79/106A - **$100+**
1C 204 - **$35+**
2N 211 - **$150+**

Page 103
2M4/S310 - **$60+**
2ML77/S323 - **$60+**
2ML104/S408 - **$60+**
2M640 - **$125+**
2ML637/S301 - **$60+**
2ML103/S150 - **$125+**
2ML110/110 - **$125+**
2ML32/S148 - **$125+**
2ML28/158 - **$125+**
2ML26/165 - **$125+**

Page 104
873 - **$60+**
285 - **$200+**
260 - **$60+**
874 - **$125+**
783 - **$400+**
784 - **$400+**
875 - **$125+**

Page 105
L746 - **$850+**
L796 - **$700+**
L743 - **$1000+**

Page 106
L1595 - **$1100+**
L794 - **$1100+**
L742 - **$1100+**

Page 107
L739 - **$1100+**
L740 - **$1100+**
L782 - **$700+**

Page 108
L1615C - **$1100+**
L1615A - **$1100+**
L1615B - **$1100+**

Page 109
L1568 - **$350+**
L1506 - **$800+**
L1474 - **$900+**

Page 110
L3106 - **$325+**
L3107 - **$325+**
L726 - **$150+**
L3132 - **$350+**
L3133 - **$350+**

Page 111
5353 - **$3500+**
5234 - **$1750+**
5409 - **$3000+**
5307 - **$3000+**
5442 - **$3000+**
5121 - **$4200+**

Page 112
5458 - **$2700+**
5219 - **$2700+**
5208 - **$2700+**
5220 - **$1600+**
5213 - **$2500+**

Page 113
All lamps - **$2500+**

Page 114
All lamps - **$4000+**

Page 115
All lamps - **$2000+**

Page 116
All lamps - **$3400+**

Page 117
All lamps - **$2600+**

Page 118
All lamps - **$3000+**

Page 119
5230 - **$250+**
6513 - **$250+**
180 - **$125+**
8615 - **$125+**
8734 - **$400+**
8734AC - **$125+**

Page 120
8734XD - **$125+**
8734 - **$400+**
8734AC - **$125+**

Back Cover
29-K-1 - **$200+**
404 S1217 - **$600+**
240-K-2 - **$250+**
180-K-5 - **$400+**
181-C-1 - **$50+**
601-K-1 - **$300+**
280-K-5 - **$500+**
405/S1218 - **$250+**

Jeannette Lamps
Group 500 - **$2000+**
Group 297 - **$1000+**
Group 800 - **$2000+**